THE DENVER BRONCOS
ALL-TIME ALL-STARS

ALSO AVAILABLE IN THE ALL-TIME ALL-STARS SERIES

The Cleveland Browns All-Time All-Stars:
The Best Players at Each Position for the Browns

The Crimson Tide Football All-Time All-Stars:
The Best Players at Each Position for Alabama

The Boston Celtics All-Time All-Stars:
The Best Players at Each Position for the C's

The New York Yankees All-Time All-Stars:
The Best Players at Each Position for the Bronx Bombers

The Boston Red Sox All-Time All-Stars:
The Best Players at Each Position for the Sox

The Pittsburgh Pirates All-Time All-Stars:
The Best Players at Each Position for the Bucs

The Green Bay Packers All-Time All-Stars:
The Best Players at Each Position for the Green and Gold

The Minnesota Vikings All-Time All-Stars:
The Best Players at Each Position for the Purple and Gold

The New York Mets All-Time All-Stars:
The Best Players at Each Position for the Amazin's

THE DENVER BRONCOS ALL-TIME ALL-STARS

THE BEST PLAYERS AT EACH POSITION
FOR THE ORANGE AND BLUE

MIKE KLIS

LYONS
PRESS

Essex, Connecticut

An imprint of Globe Pequot, the trade division of
The Rowman & Littlefield Publishing Group, Inc.
4501 Forbes Blvd., Ste. 200
Lanham, MD 20706
LyonsPress.com

Distributed by NATIONAL BOOK NETWORK

British Library Cataloguing in Publication Information available

Library of Congress Cataloging-in-Publication Data

Names: Klis, Mike, 1959- author.
Title: The Denver Broncos all-time all-stars : the best players at each
    position for the orange and blue / Mike Klis.
Description: Essex, Connecticut : Lyons Press, [2023] | Series: All-time
    all-stars
Identifiers: LCCN 2023018471 (print) | LCCN 2023018472 (ebook) | ISBN
    9781493055531 (paperback : acid-free paper) | ISBN 9781493055548 (ebook)
Subjects: LCSH: Denver Broncos (Football team)—History. | Football
    players—United States—Statistics. | Football players—Rating
    of—United States.
Classification: LCC GV956.D37 K554 2023 (print) | LCC GV956.D37 (ebook) |
    DDC 796.332092/2—dc23/eng/20230518
LC record available at https://lccn.loc.gov/2023018471
LC ebook record available at https://lccn.loc.gov/2023018472

To my mom, so she can have a fresh book for her coffee table.
And to my wife, my motivator.

CONTENTS

INTRODUCTION

Every two weeks was Dad's payday and Mom would go shopping that Friday evening at Paramount Heights grocery store, located in the township of Oswego, Illinois. Mom and Dad had six kids, so it took a while. As she shopped, I would hang out at the magazine rack and read either the latest edition of *Baseball Digest*, especially if there was a story on one of my beloved Chicago Cubs, or *Sport* magazine, which had full-page color photos.

This affinity eventually led to reading sports books like Tom Meany's *Babe Ruth* and *Baseball's Greatest Players*, the edition with Joe DiMaggio, the Babe, and Ty Cobb pictured on the cover. Then came three of my favorite sports autobiographies with such colorful titles as Joe Namath's *I Can't Wait Until Tomorrow Because I Get Better Looking Every Day*, Johnny Sample's *Confessions of a Dirty Ballplayer*, and Lance Rentzel's *When All the Laughter Died in Sorrow*. For some reason, I read Jerry Kramer's book on Lombardi before I read his famed *Instant Replay*. Jim Bouton's *Ball Four* was read a couple years after it was published, as it required a slightly more mature audience.

So I have considered writing sports books a privilege, not a chore. When first approached about joining this project, *The Denver Broncos All-Time All-Stars*, I figured, no sweat. It couldn't be too difficult to choose the Broncos' all-time starting lineup. Maybe a couple close calls here and there, but I'd pound it out as a labor of love in no time.

Then, in one of my early discussions with my first editor, Niels Aaboe, he casually mentioned something like "Some of these guys will be no-brainers, like Floyd Little. Obviously, he's going to be a starter."

Oh, yes, of course, I told Niels. He's "The Franchise." Gotta have Floyd.

I said this as Terrell Davis flashed through the back of my mind. There can only be one starter at each position, right? Floyd Little is automatically the starting running back over Terrell Davis? The back of my mind didn't think so. (You'll see my solution to this dilemma in the running backs chapter.) As I got into this project, there were so many other factors that made picking the starting lineup difficult.

The 3-4 defense versus the 4-3, for instance. The Broncos, thanks to 20-year defensive coordinator Joe Collier and the famed *Sports Illustrated* cover photo of nose tackle Rubin Carter, were at the forefront of the 3-4 defense. It not only created a numbers problem for this project—four defensive linemen and four linebackers? Yes and yes—it also created two different-type players for each position. A defensive end in the 3-4, for instance, is really a defensive tackle in the 4-3. And a 4-3 defensive end from years gone by is similar to a modern-day 3-4 outside linebacker when it comes to rushing the passer.

Then again, all defensive players in days gone by—defensive ends and outside linebackers—were ordered to stop the run, first. Sacks weren't the be-all, end-all until the mid-1980s. So what about all those great players on those iconic Orange Crush defenses in the late 1970s? They were not forgotten, even if it was easier to recall all those great Broncos players from the late 1990s through the mid-2010s.

Then there's the fullback position. It used to be the primary ball-carrying position—Jim Brown and Franco Harris were fullbacks—until the West Coast offense came along in the 1980s. Then it became a lead-blocking position. One fullback; two different types of players.

It became a far more challenging project than I'd anticipated.

And this doesn't even get into the abundance of very good players who deserved All-Time starter status, but were left out. Remember this: In a 44-season stretch from 1973 through 2016, the Broncos had more Super Bowl appearances (8) than losing seasons (7). In that same 44-season stretch, the Detroit Lions and Cleveland Browns combined for 0 Super Bowl appearances and 56 losing seasons.

The Broncos had so many good players, they went five deep with all-time greats at some positions, most notably at safety.

And yet decisions were made and explanations were provided. We don't expect you to agree with all the choices. In fact, published critiques and disagreements are encouraged. But as of the end of the 2022 season, here is one published documentation of *The Denver Broncos All-Time All-Stars*. Paramount Heights went out of business long ago. So many of the Broncos' great players live on in these pages.

HEAD COACH

The head coach who stirred the greatest fanfare in Denver Broncos history, the new boss who arrived with the most gusto, excitement, and anticipation, was not Mike Shanahan or Dan Reeves or even, given the bump from the social media era, Sean Payton.

Nor were Floyd Little or John Elway the first of the franchise's saviors. None other than Lou Saban was the first show-stopper acquisition the Broncos ever had when he was given a 10-year contract—10 years!—for a robust $50,000 a year to become Denver's general manager and head coach the day after the 1966 season ended, on December 19.

More than 50 years later, the hated Raiders shocked the NFL landscape by giving Jon Gruden a 10-year contract to lure him out of the broadcast booth and onto the sidelines. Granted, Gruden's 10-year deal was initially worth $100 million, not $500,000. Still, Saban was ahead of his time as one of the most hyped head coaches in the history of the NFL, never mind the Broncos.

Some context is needed to explain the magnitude of the Saban hire. While the Broncos were perennial American Football League doormats through their first seven seasons, Saban had led the Buffalo Bills to back-to-back AFL titles in 1964 and 1965. The Bills behind Saban and future US senator Jack Kemp went 12-2 and 10-3-1 during the regular season of those title years.

Saban was named AFL Coach of the Year both seasons.

Previously, Saban was a huge winner as a player, too, playing both center and linebacker for the Cleveland Browns when they won All-America Football Conference championships in all four years he was registered with the team, from 1946 to 1949. Saban was nothing if not a champion.

Saying there was nothing left to accomplish in professional football, Saban stunningly jumped from the Bills following his second AFL title to the University of Maryland in 1966. Ignoring the warning signs that Saban's impetuous nature could lead to ill-fated decisions, Broncos owners Gerald and Allan Phipps lured the coach back to the AFL after the 1966 season.

The Phipps brothers were tired of life in the AFL basement. Through their first seven seasons, from their AFL charter season of 1960 through 1966, the Broncos were 26-69-3. An average of 4-10 a year. In 1966, they were 4-10 again under Mac Speedie and interim coach Ray Malavasi.

The brash, outspoken, taskmaster Saban was brought in to save the franchise.

"The challenge of directing the Denver Broncos is the most stimulating assignment I have undertaken during the years I've been associated with football," Saban was quoted as saying in the team's 1967 media guide. "Our goals are twofold. We want to build a solid organization . . . and we want to win football games. The two go hand in hand. They can be accomplished."

Yes, but not by him. The Stormy Saban era was about to begin.

He did get off to an encouraging start, quickly putting together a Who's Who coaching staff that included Dick MacPherson, Stan Jones, and Sam Rutigliano. The burgeoning fan base was energized. Even though metropolitan Denver voters defeated a stadium bond issue, a group of civic leaders organized a fund-raising drive that eventually gifted $1.8 million to add a 16,000-seat upper deck and increase Bears Stadium's capacity to 50,000.

After the 1968 season, the venue was officially renamed Mile High Stadium. The Phipps brothers moved the team's headquarters and practice facilities to the Adams County suburbs.

The AFL and big brother NFL had agreed on a merger beginning in 1970. Spearheaded by the Saban hire, the Broncos were on their way to becoming a big-league franchise.

And then in his first big player move, Saban traded away Broncos cornerback Willie Brown to the Oakland Raiders. Ugh. Brown had 9 interceptions with 140 return yards in his first full season of 1964 with the Broncos, second overall, but maybe his tape was too grainy for Saban to spot the Hall of Fame talent. Brown went on to play 12 seasons with the Raiders, finished his career with 54 interceptions—still ranked tied for 21st all-time—had a memorable 75-yard, pick-six off Fran Tarkenton to clinch Super Bowl XI, and was inducted into the Pro Football Hall of Fame in his first year of eligibility in 1984.

Saban made amends nearly two months later when in the first-ever NFL-AFL common draft he selected Floyd Little, the All-American running back from Syracuse, with his No. 6 overall selection. Little became one of only eight Hall of Famers who was selected in that 17-round, 1967 draft.

But Saban seemingly tried too hard to make an impact, as before he coached his first game with the Broncos, he traded away nearly all the team's previous stars and leaders, like Lionel Taylor, Austin "Goose" Gonsoulin, Jerry Sturm, and Abner Hayes.

Saban did acquire such defensive stalwarts as Rich "Tombstone" Jackson and Dave Costa. Indeed, even during their initial 13 non-winning seasons to start their franchise history, the Broncos were never an embarrassment because they always had a physical, bring-it-every-down defense.

But overall, Saban wasn't the answer. In fact, in his first season as Denver's head coach, the Broncos finished 3-11. One game worse than the team he inherited.

And it never got much better. The Broncos followed with records of 5-9, 5-8-1, and 5-8-1 in 1970. The natives were getting restless. And then in the 1971 season-opener, the Broncos had the ball at their own 20 with 2 minutes remaining and the game tied 10–10 against the Miami Dolphins, who were at the beginning of their early-1970s dynasty. Saban called for three runs to run out the clock, and in the days where there was no overtime, took the 10–10 tie.

Afterwards, Saban explained his strategy to the media by saying "Half a loaf is better than none."

That was it for Broncos fans. Saban was officially on borrowed time. Fans started littering the field with half loaves of bread, and Saban resigned under duress after losing at home to the Bengals in the ninth game of the season. The Broncos were 2-6-1 at the time, leaving Saban's overall coaching record in Denver at 20-42-3. He served just four and a half years of that 10-year contract.

The Phipps brothers got it right with their head coach the next year, though, when they hired John Ralston. He had made his mark at Stanford, beating Ohio State and then Michigan in back-to-back Rose Bowls with Heisman Trophy winner Jim Plunkett at quarterback in 1970.

The Broncos went 5-9 in Ralston's first season of 1972—the 13th out of 13 years without a winning record for the Denver franchise—but the skid was snapped in 1973 when behind veteran quarterback Charley Johnson and one more great season from Floyd Little, the Broncos finished 7-5-2.

Ralston would post winning records in two of the next three seasons, but after going a franchise-best 9-5 in 1976, a player insurrection partly led to Ralston's firing.

Red Miller took over, and with the exception of a hiccup season here and there, the Broncos went on a 30-year run of perennial playoff contention.

Denver's head coaching stories were never dull. Miller had a successful four-year run that included the Broncos' first Super Bowl appearance. Yet, he was let go after just his fourth season and replaced by the youngest coach in the NFL, Dan Reeves. Miller's head coaching career ran into a bum-luck transition in ownership. The Phipps brothers sold the franchise to Edgar Kaiser Jr., an heir to a shipbuilding industrialist, for $29 million in February 1981.

Kaiser wanted his own coach and wanted to make a splash. Reeves had had a very good, 12-year run as Broncos head coach that included six postseason and three Super Bowl appearances. But he was let go because Pat Bowlen, who bought the team from Kaiser in 1984, couldn't wait to make Reeves's top assistant, Mike Shanahan, his head coach.

Shanahan turned down Bowlen's initial offer to head his team in 1993 and moved on to San Francisco for two years, where he had a remarkable run as offensive coordinator while learning the 49ers Way that had been established by the legendary Bill Walsh, and carried on by George Seifert. Bowlen turned to defensive coordinator Wade Phillips instead as a two-year bridge from Reeves to Shanahan.

Phillips was essentially a two-year interim. Though he posted respectable 9-7 and, with Elway injured much of the season, 7-9 records, Phillips was let go after the 1994 season when Bowlen finally was able to recruit Shanahan away from the 49ers after San Francisco pulverized the San Diego Chargers, 49–26, in Super Bowl XXIX.

While the Broncos would later have another run of successful head coaches in John Fox and Gary Kubiak in the six-year run from 2011 to 2016, there were really only three candidates in the running to become the head coach for *The Denver Broncos All-Time All-Stars.*

THE CANDIDATES

Mike Shanahan
Dan Reeves
Red Miller

DAN REEVES (1981–1992)

Got to hand it to Kaiser: He made two franchise-uplifting decisions in his mere three years as the Broncos' controlling owner. You know about how Kaiser snookered John Elway, the rookie quarterback, away from Baltimore Colts' owner Bob Irsay in 1983. Two years prior, Kaiser made the untested, 37-year-old Reeves the NFL's youngest head coach. While Red Miller didn't deserve to be fired, Reeves was superb—even if he didn't always get along with Elway and his young offensive coordinator, Shanahan.

Reeves had seven 10-win seasons and a franchise-best five division titles during his 12 years as Broncos coach.

The highlight, Reeves said at his Broncos Ring of Fame ceremony in 2014, was no surprise: the 1986 season that was capped by The Drive in Cleveland to win the AFC Championship Game in overtime.

While Reeves received Broncos immortality with his pillar at Ring of Fame Plaza, located outside the famed South Stands at Empower Field at Mile High, he had been snubbed by the Pro Football Hall of Fame, although his candidacy for Canton seemed to gather testimonial momentum from voters following his death at age 77 on New Year's Day, 2022.

After a solid eight-year playing career as a halfback with the Dallas Cowboys from 1965 to 1972, Reeves became an assistant coach to Tom Landry in Dallas before Kaiser hired him to become head coach in 1981. Kaiser sold the franchise to Pat Bowlen in 1984, but Reeves stayed as head coach and lasted 12 years, posting a 110-73-1 record with three Super Bowl appearances.

The year after he was fired from the Broncos following an 8-8 record, in 1992, Reeves immediately turned the 6-10 New York Giants he inherited into an 11-5 playoff team in 1993.

He later turned around the moribund Atlanta Falcons, leading them to his fourth Super Bowl in 1998, when he lost to the John Elway–Mike Shanahan Broncos. Yes, Reeves went 0-4 in those Super Bowls, but so did Minnesota's Bud Grant and Buffalo's Marv Levy, who long ago were inducted into the Pro Football Hall of Fame. And their four losing Super Bowls were with one team; Reeves performed the much more difficult task of taking two teams to Super Bowls.

"Unfortunately, I've been on the bad side a lot of times, but I also know how great it is when you do get on the winning side," Reeves said in 2019, when he was a coaching finalist for the Pro Football Hall of Fame, only to lose out to Jimmy Johnson and Bill Cowher. "Just to get there is unbelievable. The things you accomplish just to get in that game."

Reeves died from complications of dementia less than three weeks shy of his 78th birthday, and nearly 54 years to the day of the famed Ice Bowl. On December 31, 1967, at below-zero Lambeau Field, Reeves threw a 50-yard halfback option touchdown pass to Lance Rentzel to put the Dallas Cowboys up on the Green Bay Packers, 17–14, in the fourth quarter. Everyone knows how it ended, with Bart Starr's quarterback sneak behind Jerry Kramer's block with 13 seconds to go, giving the win to Green Bay.

Still, that iconic moment for Reeves, plus his solid playing career and outstanding coaching career, warrants his bust to be bronzed in Canton, Ohio.

"He was a great coach, I thought," said Joe DeCamillis, special teams coordinator for the Los Angeles Rams and formerly of the Broncos, said about his father-in-law. "He got the most out of his players. And he cared about his players. He helped out so many of his players that nobody knew about.

"But as good as he was as a coach, he was an even better father, grandfather, and husband. He always wanted to be around when our kids had something going on. One of the things he always said: 'You can really tell the character of a person by how he treats people who can't help him.' That's how he lived his life. He treated the cleanup people the same way he did Mr. Bowlen."

RED MILLER (1977–1980)

Miller wasn't the Broncos' first winning coach. John Ralston was. But Miller was the first Broncos head coach to lead the franchise to the Super Bowl during the Orange Crush/Broncomania season of 1977. Miller was also the first to lead the Broncos to three straight postseason appearances and the first to not have a losing record. Yet he was fired after his fourth season by new owner Edgar Kaiser Jr., who had just bought the team from the Phipps brothers, Gerald and Allan. Kaiser wanted his own head coach, and hired Dan Reeves.

Miller became the Broncos head coach in 1977 after Ralston was fired, either because 12 prominent players went to Phipps, urging his dismissal, or because the coach wouldn't give up his GM duties.

Before Ralston and Miller, the Broncos weren't exactly a laughingstock—they had too many physical defenses in their infancy for that—but poor quarterback play was a big reason why the franchise didn't have its first winning record until its 14th season of 1973. Charley Johnson wound up in the team's Ring of Fame because of his one winning season at QB.

Miller inherited a team that went 9-5 in 1976 and immediately instilled a firebrand type of leadership that helped produce one of the most iconic defenses in NFL history, when the Orange Crush, and its adoring fan base, captivated the nation. The offense was conservative—it played to its defense—but newly acquired veteran Craig Morton gave the Broncos a proven winner at quarterback.

After losing to the Cowboys in Super Bowl XII, Miller's Broncos went 10-6 and lost a playoff game in 1978 and 10-6 with another playoff loss in 1979. The team was getting a little long in the tooth in 1980, as such stalwarts as Morton, Haven Moses, Otis Armstrong, and Billy Thompson were near the end of their careers. Still, Miller had the Broncos battling to a competitive 8-8 record. Miller had enough equity built up with the Phipps brothers to survive one down year, but not with the new boss, Kaiser.

For more than 35 years Miller was easily the most unappreciated coach in Broncos history. The team finally recognized him in 2017 when he was elected into the Ring of Fame. He died at 89 from complications of a stroke two months before the ceremony, with his widow Nan accepting the honor on Red's behalf.

MIKE SHANAHAN (1995–2008)

Entering the 1997 season, the NFL wasn't as balanced between conferences as it is now, and has been for more than two decades.

The NFC had won 13 Super Bowls in a row entering 1997—by an average margin of nearly 21 points. The Broncos were sporting the largest tire tracks during that AFC rut, losing three Super Bowls by a combined 96 points.

"That was actually an interesting development at that time: What do we have to do to beat the NFC?" Mike Shanahan said years later. "And what's the difference between the NFC and AFC? Not only were we getting beat, we were getting beat pretty good."

Shanahan's Broncos cut free from the NFC stranglehold by beating the conference at its own game. It was the running game featuring Terrell Davis and the zone-blocking scheme, with a little help from quarterback John Elway in the passing game, that pushed the Broncos over the top. It was the Broncos—not Jimmy Johnson's Cowboys or Bill Parcells's Giants or Washington's Hogs—who were the more physical, pound-the-rock team.

The Broncos steamrolled the heavily favored Green Bay Packers in Super Bowl XXXII, then cruised by Dan Reeves's Atlanta Falcons to cap the 1998 season with a decisive win in Super Bowl XXXIII.

The zone-running scheme lost its prominence during the Patriots' 20-year dynastic run at the onset of the 21st century, but so many of Shanahan's assistants have brought it back in vogue within the past five years, including his son Kyle, who's had impressive success from 2019 to 2022 with the San Francisco 49ers.

"It's cool that it's recognized," Kyle Shanahan said of his dad's impact on the back-in-vogue West Coast offense. "I was always biased growing up as his son, but it was always so different watching his offenses. I always remember [when he was] a coordinator going from when I was younger all the way to my freshman year in high school, when he was with San Francisco in '94, it was always so impressive how good his offenses were. Then he came to Denver and did it as a head coach—that's all I saw.

"Even though I didn't realize that's what I was naturally studying, that's how I see football. And it's worked for so many different teams because it was different. I always knew how special his offense was, but it's cool to see everyone else give him his due."

ALL-TIME ALL-STARS HEAD COACH

Mike Shanahan was simply the most successful coach in Broncos history, with two Super Bowl titles, seven playoff seasons, and 146 wins (counting 8 in the postseason). He was elected into the Broncos Ring of Fame in 2020, and because of the COVID-19 pandemic that year, had his induction ceremony in 2021. He is on the short list of coaches up for Pro Football Hall of Fame consideration, although it will be interesting to see who gets the nod first—Shanahan or Reeves.

But for *The Denver Broncos All-Time All-Stars*, there is little doubt the team's head coach is the two-time Super Bowl winner, Mike Shanahan.

OTHERS

John Fox (2011–2014)
He only had four years as head coach, but it was a memorable term for many reasons. Fox's first year as Broncos head coach

Mike Shanahan © ERIC LARS BAKKE

was the magical season of Tim Tebow. And Fox was instrumental in making the Tebow year happen.

In that 2011 season, Fox ordered a switch to the college offense for the passing-challenged Tebow, whose other quarterback strengths of power running, inspirational leadership, and an otherworldly will to win surfaced during a six-game winning streak that featured one unlikely comeback after another. Tebow also won a playoff game that year that not only shook the stadium rafters but the surrounding city balconies.

Then Fox was instrumental in the recruitment of a seemingly broken-down free agent quarterback named Peyton Manning. Together, Fox and the recovering Manning posted regular-season records of 13-3, 13-3, and 12-4. In all Fox won four AFC West titles in his four years and guided the Broncos to the 2013-season Super Bowl. His 49-22 record makes him the winningest coach in Broncos history in terms of win percentage.

Despite this tremendous success, Fox and general manager John Elway had an acrimonious split following the 2014 season. Fox was quickly hired by the Chicago Bears—his third team in six years without taking a year off. Tension between Elway and Fox began after a shocking 2012-season playoff defeat when Fox had Manning take a knee with 31 seconds remaining in regulation and the score tied, 35–35, against the Baltimore Ravens. Fox's gut told him his team was too shell-shocked after the Ravens' Joe Flacco heaved a 70-yard desperation pass to Jacoby Jones that was misjudged by safety Rahim Moore, who went for a game-tying touchdown. The Ravens won in overtime on a field goal by rookie Justin Tucker.

The relationship between Elway and Fox was further strained after the Broncos' record-setting offense was destroyed by Seattle's Legion of Boom, 43–8, in Super Bowl XLVIII in New Jersey. Officially, Fox resigned. He was not fired, as the Broncos didn't pay him any money from the final year of his contract. But let there be no doubt Fox left the Broncos in great shape.

Gary Kubiak (2015–2016)

Elway replaced Fox with his good friend and former QB backup, Gary Kubiak. And the decision to force a coaching change was justified when Kubiak led the Broncos to the Super Bowl 50 title in his first season of 2015. Kubiak did a masterful job juggling a fading Manning with up-and-coming Brock Osweiler at quarterback. Manning and Kubiak's offense was not a good match; Manning had his worst statistical season in his one and only season with Kubiak, as he threw 9 touchdown passes against 17 interceptions during the 2015 season. But even with Osweiler coming in at midseason and playing well while posting a 5-2 record as a starter, Kubiak benched him in the second half of the regular-season finale against the San Diego Chargers and brought in Manning—to a thunderous ovation from the Broncos' stadium crowd.

Manning inspired a comeback, then stayed in as the starter through three postseason games. Denver's third Super Bowl title was mostly credited to Von Miller and its stout defense, but Kubiak's game management was near perfect, as the Broncos won 11 games by one score or less—including their first two postseason wins against Ben Roethlisberger's Steelers and Tom Brady's Patriots.

The Broncos started 4-0 the next season behind little-known QB Trevor Siemian, who had replaced the retired Manning and free agent–departing Osweiler, but then Kubiak fell ill from a transient ischemic–like stroke—his second such incident as a head coach. The first was during the 2013 season while with the Houston Texans.

With Kubiak struggling with his health the rest of the season, the Broncos slumped to a 9-7 finish, and Kubiak was forced to retire after the season for medical reasons.

Kubiak was also an 11-year offensive coordinator under Mike Shanahan in Denver, a run that included Super Bowl wins to cap the 1997–1998 seasons. Between his stints as offensive coordinator and head coach, Kubiak was one of the greatest all-around coaches in Broncos history.

OFFENSE

QUARTERBACK

There were two periods when Denver quarterbacks suffered: The first was after Elway. The second was after Peyton.

John Elway wasn't just a great quarterback during his Hall of Fame career from 1983 to 1998 with the Broncos. He went beyond stardom. His incredible rocket arm and innate scrambling ability broke the mold of the drop-back, pocket quarterback. Never before had a quarterback come out of college, as Elway did from Stanford following the 1982 season, with such enormous can't-miss hype. Johnny U. was a ninth-round pick in 1955. Joe Montana was a third-round pick out of Notre Dame in 1979. Peyton Manning and Andrew Luck came later.

Joe Namath had the hype, but largely because of his larger-than-life persona and then the record signing bonus he received out of Alabama with a team from New York in a still upstart league. A terrific passer, yes, but his bad knees prevented him from can't-miss status, especially when his best years were not with the established NFL.

Elway was the first of the one-and-onlys. His rookie year came at the height of a Denver newspaper war that was so competitive for a fresh angle with the city's first megastar, one columnist resourcefully, if infamously, wrote about the candy he gave out on Halloween.

Stats did not properly measure Elway's prowess at the quarterback position. Two eyes did. It was the otherworldly dodge and scramble left, the plant into the pigeon-toed stance, and the throw deep across the far quadrant right to Vance Johnson or one of the Three Amigos that brought awe to those who had never before witnessed such remarkable feats of strength.

It was the off-script style, and it was all those victories. Elway's 148 regular-season wins dwarfed Peyton Manning's runner-up Broncos' QB win total of 45. Elway's 14 postseason wins similarly stomped Manning's next-best total of 5. Granted, the fact that Manning needed just four seasons—12 less than Elway—to finish second in Broncos history in wins and post-season wins was itself a remarkable achievement.

But with Elway, the Broncos not only won more games than ever before, they won in exciting, final-minute fashion. He went out like John Wayne in most of the Duke's movies—on top. After substantial regular-season and AFC playoff success during his first 14 seasons, Elway proved his few remaining doubters wrong by guiding the Broncos to back-to-back Super Bowl titles in his final two seasons of 1997 and 1998.

Broncos owner Pat Bowlen waived the mandatory five-year waiting period and put Elway into the team's Ring of Fame in 1999, a few months after he retired.

The quarterbacks who followed Elway never measured up, no matter that they were pretty good in their own right.

Brian Griese, Jake Plummer, Jay Cutler, and Kyle Orton all had their moments.

Griese went to the Pro Bowl in his second year as a starter in 2000, throwing 19 touchdowns against just 4 interceptions while guiding the Broncos to an 11-5 record and a postseason appearance.

He wasn't Elway.

Plummer was a swashbuckling quarterback from the Arizona Cardinals and Arizona State who went 9-2, 10-6, 13-3, and 7-4 in his four seasons with the Broncos.

But there were no Super Bowl appearances, so he was no Elway.

Cutler nearly resembled Elway in arm strength, but his sometimes surly personality clashed with new hot-shot and temperamental head coach Josh McDaniels. Cutler was traded away before his fourth season, and before getting a chance to realize his potential.

It was Chicago where Cutler wound up in exchange for Orton, who threw for 3,802 yards and 21 touchdowns in his first season with the Broncos, but the team's collapse following a 6-0 start dropped Denver out of the playoffs.

Orton could sling it, but he couldn't win like Elway.

Which led to Tim Tebow, who seemingly had the intangibles to win like Elway, but couldn't sling it. Elway was the Broncos' first-year general manager when Tebow had his magical season of 2011, but the fire-breathing competitor from Florida wasn't the boss's kind of QB.

Tebow was dumped for Peyton Manning prior to the 2012 season.

And thus began the second magical era of Broncos quarterbacks. Cut loose by the Indianapolis Colts because of a neck injury that wasn't repaired until a third surgery and insufferable months of rehab, Manning guided the Broncos to the most successful four-year stretch in franchise history, posting regular-season records of 13-3, 13-3, 12-4, and 12-4 (Brock Osweiler went 5-2 in the final seven games of the 2015 season). The Broncos had the best record in the AFC all four years of the Manning era, so the fact they reached the Super Bowl only two of those four years meant there were two other postseason disappointments.

Still, Manning was sublime in his ability to "throw open" his receivers. Elway would see an open receiver and gun it in before the defensive back could close. Manning released the ball as his receivers were breaking away from coverage, the sometimes wobbly sphere landing in their wide-open arms.

Manning had the best single-season passing performance in NFL history during his second season with the Broncos in 2013, setting records with 55 touchdown passes, 5,477 passing yards, and 606 points (37.9 per game). Incredibly, those records still stand nine years later—even after the regular season expanded from 16 to 17 games in 2021.

As Manning began to break down physically during his final season of 2015, at the age of 39, he had help from his backup Osweiler and a Denver defense that was one of the two best in franchise history (the 1977 Orange Crush shall never be forgotten). Still, after missing seven games with a heel injury, Manning came off the bench in the regular-season finale at Broncos Stadium to thunderous applause from the home crowd, and led the Broncos to a comeback victory against the Chargers, clinching once again the AFC's No. 1 playoff seed.

This time, Manning had just enough left for a postseason run and helped the Broncos defeat the Steelers, Patriots, and Panthers to win Super Bowl 50.

Manning also retired Elway- and John Wayne–like after that 2015 season—on top. The quarterbacks who followed had little chance to satisfy the Broncos' QB-centric fan base. Osweiler surprisingly left for Houston via free agency following the Super Bowl 50 title. Trevor Siemian was a pleasant surprise as a seventh-round compensatory pick, No. 250 overall, out of Northwestern as he went 8-6 in his first year as a starter in 2016.

But Paxton Lynch was supposed to be the heir apparent to Manning. Lynch was the Broncos' first-round draft pick, No. 26 overall, in 2016. He had the arm, physical strength at 6-foot-7, and decent mobility for his size, but he didn't have the ability to make split-second decisions while 21 other players on the field were running around at full speed.

With Siemian, Lynch, and Osweiler, who had returned to Denver after it didn't work out in Houston, all struggling in

2017, the Broncos turned to Vikings' miracle man Case Keenum in 2018. Then Ravens' Super Bowl hero Joe Flacco was brought in by the Broncos in 2019, followed by second-round rookie Drew Lock. The team was built around Lock for 2020, but an off-season shutdown for the 2020 COVID-19 pandemic and an early-season shoulder injury in 2021 crimped his development.

When Elway decided he had had enough of the GM stress and was replaced by George Paton as Broncos GM in 2021, veteran Teddy Bridgewater was brought in to become the Broncos starting quarterback.

All failed to bring the Broncos back to the postseason, much less the Super Bowl. Five consecutive losing seasons, six without a playoff game, led Paton to make a bold move and acquire star quarterback Russell Wilson from the Seattle Seahawks for the 2022 season.

While expectations for Wilson are enormous, his first season was a huge disappointment, and as of this writing he is not among the candidates for the Broncos' all-time starting quarterback. For that, there are but three candidates—Elway, Manning, and Craig Morton, who was the franchise's first savior-like quarterback acquisition. In his first year with the Broncos, Morton directed the team to its first AFC Championship and Super Bowl appearance. And it came at the height of Broncomania.

THE CANDIDATES

John Elway
Peyton Manning
Craig Morton

CRAIG MORTON (1977–1982)

More than Manning after the 2011 season in Indianapolis, Morton was considered washed up following a disastrous 1976 season with the New York Giants. He threw 20 interceptions against just 9 touchdowns that year, and took 39 sacks in just 12 starts, of which 10 were defeats. In fairness, quarterbacks didn't have the means to throw the ball away as they do now, if they are outside the pocket. All intentional throw-aways prior to 1993 were 15-yard penalties for intentional grounding and loss of down. It's a big reason why the pre–free agency quarterbacks have worse touchdown-to-interception ratios—and more battered bodies—than QBs of today.

Morton—not much of a runner, as his body was beaten up as he moved into his 30s—was booed unmercifully by Giants fans. Their ill will toward him no doubt was established during his run with the rival Dallas Cowboys from 1969 to 1972, so successful that he often started ahead of the popular and future Hall of Famer, Roger Staubach.

In March 1977, Morton was traded to the Broncos for Steve Ramsey in a swap of ineffective quarterbacks. At that point, the Broncos had gone through 25 quarterbacks during their first 17 seasons, but in Morton they found their guy.

At 34, Morton brought steady leadership and impact passing to an offense that otherwise served as a complement to Denver's terrific Orange Crush defense. He had a steady regular season in 1977, throwing for 1,929 yards and 14 touchdowns against just 8 interceptions. These stats may seem modest now, but Morton was the No. 4–rated passer that year, with an 82.0 rating, while posting a 12-1 record before a left hip injury and little to play for had him playing just one three-and-out series in the final regular-season game against his former Dallas Cowboys.

The Broncos lost the game 14 finale to the Cowboys, 14–6, which would have been meaningless had it not turned out to be a preview of Super Bowl XII.

But first, in the two AFC playoff games—the first two playoff games in Broncos history—Morton threw two touchdown passes in each. He beat the Steelers, the team of the 1970s, and the Raiders, the defending Super Bowl champs, in that magical 1977 postseason.

Morton played well again in 1978, when the Broncos again won the AFC West and made the playoffs. Broncos head coach Red Miller flirted with starting the more mobile Norris Weese in 1979, but with the Broncos down, 34–10, midway through the third quarter in game 4 against Seattle, Morton was sent in.

In the span of 7.5 minutes of game time, Morton threw touchdown passes to tackle-eligible Dave Studdard, then star receiver Haven Moses late in the third quarter, and Rick Upchurch early in the fourth, to draw the Broncos within, 34–31.

Morton wasn't done. He then engineered a 40-yard touchdown drive capped by Rob Lytle's 1-yard touchdown run to give Denver a 37–34 victory in one of the greatest comebacks in NFL history.

"We got a lot of breaks," Morton said of that game for the book, *The 50 Greatest Players in Denver Broncos History*. "Upchurch made some great plays and Haven made some big plays. The defense started getting turnovers. It just turned. It wasn't just me. Defense created good field position and guys were making plays and then we just thought, 'Well, this could be fun.'"

Still, Morton had a way of creating a spark, whether for one game or for the entire Orange Crush era. His best season with the Broncos, at least statistically, was 1981. At the age of 38, Morton threw for a career-best 3,195 yards and tied his single-season best with 21 touchdowns while posting a 10-5 record as a starter.

For Broncos fans, though, Morton's signature season will always be 1977, and his signature game will always be the AFC Championship.

From the jump, Morton had an instant connection with Moses. Thus, the M & M connection.

"Haven saw the same thing I saw from his perspective down field," Morton said. "It was to where we knew what the other one was going to do."

That he played in one particular game for the Broncos, and played like a champion, was the stuff of lore.

In that first, great Broncos season of 1977, Morton famously hobbled and winced his way out of his hospital bed to play in the AFC Championship Game on a frigid January 1, 1978, at Mile High Stadium. Not only play, but throw two touchdown passes to Moses in a 20–17 win against the hated and defending champion Oakland Raiders. The Broncos were going to the Super Bowl.

Broncomania was never more manic.

"Now all the information came out after the game, and as history has gone on, I know what happened," said Broncos cornerback Louis Wright. "But then I did not know. I knew he was hurt and might not play. Norris Weese was taking all the snaps and we thought Norris was going to be the quarterback. And then all the sudden there was Craig. I didn't know what I know now. I know he played, but now that I know the circumstances of how he played, it was pretty incredible."

A week earlier, Morton had thrown two touchdowns without an interception in the Broncos' 34–21, first-round AFC playoff win against the Pittsburgh Steelers, then went to the hospital to spend a week battling an infection. Blood kept building up in the hip and doctors had trouble draining it. It left his leg grotesquely discolored from the upper left hip down to his knee. Weese took the first-team practice snaps that week and most of the Broncos players figured he would play in the AFC Championship Game against the Raiders.

Although accounts said Morton left the hospital on Thursday, he remembered leaving the hospital on Sunday morning, the day of the game, and being driven to Mile High by a friend, Oren Hawley. Morton's condition was kept hush-hush for the upcoming epic battle against the hated Raiders, with the media reporting little about it during the week.

Regardless of when he was released from the hospital's care, they don't make 'em as tough as Craig Morton anymore. He was the son of a World War II veteran who fought Japan in the New Guinea operation.

Having passed up the chance to sign with the Detroit Tigers or New York Yankees in the pre-draft Major League Baseball era, Morton instead wanted to play quarterback at nearby Cal, where he was a two-and-a-half-year starter for head coach Marv Levy and a staff that included Bill Walsh and Mike White. Morton broke all of Cal's passing records for some pretty bad teams.

He showed enough to become the No. 5 overall pick by the Cowboys in the 1965 NFL Draft—after the Chicago Bears took Dick Butkus with the No. 3 overall selection and Gale Sayers at No. 4. That the Cowboys took Morton with their first pick was a mild surprise considering they already had a good young quarterback in Don Meredith, who had just finished his fifth year in the league, second as a starter.

Morton would sit four years behind Meredith before the latter surprisingly retired at age 31 while coming off three consecutive Pro Bowl seasons.

In 10 years with the Cowboys, Morton fell between Meredith and Roger Staubach. Morton was 10-2-1 as a starter in 1969 and 8-3 in 1970, when his Cowboys finally made it through the NFL playoffs and played in the first merged-league Super Bowl, or Super Bowl V.

Cowboys coach Tom Landry infamously had Morton and Staubach alternate plays for a week 7 game against the Chicago Bears in 1971. It didn't work, and Staubach became the quarterback for the rest of the season. Morton went 10-4 in 1972 after Staubach suffered a separated shoulder.

"Boy, we had great competitions," Morton said. "It switched every year, it seemed like. He's still one of my great friends. We were always really good friends, but boy, we were competitors. The competition never got in the way of our friendship."

Midway through 1974, Morton asked for—and was granted—a trade when he was again replaced by Staubach at the halfway point. But his two and a half seasons with the Giants were miserable, as Morton played down to the level of his team.

After the 1976 season, Giants head coach John McVay— who later became enormously successful while helping to build the San Francisco 49ers into a dynasty from 1982 to 1994— informed Morton on March 7, 1977, that he had been traded to the Broncos in exchange for quarterback Steve Ramsey, and a draft pick.

"I said 'Thank you very much,' " Morton said. "I was so relieved."

The Broncos had gone a franchise-best 9-5 in 1976, but 12 of their veteran players—nicknamed the Dirty Dozen—led a revolt against head coach John Ralston. Broncos owner Gerald Phipps supported Ralston, although the coach resigned in part because of his players' actions. Phipps replaced Ralston with Red Miller, who had been offensive line coach the previous four seasons with the New England Patriots.

The fiery Miller was well received. Morton's arrival drew mixed feelings.

"We were skeptical," said Rick Upchurch, who was coming off a punt return season for the ages in 1976. "We're saying, wait a minute. You're bringing in a guy that's been in the league, what, 12, 13 years already? And he's not in the best of health. People who saw him were like, 'Check his legs out.' But what you couldn't account for was his savvy, his smarts, and his ability to throw the ball in the right place."

Others were more enthusiastic from the jump.

"When we got Craig, I was glad, because he had experience," said nose tackle Rubin Carter. "And that means a lot. He had been there. He took his bumps and bruises but he was still there and he still had his mental capability and he was able to run an offense and run a team and be able to make audibles at the line of scrimmage.

"I felt good about it. Until then, we had young guys at the quarterback position. Craig gave us a chance. Don't turn the ball over. You know, let the defense win the game."

"He was the missing ingredient," said Broncos safety and captain Billy Thompson. "He had an immediate connection with Haven. It was a tremendous year for both of them."

PEYTON MANNING (2012–2015)

To fully appreciate the impact Peyton Manning had during his four years with the Broncos, look at how the team struggled in the five years before he arrived, and the seven years after he retired.

During his term in Denver, the quarterback led the Broncos to their winningest four-year stretch in team history, posting records of 13-3, 13-3, 12-4, and 12-2 from 2012 to 2015. There were five consecutive non-winning seasons before Manning arrived (7-9 in 2007, followed by 8-8, 8-8, 4-12, and 8-8). There have been seven consecutive non-playoff seasons since Manning hung it up, including six in a row with a losing record

(5-11, 6-10, 7-9, 5-11, 7-10, and 5-12)—the worst six-year stretch in the Broncos' past 50 years.

Not surprisingly, Manning was elected into the team's Ring of Fame and the Pro Football Hall of Fame in his first year of eligibility for each honor.

There were two biographical books to Manning's NFL career. The first was a 14-season stay with the Indianapolis Colts, where he was the No. 1 overall draft pick in 1998, won four of his record five MVP awards, threw a then-NFL-record 49 touchdown passes in 2004 that broke the mark set 20 years earlier by his childhood hero Dan Marino, and led Indianapolis to a Super Bowl XLI victory to cap the 2006 season.

But when Manning missed the entire 2011 season because of a neck injury that required three surgeries before he could get back on the field, the Colts were so bad without him that they tumbled into the No. 1 overall draft pick at the exact time once-every-generation quarterback prospect Andrew Luck was coming out of college. Manning was released to free agency.

Hurt in more ways than one, the battered, free-agent Manning wound up signing with the Broncos, who gambled the quarterback could rebound from his dramatic neck injury.

"I certainly had concerns, and looking back you can definitely say I was not 100 percent confident," Manning said in a 2021 interview with 9NEWS. "The only thing I was 100 percent confident in is I wanted to try. I wanted to give it a go. I knew it was going to be tough, playing in a new physical state after these neck problems and nerve problems that it had caused in my right arm. Learning a new system, learning timing with new receivers. It was a challenge in and of itself.

"But I wanted to give it a go. And Denver was the best place for me. They were very adaptive, welcoming. Greek [head trainer Steve Antonopulos] and the training staff had a great rehab plan. The coaches said, We'll take some of your plays in Indianapolis and mesh it with some of our plays and really make you feel comfortable. That was not the case that all teams were presenting. Those were big reasons why I ended up choosing Denver, and [I'm] really glad it worked out the way it did. I started feeling better, started feeling more confident throughout that season, and got my edge back a little bit and was able to have four wonderful years here with the Broncos."

His four years in Denver cemented his greatness.

Manning and the Broncos took a few games to get rolling as they were 2-3 to begin his initial season of 2012. He and the Broncos were then trailing 24–0 at halftime at San Diego in game 6. But just as it appeared the Manning Era in Denver would begin 2-4, Peyton and the Broncos rallied for 35 unanswered points in the second half, igniting an 11-game winning streak to finish the season.

Although the Broncos were stunned by Baltimore in their second-round playoff game, Manning bounced back in 2013 to record the best regular season by a quarterback in NFL history. Manning threw for 55 touchdowns and 5,477 yards that year to obliterate passing records that still stand going on 10 years later. He picked up his record fifth MVP award, then guided the Broncos to AFC postseason home wins against the Chargers and New England Patriots.

Unfortunately for Manning and the Broncos, they didn't have it from the opening horrific snap in Super Bowl XLVIII, as they were trounced by the Seattle Seahawks in a game played at MetLife Stadium in New Jersey.

Manning got off to a torrid start again in 2014, setting the all-time career TD pass record along the way, but a quad injury hindered him in the final two months.

Manning and the Broncos finished the job in 2015. He led the team to a 7-0 start, but a heel injury suffered in a game 8 loss at Indianapolis rendered Manning ineffective in a game 9 home loss to Kansas City.

Broncos head coach Gary Kubiak replaced Manning in the second half of the Chiefs' loss with Brock Osweiler, who played well throughout in the final seven games. But with the Broncos trailing and sputtering in the second half of the season finale against the Chargers, Kubiak in the third quarter replaced Osweiler with Manning, who entered to a thunderous standing ovation from the Denver crowd.

The Broncos rallied to beat the Chargers to capture the No. 1 playoff seed, then won home playoff games against the Steelers and, for the second time in three years, the Patriots in the AFC Championship Game. In the upset win against the Pats, Manning threw two early touchdown passes to tight end Owen Daniels and Denver's terrific defense made it hold up.

A historic individual performance by outside linebacker Von Miller and the Denver D pushed the Broncos past favored Carolina in Super Bowl 50. Manning didn't have his best game, but he started each half with field goal drives, and, to a man, the Broncos said they couldn't have won it all without his leadership.

Manning retired after the 2015 season, but he and his wife Ashley and twin children Marshall and Mosley have made their home in the Denver area. He became the 35th member of the Broncos Ring of Fame when he was inducted in 2021.

JOHN ELWAY (1983–1998)

From the moment he entered the NFL, John Elway was a showstopper, a headliner who helped sell publications both nationally and locally, where he ignited a two-newspaper city into a full-fledged war.

The No. 1 overall draft pick in 1983, Elway refused to play for the Baltimore Colts, insisting he would play minor-league baseball for a year with the Yankees and reenter the draft rather than play for owner Bob Irsay and coach Frank Kush. Fortunately for the Denver Broncos franchise and the league itself, Irsay had a good relationship with Broncos owner Edgar Kaiser Jr. and worked out a trade.

The Colts got a very good player in guard-tackle Chris Hinton, the No. 4 overall selection in the same 1983 draft in which Elway was No. 1. Hinton went to six Pro Bowls in his seven seasons with the Colts, and he was also a four-year starter with Atlanta before finishing up his career with two years in Minnesota. But Hinton—along with quarterback Mark Herrmann and the following year's first-round draft pick, which turned out to be right guard Ron Solt—didn't offset one John Elway.

In Elway's 16-year playing career, he led the Broncos to five Super Bowl appearances. He threw for 300 touchdowns and 51,475 yards to rank third (behind Dan Marino and Fran Tarkenton) and second (behind Marino) in both categories when he retired following the 1998 season. All the while, Elway demonstrated a flair for the dramatic, not only with his playing style, but also his ability to rally late for improbable wins. In all, he had 31 fourth-quarter comebacks and 40 game-winning drives in the final minutes.

For all his accomplishments, he had two seminal moments: One was dubbed "The Drive," and the other, "The Helicopter."

"The Drive put me on the map," Elway said. "That was my coming-out party. That legitimized me in big games. The Helicopter kind of helped win the championship, because of the mentality and the energy it created."

First, The Drive. In Elway's fourth season of 1986, he carried the Broncos to the AFC Championship Game where the foe was Bernie Kosar and the Cleveland Browns. There were 79,973 rabid Browns fans packed in at the old Cleveland Municipal Stadium. The home crowd thought sure their team was heading to the Super Bowl when Kosar hit Brian Brennan for a go-ahead 48-yard touchdown pass with less than 6 minutes remaining, and the ensuing kickoff was bobbled enough to pin the Broncos back at their own 2-yard line.

At least the end zone where the Broncos huddled up during a long TV timeout was opposite the hostile Dawg Pound.

"Okay, boys," Broncos left guard Keith Bishop told his huddle mates, "we've got 'em right where we want 'em."

At least that was the cleaned-up version of Bishop's motivational speech. Down 20–13 with 5:32 remaining, Elway—his orange jersey and white pants caked in mud on the cold, wet afternoon—engineered a 15-play, 98-yard march that he finished off with a third-and-1, 5-yard bullet to Mark Jackson for the game-tying touchdown with just 39 seconds remaining in regulation. The key play of The Drive was a 20-yard completion to Jackson to convert a third-and-18 with 1:47 remaining.

In typical Elway fashion, there was a little bit of everything in The Drive: Two scrambles for 20 yards, three incompletions, a sack, and 6 completions for 78 yards and a touchdown. Game tied, 20–20. The game was then won on a short Rich Karlis field goal in overtime.

The victory brought Elway to the Super Bowl for the first time. Unfortunately for him, it would be the first of three consecutive Super Bowl blowout defeats. Each loss became more humiliating than the last. Against the Giants in XXI, the Broncos were up 10–9 at halftime, but got trounced in the second half, falling behind, 39–13, before Elway hit Vance Johnson for a consolation, 47-yard touchdown pass in the final minutes.

The next year, after The Fumble by the Browns' Earnest Byner helped Elway's Broncos win their second consecutive AFC Championship, Elway struck quickly, connecting with first-round rookie Ricky Nattiel—one of the famed Three Amigos—for a 56-yard touchdown heave to cap the opening drive of Super Bowl XXII. A short Karlis field goal off the second possession gave Denver a 10–0 lead heading into the second quarter.

At which point the game turned into an unmitigated disaster.

Washington quarterback Doug Williams threw an 80-yard touchdown pass to Ricky Sanders seconds into the second quarter, igniting a 35-point onslaught in a 13-minute span. The Broncos came away with a 42–10 shellacking. Elway played poorly after the first quarter, throwing 3 interceptions.

Two years later, Joe Montana and the San Francisco 49ers obliterated the Broncos, 55–10. Again, Elway pressed to do too much, completing just 10 of 26 for 108 yards, with 2 more interceptions. Suddenly, Elway was dealing with the rap he couldn't win the Big One. He had completed just 46 of 101 passes combined in his first three Super Bowls, with 2 TD passes against 6 interceptions.

It would be nine years later that Elway and the Broncos got another chance at the Super Bowl, this time with Mike Shanahan as head coach, Terrell Davis at running back, and offensive line coach Alex Gibbs with his zone-blocking scheme. Again, Elway dealt with Super Bowl nerves. His Super Bowl XXXII opponents were Reggie White, LeRoy Butler, Brett Favre, and the Green Bay Packers. Thanks to an NFC run of 13 consecutive Super Bowl victories—three of which involved blowouts of the Broncos—the Packers were 11- to 12-point favorites.

Carrying with him the burden of three difficult Super Bowl losses, Elway was only 12 of 23 for 126 yards with an interception in the end zone that erased a great scoring chance. There was an early second-quarter 1-yard touchdown run in which Elway had fullback Howard Griffith wide open in the end zone for an easy flip. But Elway was still a bit uptight and kept it himself for the score.

Late in the third quarter, though, Elway lifted his team with an iconic play that will be forever immortalized in Super Bowl history. The Helicopter. The game was tied, 17–17, with a little more than 2 minutes remaining in the third quarter and the Broncos were facing third-and-6 at the Packers' 12-yard line. Shanahan called a play that supposedly was 100 percent guaranteed to work against a certain coverage. Only when Elway got to the line, the Packers weren't in the coverage Shanahan had emphatically predicted.

From the snap, Elway determined he was going to drop back, then step back up into the pocket and take off. The escape lane opened inside Reggie White's wide pass rush off Elway's right side. As Elway neared the first-down mark, he leaped forward as three Packer defenders converged. All three—linebacker Brian Williams, safety Butler, and another safety, Mike Prior—hit Elway while the quarterback was airborne. Elway spun and landed safely a good 2 yards past the first-down marker.

The play not only set up first and goal from the 4—Davis took it from there, scoring the go-ahead touchdown—the sacrificial effort from a 37-year-old star energized the Broncos.

"He got up and was like, 'Is my helmet on? Am I still in one piece?'" said tight end Shannon Sharpe. "And when he raised his hand, I'm like, 'We're going to win this game. We've got them now.' Because we saw that from *that* guy. So anything less from you was unacceptable."

The Broncos broke their Super Bowl slump by going on to beat the Packers, 31–24. Elway and the Broncos franchise had won the Big One.

Denver was an even better team in 1998, starting 13-0 despite a stretch where Elway was injured and missed four games. The Broncos then waltzed through the postseason, whipping the Dolphins, 38–3, in a second-round playoff game, the Jets, 23–10, in the AFC Championship—Elway's final home game—and then crushing the Atlanta Falcons and Elway's former head coach Dan Reeves, 34–19. It wasn't that close.

A relaxed Elway, 38 years old and all but certain he was playing in the final game of his illustrious career, completed 18 of 29 passes for a whopping 336 yards—of which 80 came on a roll right, heave down the left seam bomb to Rod Smith. An Elway 3-yard touchdown run gave the Broncos an insurmountable 31–6 lead with less than 12 minutes remaining.

For his superb play, Elway was named the Super Bowl XXXIII MVP. Back-to-back Super Bowl titles. What a way to go out.

STARTER

Not only is Elway the Broncos starting quarterback on *The Denver Broncos All-Time All-Stars*, he's the No. 1 player in franchise history. Statistics don't properly measure Elway's greatness. He didn't throw for the highest completion percentage. His TD to INT ratio is down the list among the all-time greats. But Elway had a knack not only for winning, but winning when the game seemed lost.

Down 6 with 2 minutes to go, ball on his own 20, a typical Elway drive might start something like this: three incompletes, fourth-down scramble for a first down. Then two more incompletes, followed by a third-down, 25-yard howitzer from left side to far right side. So he's 1 of 6 passing, but it's now first down at the opponents' 40.

Elway led the Broncos to five Super Bowls. Next is Manning with two. Elway won two Super Bowls. Manning is next with one. This project may be updated 50, 75, 100 years from now. It would be a surprise if Elway isn't still the best player in Broncos history.

John Elway © ERIC LARS BAKKE

OTHERS

Frank Tripucka (1960–1963)

He was the first Broncos quarterback and the first in AFL/
NFL history to surpass 3,000 passing yards in a single season,
which he did in the Broncos' inaugural season of 1960. Because
Tripucka, who threw his first NFL pass in 1949 for the Detroit
Lions, brought such respectability to an otherwise ragtag col-
lection of Broncos in their initial seasons of 1960 through

1963, he was the first player in team history to have his number retired. Tripucka later let Peyton Manning borrow his No. 18 from 2012 to 2015.

But the retired number honored with a banner that hangs at Empower Field at Mile High belongs to Tripucka.

Marlin Briscoe (1968)

Another history-making Broncos quarterback was Briscoe, who in 1968 became pro football's first Black starting quarterback. (Willie Thrower was the first Black QB to play, when he came off the bench for the Chicago Bears in a 1953 game. Fritz Pollard was a quarterback for the Akron Pros as the NFL was formed in 1920, but quarterback was really a running back position in the league's infancy stage.)

Briscoe in his five starts for the Broncos threw for 1,589 yards off just 93 completions—a league-best 17.1 yards per completion—with 14 touchdown passes against 13 interceptions. He also rushed for 308 yards on 7.5 yards per carry and 3 more touchdowns, a dual threat that earned him the nickname "The Magician."

Alas, Broncos coach Lou Saban didn't think the 5-foot-10, 177-pound Briscoe could play NFL quarterback long-term. When Briscoe found out Saban had acquired Pete Liske to become the Broncos QB in 1969, Briscoe asked for, and was granted, his release. He was picked up by the Buffalo Bills, where he became a Pro Bowl, 1,000-yard receiver in 1970 and helped the Miami Dolphins win back-to-back Super Bowls in 1972 and 1973.

The Broncos now have a diversity intern coaching position named after Briscoe.

Charley Johnson (1972–1975)

Another Broncos quarterback who is in the team's Ring of Fame is Charley Johnson. Although a longtime St. Louis Cardinal, Johnson at the then-advanced age of 35 led the Broncos to their first-ever winning season in 1973—the 14th season in franchise history—guiding them to a 7-5-2 record. Johnson went 6-5-1 in 1974 before injuries limited him to just six starts in 1975, his final season. Although other Broncos quarterbacks had far better stats and records and were not elected into the Ring of Fame, delivering the team's first winning season immortalized Johnson.

Jake Plummer (2003–2006)

Only Peyton Manning had a better winning percentage (.789, 45-12) than Plummer's .722 (39-15) as a Broncos starting quarterback. In his four Broncos seasons, Jake The Snake averaged 2,908 passing yards, 18 touchdown passes, and 12 interceptions a season—above-average numbers for the times.

Yet Plummer was foremost a winner. He had a different way of viewing the quarterback role in the ultimate team sport. His teammates loved him in part because he despised being singled out as more important than anyone else. While he could be a polarizing figure to the Broncos fan base and media, no one could deny he was a tremendous athlete who despite his average arm strength relative to the NFL level was an incomparable winner.

His 39-15 record with the Broncos was third best among NFL quarterbacks who played in that four-year period, trailing only Tom Brady and Peyton Manning. That's it. Brady and Manning.

Place Plummer as the fourth-best quarterback in Broncos history, trailing only John Elway, Manning, and Craig Morton.

Tim Tebow (2010–2011)

Just as Briscoe deserves mention for his historical season of 1968, Tebow is worthy of notice for his incredible and improbable 2011 run that captivated the nation. After his first miraculous victory at Miami—a game in which the Broncos were trailing 15–0 with 3 minutes remaining against the Dolphins, only to win, 18–15, in overtime—a fan captured Tebow in a one-kneed prayer stance, right knee supporting his right hand supporting his bowed head—and mimicked it with friends in a social media post.

Never has a social media post gone more viral. Over the next two months, everyone was "Tebowing." Tebow led the Broncos to six straight wins, carrying the team from its 1-4 start when he took over for Kyle Orton as the Broncos starting quarterback, to 8-5. A three-game losing streak to finish the season wasn't enough to prevent the Broncos from winning the AFC West on a tiebreaker.

Although Tebow played poorly in those final three games, he rallied to throw for 316 yards in a first-round playoff upset win against the Pittsburgh Steelers. Tebow's 80-yard touchdown strike to Demaryius Thomas on the first play of overtime is unquestionably the most exhilarating single play in Broncos history.

Tebow only completed 47.3 percent of his passes in his two part-time seasons with the Broncos, but he proved that you don't have to be a great passer—or even an average passer—to be a great quarterback. Tebow's physical brand of quarterback didn't hold up in the Broncos' second-round playoff game at New England, where he suffered a ruptured spleen—one reason why John Elway as general manager decided to pursue a quarterback named Peyton Manning in free agency.

After Manning signed with the Broncos in March 2012, Tebow was traded the next day to the Jets. Tebow never really got a chance to play NFL quarterback again. But his 2011 season will always have its memorable place in the annals of Broncos history.

LEFT TACKLE

Gary Zimmerman doesn't need a rule to stay quiet. A policy among offensive linemen, even if he helped create and administer it, is not why he is a silent type.

Zimmerman was Theodore Roosevelt's kind of left tackle: "Speak softly and carry a big stick." Zim wasn't John Elway's first blindside protector, or his last. But he may have been his favorite, as evidenced by Elway riding his motorcycle up to Sturgis, South Dakota, for the annual summer bike rally that Zimmerman was attending in 1998.

Zimmerman had first retired in 1997 only to change his mind and return in time for the second game of the season. He played four games at right tackle, then moved to his customary left tackle position, where he helped clear the way for the Broncos to win their first-ever Super Bowl and for running back Terrell Davis to romp through the Packers' defense on his way to Super Bowl XXXII MVP.

There was a report after the Elway visit to his good friend in Sturgis that Zimmerman would return again for 1998. But with Zimmerman's shoulder beat up and the desire to became a full-time dad and husband tugging at his heartstrings, not even Elway could bring Zim back for one more year.

Naturally, Zimmerman's official decision to retire came without comment. It was because of Zim that Broncos offensive linemen either stopped talking to the media—or would get fined through the Kangaroo Court.

"Brian Habib and I were with the Vikings and we kind of started it there, and we carried it over," Zimmerman said in the fall of 2022. "I think Alex [Gibbs] made it official and brought the Kangaroo Court along."

The code of silence among Denver offensive linemen lasted a good 20 years until Broncos blockers were finally allowed to speak publicly without fear around the time quarterback Peyton Manning took charge, from 2012 to 2015. It wasn't anything Manning ordered or recommended. It was just that Manning thought his offensive linemen deserved all the credit they could get. And speaking to the media is a good way to get positive publicity.

But again, it wasn't an ad hoc policy that prevented Zimmerman from talking. He just wasn't much of a talker. Nor was another great left tackle in Broncos history, Ryan Clady. The team's first-round draft pick, No. 12 overall, in 2008, Clady was a second-team All-Pro as a rookie, and first-team All-Pro in his second season of 2009.

Clady was highly decorated in his seven playing seasons with the Broncos—three All-Pro selections and four Pro Bowls. But through an incredible stroke of misfortune, he suffered season-ending injuries early in the Broncos' two Super Bowl appearance years of 2013 and 2015.

Clady was as soft-spoken as he was large and agile. Some of his reserve was out of sadness from his mom dying suddenly of a heart attack at 53 years young, when Clady was 13 years old and in eighth grade.

"When Mom died, it was such a shock," he said. "I was kind of quiet and reserved before she died, and then I was even quieter after that. I hardly spoke to anybody. It took me, I would say, at least two years to get over it. I was sad, I guess, is how you would put it."

There were three other left tackles who deserved at least second-level consideration as among the best in Broncos history: Garett Bolles, Claudie Minor, and Dave Studdard. But at the time of this writing, Bolles needed one or two more good seasons to qualify as a finalist. Studdard was a four-year starter on the right side to begin his career before switching to left tackle, where his five-year run essentially ended with a major knee injury in Super Bowl XXII against the Washington Redskins (now Commanders). Minor spent seven of his nine seasons, from 1974 to 1982, at left tackle, blocking primarily for quarterback Craig Morton.

But there were two left tackles who stood out above the rest:

THE CANDIDATES

Gary Zimmerman
Ryan Clady

GARY ZIMMERMAN (1993–1997)

As he has since he retired following the 1997 season, Zimmerman and his wife Lisa spend their time outside Bend, Oregon, managing a 40-acre timber farm.

"I stay pretty busy whether I want to or not," he said in September 2022.

One daughter, Lindsay, works for a biomedical research company in Hawaii. Another daughter, Kelsey, worked several years for the Broncos before moving on to a start-up energy company in Denver in 2021.

Gary Zimmerman began his professional career by playing two years for the Los Angeles Express of the USFL. After playing guard and center at the University of Oregon, Zimmerman became a left tackle when the Express starter suffered an injury. He only played two years for LAX before the USFL folded, but it was just long enough to change his life.

"The USFL was probably the most important piece of my career because I learned how to play tackle," Zimmerman said. "I was never a tackle before. I was a center-guard. So I never played one snap of tackle, and I went to the LA Express and our left tackle got hurt in the first or second game, so I instantly became a left tackle. So I got two years of training in the USFL and that kind of groomed the course for me."

The adjustment between center-guard and tackle?

"It's huge," Zimmerman said. "The center and guard play in a bunch, so a guy has to go straight through you, whereas a tackle, they can go around you, through you, cut inside on you.

"The tackle position, they always say you're on an island, because you're out there by yourself. The tackle is more an angles type of game, whereas center and guard is more about strength. You're firming up the pocket, where the tackle is containing the pocket. There's a huge difference when you're making the change."

After the USFL shut down, Zimmerman was left with his rights owned by the New York Giants. To suggest Zim is a New York kind of guy is like saying *Yellowstone*'s John Dutton is open to real-estate development growth around his ranch in Montana.

Refusing to play in New York, Zimmerman accepted a trade to the Minnesota Vikings. And this is where his Pro Football Hall of Fame career began. He was a four-time Pro Bowler and two-time All-Pro with the Vikings, even if he became increasingly discontented with the media, and then-franchise ownership's penny-pinching ways.

According to Zimmerman, a story following a loss badly took his quote out of context, forcing him to apologize to his teammates and causing him to ban further interviews with the media.

A fine system was established for blockers who were quoted. Even Zimmerman let his guard down while he thought he was retired in 1997.

"I think I might have set the record," Zimmerman said. "The year I held out they fined me eight grand. I don't know if anyone passed me, but I held the record there for a while."

As for the Vikings' ownership consortium, dismay grew into contempt when after the 1992 season, Zimmerman sought to restructure his contract so that he could receive an advance on deferred money, for tax reasons. The ownership's response insulted Zimmerman and he let it be known he would never again play for the Vikings. He wound up getting dealt to the Broncos prior to the last preseason game of 1993.

"I'm grateful I got the opportunity to see the other side of the NFL, where it wasn't about dollars," Zimmerman said. "It was playing for somebody who wanted to win. There's quite a difference between playing for bean counters and guys that want to win. I'm just glad I got a chance to see both sides."

He made the Pro Bowl in four of his five seasons with the Broncos, and three times earned All-Pro honors. He made the NFL's All Decade team in the 1980s, thanks to his work with the Vikings, and in the 1990s, because of his time with the Broncos. Zimmerman is one of only 29 players who have made two All Decade teams.

In 2008 he was inducted into the Pro Football Hall of Fame. Unlike baseball's hall, football doesn't ask its members to enter immortality attached to a certain team. But Zimmerman tells everyone who asks that he's in as a Bronco, not a Viking.

RYAN CLADY (2008–2015)

Entering the 2008 NFL Draft, then Broncos' football operations boss and coach Mike Shanahan zeroed his sights on one of three left tackle prospects for his No. 12 overall pick in the first round—Clady, Chris Williams, and Brandon Albert.

Shanahan picked the correct one in Clady, who came out of Boise State. Williams never did emerge as a left tackle. Albert was a two-time Pro Bowler, but his first honor didn't occur until his sixth season. Clady was not only a four-time Pro Bowler, he and former center Tom Nalen are the only Broncos offensive linemen who were twice named first-team All-Pro.

Although Clady was 6-foot-6, 309 pounds, Shanahan couldn't stop talking about his incredibly nimble feet.

"It was mostly God-given," Clady said. "But also playing basketball growing up in our area, I was always the biggest guy, and I had to guard all these guys smaller than me who were athletic and could really move."

Clady also benefited from long arms, especially as a blind-side pass protector. Clady's arms are 36.75 inches long. By comparison, Cleveland's Joe Thomas, who is widely considered the best left tackle of the 21st century, had 32.5-inch arms—4.25 inches shorter than Clady's reach.

"That's what made him tough was those long arms," DeMarcus Ware, one of the best pass-rushers in NFL history, once said of Clady. "You think you have him beat and—hey now!—he'd reach out and get you."

Clady never missed a game in his first five seasons, a streak of 80 consecutive games, but then came an unfortunate spate of season-ending injuries in the Broncos' two Super Bowl runs of 2013 and 2015. He was sidelined with a foot injury in the second game of Peyton Manning's historic passing season of 2013, and he tore an ACL on the first day of minicamp and missed the Broncos' entire Super Bowl 50 season of 2015.

"Looking at it now that I'm done, I was blessed to go to those Pro Bowls and have the success I had in the league," Clady said. "At the time, it was frustrating. After the first five years it became realistic that I had the potential to be a Hall of Famer, or at least play 12 years or so and be on the cusp of that.

"In the heat of the moment, it was a little disappointing and frustrating with the injuries, but looking back on it now, I couldn't ask for more."

If not for misfortune with injuries, Clady may well have played a few more years, and his retirement would have started a five-year countdown to the Pro Football Hall of Fame.

Although drafted for the zone-blocking scheme, Clady only got to play one year in his preferred system, as Shanahan was fired after the 2008 season. In 2015, when Gary Kubiak brought the zone-blocking system back to Denver, Clady tore his ACL on the first day of organized team activities (OTAs).

Although not ideally suited for the power-gap blocking system preferred by head coaches Josh McDaniels and John Fox, Clady nevertheless helped Willis McGahee, Tim Tebow, and the Broncos lead the NFL in rushing in 2011.

The Broncos tried to bring Clady back on a pay cut in 2016, but he wound up signing with the New York Jets and played nine games before he suffered a shoulder injury that required surgery.

"There was wear and tear in there, and then I really hurt it, like, in the third game [of the 2016 season with the Jets]," Clady said. "When I woke up from surgery and the way it felt, I said, 'Man, I'm done.'"

His career was extraordinary given that he didn't really start playing football until his high school years.

"I played once when I was 10 and I'll be honest with you, I didn't really like it," Clady said. "I wasn't good at it, and I had to lose a bunch of weight just to play. It was brutal. I didn't play again until sophomore [year] in high school, and then it was all she wrote after that."

Clady had another calling in his youth. The oldest of four children, Clady from the time he was in eighth grade had to help his father Ross raise his siblings after his mom Sharon died suddenly of a heart attack at 53 years young.

"It happened fast," Clady said. "I think she definitely would be proud. I think about her a lot in December, around Christmas, and her birthday was the 16th."

Clady was a defensive lineman at Eisenhower High School in Rialto, California, but he played left tackle for coach Dan Hawkins at Boise State.

Clady is tied with Marv Montgomery as the highest-drafted Broncos offensive lineman who played with the team. Chris Hinton was the No. 4 overall selection in the 1983 draft but never played for the Broncos, as he was traded six days later for John Elway.

The highlights of Clady's career with the Broncos?

"One of the best was that first year with Peyton," Clady said, referring to the 2012 season when the Broncos finished with 11 consecutive wins. "It started off kind of rocky, but then that turned out to be a fun year.

"And then playing with Tebow, that was fun, because we weren't supposed to get to the playoffs and then we definitely weren't supposed to beat Pittsburgh. I didn't know the line, but I know we were definitely a big underdog."

The Broncos were 8-point home underdogs in the first round of the 2011-season AFC playoffs but wound up stunning the Steelers in overtime. Not known for his run blocking, Clady proved his all-around talent that season when he helped Tebow and running back Willis McGahee and the Broncos offense lead the NFL in rushing.

"You're going to get a lot better at run blocking when you're doing it 40, 50 times a game," Clady said. "That was one of the better lines we had, and I think that was a big reason Peyton came. We were playing very well that year as an offensive front."

STARTER

There were other fine left tackles, but Zimmerman and Clady were in a class of their own. The one chosen to start for *The Denver Broncos All-Time All-Stars*? We'll let the Pro Football Hall of Fame work as the tiebreaker. Zimmerman's bust is bronzed.

Gary Zimmerman is the Broncos starting left tackle.

OTHERS

Claudie Minor (1974–1982)

A third-round selection out of San Diego State in the 1974 NFL Draft, Minor started the first 98 games over six and a half seasons in his Broncos career, and he missed just four games through his first eight seasons.

He was a nine-year starting tackle for the Broncos—seven at left tackle (1974–1975, 1978–1982) and two at right tackle (1976–1977).

Garett Bolles (2017–2022)

With another year or so, Bolles would have joined Zimmerman and Clady as a finalist for all-time starting left tackle. A first-round pick, No. 20 overall, out of Utah in the 2017 NFL Draft, Bolles was an immediate starter but struggled mightily through his first three seasons. He persevered, though, and in 2020 was a second-team All-Pro and received a four-year, $68 million contract extension that made him the highest-paid offensive lineman in Broncos history.

Through his first five seasons, Bolles started 77 of a possible 81 games at left tackle.

Dave Studdard (1979–1988)

Here was Elway's first blindside protector. Selected in the ninth round out of Texas in the 1978 draft by the Baltimore Colts, he was waived following his rookie training camp, sat out a year, and signed the following 1979 season with the Broncos. Where he instantly became a starter at right tackle. After four years of starting on the right side as a tackle and guard, Studdard became the Broncos starting left tackle in 1983, Elway's rookie year. He was a mainstay on the left side until suffering a torn ACL in Super Bowl XXII following the 1988 season. A good athlete, Studdard caught four passes in his career, two for touchdowns.

Jim Perkins (1962–1964)

Drafted out of the University of Colorado by both the NFL Philadelphia Eagles in the 7th round and in the 21st round by the AFL Broncos, Perkins started his first three seasons for the Broncos at left tackle. Those turned out to be his only three seasons. He suffered a knee injury that bothered him in the 1965 training camp, a time when injuries drew no mercy from football coaches. A realtor in the off-season, he retired from football in 1965 and went on to become a successful businessman and family man.

Sam Brunelli (1966–1971)

A three-year letterman and mathematics and physical education major at Northern Colorado, Brunelli was a teacher for one year at Greeley West High School, then asked the Broncos for a tryout prior to the 1966 season. He spent most of that year on the taxi squad, but played in the final two games, then became a four-year starter at left tackle from 1967 through 1970. A knee injury in the final game of 1970 contributed to his move to right guard, but he suffered a broken leg in game 5 of the 1971 season.

Tony Jones (1997–2000)

Jones played eight years at tackle for the Cleveland Browns, then one year for the Baltimore Ravens before the Broncos acquired him prior to the 1997 season for a second-round draft pick. Initially, Jones was to play left tackle in place of the retired Gary Zimmerman. When Zimmerman returned, Jones was shifted to right tackle. Zimmerman retired for good after the Broncos' Super Bowl XXXII title in 1997, prompting Jones's shift back to left tackle for the 1998 season, Elway's last, when the Broncos went back-to-back. Jones was named to the Pro Bowl that year and started two more years at left tackle. He was cut for salary-cap reasons prior to the 2001 season after 13 years in the NFL.

Matt Lepsis (1998–2007)

A former Colorado Buffaloes' tight end, Lepsis started five seasons at right tackle, then four seasons at left tackle, from 2004 through 2007. His best season was 2005, when he helped quarterback Jake Plummer and the running back duo of Mike Anderson and Tatum Bell push the Broncos to a 13-3 regular-season record, second-round playoff win against New England and a home AFC Championship Game. He retired the day after the 2007 season, setting up the Broncos to select Ryan Clady with their first-round draft pick a few months later.

LEFT GUARD

There are two left guards who became part of John Elway lore.

And in 1983, Elway's rookie year, those two guards, Keith Bishop and Tom Glassic, played messenger guard, the one who shuttled the plays in from coach Dan Reeves to the huddle.

Glassic had been the Broncos starting left guard for seven seasons, from 1976 to 1982, before he was nudged out by Bishop for the beginning of the 1983 season. But in game 13 at San Diego's Jack Murphy Stadium on November 27, 1983, it was Glassic who was in at left guard when he felt a tap on his behind.

It was Elway. The not-yet-superstar rookie quarterback was so flustered that day from the three interceptions he'd thrown and the four sacks he couldn't escape in a 31–7 loss to the Chargers that he'd accidentally and absentmindedly lined up behind Glassic at left guard. Glassic reached back and tapped Elway and told him about his mistake. Elway nonchalantly stepped over to center Bill Bryan, but the embarrassment didn't escape the cameras or the press.

Elway was simply too enormous as one of the most-hyped, can't-miss quarterbacks to ever come into the league. And in the 1986 AFC Championship Game at Cleveland, Elway began to live up to his billing.

This was the moment: Bishop's turn to become part of the Elway legend.

Browns quarterback Bernie Kosar had thrown a 48-yard touchdown pass to receiver Brian Brennan with less than 6 minutes in regulation to give home-team Cleveland a 20–13 lead. Winner goes to the Super Bowl. When Broncos returner Ken Bell muffed the kickoff, leaving Elway and the offense to start at their own 2-yard line, with 5 minutes, 32 seconds remaining, visiting Denver appeared doomed.

"We got 'em right where we want 'em," Bishop said in the huddle during a lengthy TV timeout. At least that was the cleaned-up version that first hit the press. The full, unfiltered version of Bishop's inspirational message included a bit more language.

"We're in the huddle, we're waiting, and we're looking at the Browns," Bishop said 21 years later for the book *50 Greatest Players in Denver Broncos History*. "And several of the Browns were good friends of mine. They're all standing in their defensive huddle and they're all laughing. And I said, "[Bleep] them [bleep, bleeps], we've got those [bleeps] right where we want them."

Perhaps not the first time a famous quote was cleaned up for posterity.

"They left some words out of it," Bishop said.

Thus started The Drive. Fifteen plays and nearly 5 minutes later, Elway finished the 98-yard march with a touchdown pass to Mark Jackson, tying the game, 20–20. A Rich Karlis field goal in overtime won it, and Elway was going to his first of five Super Bowls.

"And if we hadn't driven and scored, nobody would have heard anything about it," Bishop said about his tension-breaking message. "Then you go back and watch that damn thing and you watch some of the throws he made. And the toughness. The hits he would take. I mean, it was cold, you're tired, and he takes hits like that and he keeps on keeping on."

Glassic was the starting left guard in the Broncos' first Super Bowl appearance, to cap the Orange Crush season of 1977. Bishop played in three Super Bowls—1986, '87, and '89—all losses. Mark Schlereth was the starting left guard in the Broncos' first two Super Bowl victories to cap the 1997 and 1998 seasons.

A fourth left guard, Ben Hamilton, never played on a Broncos team that reached the Super Bowl. All he did was help block for 1,000-yard rushers.

Bishop, Schlereth, Glassic, and Hamilton are the four players under consideration for the Broncos' all-time starting left guard.

Bishop played 8 of his 10 seasons with the Broncos at left guard, starting 7. Glassic played 8 seasons at left guard for the Broncos, starting 7. Schlereth played and started 6 seasons at left guard for the Broncos. Hamilton spent 9 seasons with Broncos, playing and starting in 7 of them.

It's difficult to compare because Bishop and Glassic played in the more physical gap-blocking scheme while Schlereth and Hamilton were in the more athletic, zone-blocking scheme. But this book isn't about schemes or systems. It's about the players. The starter at each position—in this case, the left guard position—for *The Denver Broncos All-Time All-Stars.*

THE CANDIDATES

Keith Bishop
Mark Schlereth
Tom Glassic
Ben Hamilton

KEITH BISHOP (1980–1989)
Drafted in the sixth round out of Baylor in 1980, Bishop played quite a bit on special teams and as a backup right guard and center his rookie season. He might have been good enough to start, but his old-school offensive line coach, Whitey Dovell, didn't believe in starting rookies.

The next year, in the first preseason game, Bishop suffered a ruptured peroneus tendon in the bottom of his right foot, ending his second season of 1981 before it began.

He returned in 1982 as a left guard.

"Which I enjoyed more," Bishop said. "For a right-handed quarterback it's the blind side, a little more responsibility for doing things. So it made the position a little more fun."

He became a full-time starter to start the 1983 season—Elway's rookie year—and Bishop stayed there until injuries forced him to part-time duty late in his final season of 1989.

"Bish was the more physical left guard," said Elway, who played with three of the finalists—Bishop, Schlereth, and Glassic. "He was more physical and he was the leader of that offensive line. Bish is such a nice guy, but he was a tough son of a gun between the lines."

The 1986 season may have been Bishop's best season professionally—his first Pro Bowl and the Broncos' first Super Bowl appearance of the Elway era—but it was also one of his most difficult years personally. He lost both of his parents that year, two months apart.

"That's when all my hair went gray and started falling out," Bishop said. "John really helped me through that."

And Bishop was always there for Elway. A captain for seven consecutive seasons and a Pro Bowler again in 1987, Bishop knew after the Broncos had reached their third Super Bowl in four years in 1989 that his body couldn't hold up anymore. He went back to Baylor and became a full-time, 33-year-old student over two semesters. He took the necessary 27 credit hours he needed to graduate with a degree in education, which allowed him to take a job as a field agent for the Drug Enforcement Agency.

In 2012, Bishop retired from his second career and started a third: vice president of security for the Broncos. He had a connection. Elway was entering his second season as the Broncos general manager. Bishop was hired to oversee the team's entire security group. His job is to work with local, state, and federal law enforcement as well as fire departments, emergency response personnel, military, and the intelligence community to help safeguard the organization.

After seven years of protecting Elway on the football field, Bishop later spent nine more years, from 2012 to 2020, serving as Elway's bodyguard on game days.

Elway retired as GM following the 2020 season, but Bishop remained head of Broncos security at the time of this writing, which was after the 2022 season.

MARK SCHLERETH (1996–2000)
Nicknamed "Stink," Schlereth was an accomplished offensive lineman before he got to Denver, as he was six-year starting right guard for Washington's second wave of Hogs. During his time in Washington, Schlereth was a Pro Bowler and Super Bowl champion in 1991.

A free agent in 1995, Schlereth signed a three-year, $2.4 million deal with the Broncos primarily because they were the only team that didn't flunk him on his physical exam. By then, he had undergone 9 of his 20 knee surgeries and had overcome a bout of Guillain-Barré syndrome.

The Bears and Falcons brought Schlereth in for a visit but didn't pass him on the physicals. The Broncos knew what they were getting—a knee-ravaged guard who could still play football. With the Broncos, Schlereth played in 89 of a possible 104 games, even though he underwent 11 more knee surgeries in his six years in Denver, and in all had 29 surgeries during his career.

"It got to where it was a surgery of the week for him," Elway said. "Mark was a real smart player. He was a little more athletic, and he was an intelligent player who knew the techniques on how to square up a defensive tackle."

The highlights for Schlereth were the 1997 and 1998 seasons, when the Broncos won back-to-back Super Bowls on the strength of their zone-blocking scheme that made a postseason hero of running back Terrell Davis. Schlereth was a Pro Bowler for a second time in 1998, the year Davis rushed for 2,008 yards and was the NFL's MVP.

In the next two seasons, Schlereth and the Broncos offensive line helped make a 1,159-yard rusher out of rookie Olandis Gary, who filled in for the injured Davis starting in game 5 of the 1999 season, and a 1,483-yard rusher out of 27-year-old rookie Mike Anderson, who filled in for the injured Gary in game 2 of the 2000 season.

Listed as a 278-pound guard when he first arrived in Denver in 1995, Schlereth had bulked up to 287 during the Super Bowl years—still small by today's 300-pound minimum standards.

Schlereth retired as a player in the spring of 2001 and has since built a mini empire as an NFL analyst, a green chili distributor, a Denver sports talk radio host, husband to Lisa, and father of three—actress Alexandria, model Avi, and former major-league pitcher Daniel.

TOM GLASSIC (1976–1983)

It's difficult to compare Bishop and Schlereth because of the differing systems they played in. And it's difficult to compare Glassic to either of those two guards because of eras. Glassic graduated from the University of Virginia as a Dean's List English major and a 254-pound guard.

Good enough for the Broncos, who selected him in the first round of the 1976 NFL Draft, No. 15 overall. An extremely smart, quick, and technically sound player, Glassic started all 98 games, including the postseason, that he played in through his first seven seasons with the Broncos. He then shuffled in plays with Bishop in his final season of 1983.

For a three- or four-year period Glassic was considered one of the NFL's best pulling guards, although he never made a Pro Bowl in an era that included such future Hall of Fame left guards as Gene Upshaw, John Hannah, and multiyear Hall of Fame finalist Bob Kuechenberg.

BEN HAMILTON (2002–2006, 2008–2009)

A fourth-round draft pick out of Minnesota, Hamilton was essentially redshirted his rookie season of 2001, as he was inactive for all 16 games. Another key blocker in the zone scheme, Hamilton then started 84 consecutive games, including the postseason, over the five-year stretch from 2002 to 2006. The streak began when he started 7 games at left guard, then became the starting center in place of the injured Tom Nalen for the final 9 games.

Hamilton went back to left guard in 2003 and stayed there until a serious concussion issue forced him to miss the entire 2007 season. He returned and played for two more years, starting 104 games in all for the Broncos, 95 at left guard, before moving on to play one more season with the Seattle Seahawks in 2010.

During his seven years as the Broncos left guard, Hamilton blocked for four different running backs, who rushed, for a combined five 1,000-yard seasons—Clinton Portis in 2002–2003, Reuben Droughns in 2004, Mike Anderson in 2005, and Tatum Bell in 2006—and three decent quarterbacks in Jake Plummer, Jay Cutler, and Kyle Orton.

After his playing career, Hamilton went to the University of Denver to get his master's degree in curriculum and instruction, then started his teaching career in the mathematics department at Valor Christian High School (Highlands Ranch, Colorado) in 2013. Hamilton also coached football for Valor under head coach Ed McCaffrey, and in 2022 became offensive line coach at Ponderosa High School in Parker, Colorado.

STARTER

Elway decided the close battle between Bishop and Schlereth. Bishop played longer for the Broncos than Schlereth and had one more Pro Bowl (two to one). Interestingly, the Broncos are still very much part of both of their lives—Bishop works and protects the team; Schlereth talks about the team on a daily basis on 104.3 The Fan.

OTHERS

Zane Beadles (2010–2013)

Terrific in space as a pulling left guard, Beadles was the Broncos' second-round selection after Demaryius Thomas and Tim Tebow in the 2010 draft. Beadles never missed a game in his four seasons with the Broncos, and helped protect Peyton Manning during his record-setting passing season of 2013. Manning threw for 55 touchdown passes and 5,577 yards that season, records that still stand. The Broncos won the AFC Championship but got blown out for a fifth time in the Super Bowl, this time by Seattle.

Larron Jackson (1971–1974)

For his time, Jackson was a large left guard at 6-foot-3, 270 pounds, but he was quick for his size. He started 44 games in four seasons for the Broncos, occasionally kicking out to left tackle to fill in for the injured.

Dalton Risner (2019–2022)

From the rural Colorado town of Wiggins, Risner was a right tackle at Kansas State who the Broncos took in the second round of the 2019 draft, immediately converting him to their starting left guard. He missed just four starts in his four years with his home-state team before the Broncos allowed him to hit free agency in March 2023.

George Goeddeke (1967–1971)

A starting center at Notre Dame, Goeddeke started five games at left guard for the Broncos as a rookie in 1967. In 1968 he blocked for Marlin "The Magician" Briscoe, the first Black starting quarterback in AFL history, and The Franchise, Floyd Little, at running back. Goeddeke was an AFL All-Star in 1969. He became the Broncos starting center in 1971, then suffered an injury that forced him to miss most of his final season of 1972.

CENTER

When first considering the Broncos' all-time starting center, it seemed futile to consider any candidate other than Tom Nalen.

Not only is Nalen the undisputed best center in Broncos history, he is their all-time best offensive lineman, period. True, Gary Zimmerman is a Hall of Famer and former Broncos offensive lineman. But Nalen was more decorated with Pro Bowls and All-Pros while wearing the orange and blue for his entire 14-season career. Zimmerman was a Bronco for five seasons.

But in 2019, when the NFL was celebrating its 100th season, the Broncos came up with their Top 100 players, and three bona fide centers made the list: Nalen, Billy Bryan, and Larry Kaminski. Two other Top 100ers, Keith Bishop and Jerry Sturm, played more guard than center.

If Bryan and Kaminski joined Nalen among the top 100 Broncos, their case for all-time starting center deserves to be told.

THE CANDIDATES

Billy Bryan
Larry Kaminski
Tom Nalen

BILLY BRYAN (1977–1988)
A fourth-round draft pick out of Duke in 1977, Bryan became the Broncos starting center from the first game of his second season in 1978, and remained the snapper for Craig Morton and

then John Elway through the 1988 season. Bryan started 151 of his 153 career games as a 255-pound center. He was scheduled to start for a 12th consecutive season in 1989 when he suffered a season-ending torn ACL during a training camp practice in early August. It was his second season-ending knee injury in three years, and in the spring of 1990 Bryan decided to retire.

One factor was his replacement, Keith Kartz, who proved to Bryan himself during the 1989 season that the Broncos were in good hands.

"I wanted to come back at first, but seeing Keith have a super year changed my mind," Bryan told the Colorado Springs *Gazette Telegraph* at the time of his retirement. "I was in a lot longer than I anticipated. It's been a lot of good years. I want to go out with a smile. I've got nothing but good memories. I always played when I was called."

LARRY KAMINSKI (1966–1973)

Even though he was quarterback Bob Griese's starting center for three years at Purdue, and was all–Big Ten as a senior, Kaminski went undrafted in 1966—no doubt because at 240 pounds, he was considered too small even for the late 1960s. After his college football career, Kaminski was going to use his degree in industrial management to start a business career when Broncos coaches Mac Speedie and Ray Malavasi called to give him a chance to make the team.

Kaminski's smarts and agility made him the Broncos starting center from game 1 of his 1966 rookie season, and he stayed the team's starting center more or less for eight seasons. Kaminski played in the AFL All-Star Game after the 1967 season.

"The thing that I'm really proud of is that I made it eight years and I had a lot of coaches," Kaminski told his hometown Steamboat Springs newspaper, the *Steamboat Pilot & Today*, after he was included among the Broncos' Top 100 players in 2019. "I had a lot of coaches and every coach that came in thought I was too small, and they brought in somebody bigger. But every year, I managed to make the starting lineup."

After his playing days, Kaminski did establish a business career, owning an Anheuser-Busch distributorship which he eventually turned into a family business with his two sons. Kaminski and his wife settled in Steamboat Springs, where Larry also ran a fish business for a time.

TOM NALEN (1995–2007)

A seventh-round draft pick out of Boston College in 1994, Nalen spent the first half of his rookie season on the Broncos practice squad. He was then called up to the active roster and started game 9 at left guard in place of an injured player. He finished out the year as a backup before becoming the starting center from the first game of 1995 until he tore his right biceps in game 5 of the 2007 season, which turned out to be the final game of his career.

In those 13 seasons, Nalen helped the Broncos amass the most rushing yards (29,131) and most individual 100-yard games (93) while tying for the most individual 1,000-yard seasons (11) in the NFL. Whether it was Terrell Davis (four times), Olandis Gary, Mike Anderson (twice), Reuben Droughns, Clinton Portis (twice), or Tatum Bell, Broncos running backs consistently rushed for 1,000-yard seasons thanks to lanes opened by the Nalen-anchored offensive line.

And there is more evidence that it was Nalen who was at the center of all of that Broncos rushing success. The Broncos did not have a 1,000-yard rusher in the three seasons before Nalen became their starting center. And they did not have a 1,000-yard rusher in the 2007 season in which Nalen went down with a torn right biceps in game 5. Nor in the five seasons after did the Broncos have a 1,000-yard rusher.

Among Broncos offensive linemen, Nalen earned the most Pro Bowl berths with five, followed by Ryan Clady's four, Gary Zimmerman's three, Keith Bishop's two, and several with one.

Although he has received little support for the Pro Football Hall of Fame at the time of this writing, Nalen was inducted into the Broncos Ring of Fame in his first year of eligibility, in 2013. Besides his franchise-most five Pro Bowls among blockers, Nalen was also a first-team All-Pro in 2000 and 2003—when he was also selected as the NFL's Offensive Lineman of the Year—and a second-team All-Pro in 2002.

The signature moment for Nalen was Super Bowl XXXII, the first of Denver's back-to-back world championships. The Broncos had the lightest offensive line in the NFL with an average of 290.2 pounds, and Nalen was the lightest of them all, at 286.

The Broncos had been blown out in their previous four Super Bowls, and the expectation was that their lighter-sized line would get blown out again by the defending Super Bowl–champion Green Bay Packers, who were 12-point favorites largely because defensive end Reggie White and nose tackle Gilbert Brown were considered mismatches.

White is arguably the best defensive end in NFL history. Brown was one of the NFL's most popular players in 1997, in a manner similar to the likability William "The Refrigerator" Perry had in 1985. Brown was listed at 345 pounds, but he was probably closer to 375.

On nearly every snap, Brown was lined up directly across from Nalen.

White was held to one tackle. Nalen abused Brown through techniques and angles. Brown wore down into a fatigued tub of non-factor in the fourth quarter.

Running back Terrell Davis rushed for 157 yards and 3 touchdowns off 30 carries, and was the Super Bowl MVP as the Broncos upset the Packers, 31–24.

Yet Nalen never did get the credit he deserved nationally because of the belief the sum of the Broncos' zone-blocking system was greater than its individual parts. As someone who always seems to be conflicted anyway, Nalen both understands those who credit the system in one sense but believe it was an overrated factor in the team's success in another.

"[Offensive line coach] Alex Gibbs was here and didn't mind the fact that I was 280 pounds," Nalen said. "I know a lot of teams—you look at Dallas at that time—I wouldn't have been able to play for that team. I fit the ideology of the coaching staff.

"The whole zone-blocking thing is kind of crazy to me, because every team has run it. Obviously Alex had a big imprint on how many times we'd run it during the game, but to be honest, we ran the same play over and over until teams stopped it. It just happened to be a zone play."

STARTER

Tom Nalen, in one of the easier decisions for this project.

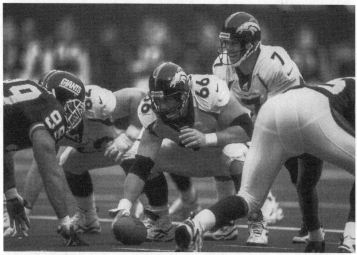

Tom Nalen (#66) © ERIC LARS BAKKE

OTHERS

Keith Kartz (1989–1993)

Undrafted out of Cal in 1986, Kartz caught on with the Broncos replacement team in 1987 and stayed on as a backup tackle once the work stoppage ended. When left tackle Dave Studdard went down with a knee injury during Super Bowl XXII, Kartz filled in.

Kartz then replaced the injured Stefan Humphries for 12 starts at right guard in 1988, before replacing the injured Bryan at center for all 19 games, counting 3 in the postseason, in 1989.

He remained the Broncos starting center until an accident during a Broncos–sponsored charity ski event in February 1994 left him with a completely torn medial collateral ligament and posterior collateral ligament to his right knee. It was initially reported that Kartz would miss five months and return in time for training camp, but he wound up having five operations on the right knee, missed the entire 1994 season, and was cut in 1995, replaced by an up-and-coming center named Tom Nalen.

Matt Paradis (2015–2018)

A sixth-round draft choice out of Boise State in 2014, Paradis spent his rookie year on the Broncos practice squad, then began an Iron Man streak of making every snap for 57 consecutive games over three and a half seasons before he suffered a broken fibula that ended his "contract year" of 2018.

In his first season as a starting center, Paradis snapped to Peyton Manning through a 7-2 start, then Brock Osweiler over a 5-2 run to finish the regular season, then to Manning again during the Broncos' 3-0 postseason march to winning Super Bowl 50.

Paradis dealt with hip injuries that kept him from practicing—but never missing a game snap—in 2016, toughness that earned him the team's Ed Block Courage Award.

After the 2018 season, Paradis was let go to free agency where he signed a three-year, $27 million contract with

Carolina. He played out that contract, although he again suffered a season-ending injury in game 9 of 2021, which was the last game of his career.

Jerry Sturm (1961–1966)

After two years of playing up front for Calgary in the Canadian Football League, Sturm brought his versatility to Denver in 1961. He was named to the AFL All-Star team in 1964 as a center and in 1966 as a left guard. He also played offensive tackle and fullback with the Broncos. That's right, in 1961, Sturm had 8 carries for 31 yards and added 2 receptions.

As much as his football prowess, Sturm drew attention for his virtue that helped stymie a game-fixing scheme.

While playing for the Houston Oilers in 1971, Sturm was approached by a former Broncos player who offered a $10,000 bribe if the center would mess up snaps on kicks and to the quarterback in a December 1971 game against the Pittsburgh Steelers.

Sturm turned in the bribe offer to Houston head coach Ed Hughes, who went to the NFL, who went to the FBI.

Upon retirement, Sturm owned and operated "The South" restaurant, a popular Mexican-American eatery, in Englewood, and three other Denver-area establishments.

And yet, Sturm, who died in 2020 at age 83, had other priorities.

"He golfed every day of his life," said his son Brett. "He always said golf was number one, he told my mom she was number two [he laughed], and the restaurant was number three. We used to always joke about that."

Jerry Sturm was a scratch golfer and even in his advanced years he kept his handicap below a five until health problems forced him to stop playing. Brett grew up on a house sitting just off the second hole at the Columbine Country Club.

"He was trying to make the Tour for a while after his NFL career," Brett said. "Everyone who knew him knew he loved his Coors Light and he loved his golf."

Brett said his dad counted former NFL quarterback Billy Kilmer as his best friend. Former Broncos teammates Goose Gonsoulin and Bud McFadin were also close friends. Sturm also golfed many rounds with former Broncos quarterbacks John Elway and Gary Kubiak over the years.

Jerry Sturm and his wife Deborah were together 45 years, married for 43. They had one son, Brett, who played at Heritage High School and San Diego State University from 2002 to 2006. Brett went to training camps with Seattle and Tampa Bay and had tryouts with Houston and the Broncos.

"I tried to follow [in] my father's footsteps to the NFL, but I was in and out of four NFL camps and kept getting cut," Brett said. "Pops was the one who had the amazing career."

Bobby Maples (1972–1978)

Now here was an athlete. Maples was an all-conference quarterback his freshman year at Baylor, then switched to linebacker as a sophomore. He was drafted as a linebacker in 1965 by the Houston Oilers in the fourth round, then switched to center and long snapper in his second season of 1966.

A six-year starter for the Oilers, Maples was claimed off waivers by the Pittsburgh Steelers in 1971, played sparingly, then was traded to the Broncos prior to the 1972 season. Primarily a long snapper his first season in Denver, Maples was the Broncos' full-time starting center from 1973 to 1976, and long-snapped in 1977–1978, although he did start five games at center in his final season of 1978.

A year after he retired he was diagnosed with Hodgkin's disease and eventually passed away from complications of the disease in 1991, at the age of 48.

RIGHT GUARD

If you bothered to rank the starting football positions 1 through 22 in terms of notoriety and acclaim, right guard might come in No. 22. Jerry Kramer had to write best-selling autobiographies—and throw the most famous block in NFL history—to bring some attention to the right guard position.

Otherwise, there are 21 other positions, offense and defense, that receive more recognition.

The offensive tackle positions receive the spotlight for the way they block the opponent's best pass-rushers. The center gets notice for his smarts as the quarterback of the offensive line. The left guard gets to pull out in space and occasionally receives the announcer's praise for his athleticism on screens and trap plays.

The right guard is generally a down-and-dirty mauler buried inside a scrum.

The Broncos have had a few unsung standouts at the position. But guess how many Broncos right guards have been named to the AFL All-Star, Pro Bowl, or All-Pro teams?

One. Louis Vasquez, in 2013. And he only played three seasons for the Broncos, two and a half at right guard.

Otherwise, there have been plenty of Broncos left guards (Keith Bishop, Jerry Sturm, Ken Adamson, Mark Schlereth, Zane Beadles), centers (Tom Nalen, Sturm, Casey Wiegmann, Larry Kaminski), and tackles (Eldon Danenhauer, Gary Zimmerman, Ryan Clady, Tony Jones, Mike Current) who received individual honors.

But only Vasquez received a Pro Bowl and All-Pro honor among right guards, and that was just once, in 2013, when the Broncos recorded the best offensive season in NFL history, scoring 606 points (37.9 per game).

That doesn't mean there weren't multiple candidates to choose from for the honor of starting right guard on *The Denver Broncos All-Time All-Stars*.

THE CANDIDATES

Paul Howard
Brian Habib
Dan Neil

PAUL HOWARD (1973–1986)

Howard's 14 seasons with the Broncos are tied for fourth all-time among Broncos players, behind only John Elway (16), Jason Elam (15), and Tom Nalen (15). Howard's 187 games played rank fifth in Broncos history, behind only Elway, Elam, Nalen, and Tom Jackson. All of those men but Howard are in the Broncos Ring of Fame.

Howard should have had more than 147 starts, but he was never a favorite, to put it mildly, of head coach Dan Reeves.

"Paul was the kind of guy, he loved to tie one on, on Thursday night," said Dave Studdard, who was mostly a Broncos offensive tackle starter in the 1980s. "He'd sleep in on Friday and come to practice on Saturday. He did that a couple times. And Dan [Reeves] would say, 'We're going to let you guys decide if he should play or not.'

"We were like, 'Are you kidding me? Are you stupid?'"

Of course, Howard's teammates wanted to go to battle with him when it mattered most, which was game day.

"Paul would tell us, 'You know I do this every once in a while, but I'm the kind of guy who is going to kick the [bleep] out of everybody on Sunday,'" Studdard said. "And he did. He'd get a game ball—he'd get, like, five of them after he came from drinking, and on Sunday he'd beat the snot out of everybody."

It was a different time. Reeves didn't dare cut Howard. Mad as Reeves would get at his right guard, much as he threatened him with his job, Howard was simply too good of a right guard—honor snubs be darned—to let him go.

"He was strong as a bull for one thing," Studdard said.

So massively strong that Howard's nickname was Bunsy, short for Paul Bunyan.

Studdard was usually a tackle, but one year, in the strike-shortened season of 1982, Studdard started all nine games at right guard only to be replaced by Howard, who played the second half of all nine games at right guard. Again, Reeves thought he was punishing Howard.

"Paul and I would talk about it, how it was the easiest season either one of us [had] had on our bodies," Studdard said. "One half of nine games."

Howard was once sucker-punched below the belt by the Steelers' Mean Joe Greene in the 1977 AFC Divisional Game. The blow was not only below the belt but well after the play. Broncos coach Red Miller chewed out Steelers head coach Chuck Noll after the game.

The Broncos beat the Steelers that day to advance to the AFC Conference Championship, where they beat the Raiders to advance to the franchise's first-ever Super Bowl.

Howard, who passed away in December 2020 at age 70, started his last game for the Broncos in the 1986-season play-offs, a second-round win against New England. But in the final three postseason games that year, including a Super Bowl XXI loss to the New York Giants, Reeves finally benched Howard for Mark Cooper. A second-round draft pick in 1983, Cooper essentially played behind Howard for four seasons before Reeves gave the up-and-comer his chance.

Howard was 36 and beat-up and called it good.

DAN NEIL (1997–2004)

A *Parade* All-American high school selection from Cypress Creek, Texas, Neil started four years for the Texas Longhorns, then became the Broncos' third-round draft pick in 1997. He played in only three games as a rookie, mostly on special teams, as groin surgery late in training camp, and veteran Brian Habib, kept Neil inactive or sidelined through the Broncos' first Super Bowl championship season.

Neil then started all but two games over the next five seasons, beginning with the Broncos' Super Bowl XXXIII championship team, to cap the 1998 season. Neil would start two more seasons in 2003–2004 before injuries beat him down. He had nine surgeries on his left knee alone during his career.

Neil and center Tom Nalen, who both played at around 285 pounds, were mainstays on the Broncos' vaunted zone- and cut-blocking offensive line that cleared the way for the likes of Terrell Davis, Olandis Gary, Mike Anderson, Clinton Portis, and Reuben Droughns to have 1,000-yard seasons.

A few years after football, Neil ran for the Texas House of Representatives as a Republican only to lose by four votes to the Democratic incumbent.

BRIAN HABIB (1993–1997)

After four seasons as Gary Zimmerman's teammate with the Minnesota Vikings, Habib signed with the Broncos as a free agent and became Zimmerman's teammate for five more years in Denver. Zimmerman says it was Habib who started the Denver offensive linemen's policy of not talking to the media, as Habib brought his no-talk stance over from his Vikings' days. Zimmerman gladly partnered with his good friend Habib to shut out the media.

Habib started 74 consecutive games over his first four and a half seasons with the Broncos, missed 2 games in the midst of the 1997 season, then returned to start 10 more to finish that year, including all 4 postseason games that led to the Super Bowl XXXII championship.

Habib was instrumental in helping to steamroll the Packers' 345-pound (cough, cough!) defensive tackle Gilbert Brown in Super Bowl XXXII, a performance that helped running back Terrell Davis capture the Super Bowl MVP award.

Habib was the largest of the Broncos' offensive linemen at 6-foot-7, 293 pounds (Zimmerman, the left tackle, was 6-6, 294) for a front that otherwise was considered the smallest in the NFL. That Habib could move in the zone-blocking system despite his size was a testament to his athleticism, which helped him become a high school state record holder in swimming, as well as football and basketball.

With third-round rookie Dan Neil behind him, Habib was allowed to become a free agent after the 1997 season, and he wound up starting two more years for the Seattle Seahawks.

STARTER
Paul Howard. Hard to beat a 13-year starter who was always dependable on game days, if not always the Friday before.

OTHERS

Chris Kuper (2008–2012)
Had it not been for a career-ruining dislocated ankle in the final game of the 2011 season, Kuper may have eventually become the best right guard in Broncos history. He

was certainly among the most talented. Selected in the fifth round of the 2006 draft that was one of the best in franchise history—quarterback Jay Cutler went in the first round, tight end Tony Scheffler in the second, and receiver Brandon Marshall and pass-rusher Elvis Dumervil were selected in the fourth—Kuper was essentially redshirted his rookie year, as all Broncos' offensive linemen were during that time.

Kuper then played in all games, starting the final 11, at left guard in 2007. He then moved to right guard in 2008, where he began a four-year run of starting all but two games. He helped quarterback Kyle Orton throw for 3,600-plus yards and 20-plus touchdowns in both 2009 and 2010, then shifted styles to help the Broncos lead the NFL in rushing behind Tim Tebow and Willis McGahee in 2011.

After his gruesome ankle injury, Kuper played sparingly in 2012–2013, and even made it back to the starting lineup on occasion, but the discomfort never allowed him to regain form. Upon retirement, he quickly got into coaching, starting at the bottom with the Miami Dolphins before becoming the Broncos assistant offensive line coach for three years. In 2022, Kuper became the head offensive line coach for the Minnesota Vikings, who went 13-4 in his first year.

Louis Vasquez (2013–2015)

A four-year starter for the San Diego Chargers, Vasquez became a free agent and signed a four-year, $23.5 million deal with the Broncos. A large, powerful blocker at 6-foot-4, 330 pounds, Vasquez was an immediate success in Denver as he was named first-team All-Pro in 2013, when Peyton Manning set the single-season passing records for touchdowns (55) and yards (5,477). Those records, as well as the Broncos' 606 points scored, were still standing through the 2022 season, even though the NFL expanded its season from 16 to 17 games beginning in 2021.

After 2013, Vasquez was occasionally moved out to right tackle as the team continued to struggle to fill the position. After helping the Broncos reach Super Bowl XLVIII in 2013, Vasquez started on the Broncos' Super Bowl 50 winning team, even though his power-blocking style wasn't a great fit once coach Gary Kubiak brought the zone-blocking system back to Denver.

Battered more than he let on, Vasquez was released a month after the Broncos' Super Bowl 50 triumph, and he retired without fanfare at age 29 for health and family reasons.

Bob "Spud" McCullough (1962, 1964–1965)

A two-time high school All-American from Helena, Montana, and a starting guard and linebacker on the Colorado Buffaloes' Big Eight Conference Championship team in 1961, McCullough was considered a long shot to make the Broncos as an undrafted rookie linebacker in 1962. But during a preseason drill, the Broncos offensive line coach, Jim Martin, liked what he saw from McCullough and brought him over to the offensive side of the ball.

McCullough started all 14 games as a 6-foot-2, 230-pound rookie right guard in 1962, switched to become the starting left guard in 1963, before returning to starting right guard for the 1964 and 1965 seasons, when he got his weight up to about 250.

After retiring, McCullough finished his college degree in marketing, then became a stockbroker in Denver for 12 years before moving to Spokane, Washington, where he lived for two decades before settling back home in Helena.

In 2019 he was inducted into the Montana Sports Hall of Fame.

Tommy Lyons (1972–1974, 1976)

Raised in Atlanta and earning his undergrad degree while playing at the University of Georgia, Lyons was the Broncos'

14th-round draft pick in 1971. Lyons started 49 consecutive games for the Broncos at one point, the first 36 at right guard, before switching to left guard. In 1973 he helped the Broncos post their first-ever winning record (7-5-2).

After starting all 14 games back at his more familiar right guard position in 1976, Lyons retired to finish up his medical degree, which he received from the University of Colorado in 1977. (Lyons had studied medicine simultaneously while playing for the Broncos.)

He was a practicing ob-gyn in Athens for 12 years, becoming one of the nation's leading experts in women's health care.

RIGHT TACKLE

Somewhere in time, right tackle became the stepbrother to the more glamorous left tackle position.

Maybe it was Giants outside linebacker Lawrence Taylor coming from the right side of the defense that made the left tackle position of greater importance. The 2009 blockbuster movie *The Blind Side* didn't hurt the perception that left tackles were more valuable than right tackles.

The bank accounts followed. Even in 2022, when a high percentage of edge-rushers like Von Miller, the Bosa brothers, and the Watt brothers come from the left side of the defense, the four highest-paid offensive tackles, and 7 of the top 10, play on the left side.

It didn't use to be that way. Forrest Gregg is widely considered the best offensive tackle of all time. He played the right side. So did the likes of Dan Dierdorf, Rayfield Wright, Jackie Slater, and Ron Mix.

At least right tackle never threatened extinction like the fullback position. Hard to believe Jim Brown, Jim Taylor, Larry Csonka, Cookie Gilchrist, and John Riggins were fullbacks. Only tailbacks get the ball now.

Manifesting the right tackle oddity over the past decade, it has easily been the most difficult position for the Broncos to fill. We're talking 10 different starters in the 10-year period from 2013 to 2022.

The Broncos' season-opening, right tackle starters in succession the past decade: Orlando Franklin (2013), Chris Clark

(2014), Ryan Harris (2015), Donald Stephenson (2016), Menelik Watson (2017), Jared Veldheer (2018), Ja'Wuan James (2019), Elijah Wilkinson (2020), Bobby Massie (2021), and Cam Fleming (2022).

That's not a right tackle. That's a swinging gate. Next.

Before then, the Broncos had three right tackles who were among the most dependable in their day—Eldon Danenhauer starting with Denver's inaugural season in 1960; Mike Current, who followed Danenhauer for an extended run; and Ken Lanier, who protected John Elway through the first half of the Hall of Fame quarterback's career.

As we picked the Broncos' all-time starting lineup, it was tempting to simply list the two best offensive tackles overall—Gary Zimmerman and Ryan Clady—even though both were left tackles. But the left and right tackle positions are so different in the type of skill sets they require, we couldn't drop one for the other.

For this project, *The Denver Broncos All-Time All-Stars*, right tackle got its due.

THE CANDIDATES

Eldon Danenhauer
Mike Current
Ken Lanier

ELDON DANENHAUER (1960–1965)

Anyone who doesn't think professional football puts business first, and family, second, isn't familiar with the Danenhauer story.

In 1960, Bill Danenhauer was already a member of the Denver Broncos' inaugural team when he recommended to his coaches they give his younger brother Eldon a tryout. Bill Danenhauer was a defensive end who had played for the NFL Baltimore Colts in 1956–1957 before catching on with the

Broncos. Eldon Danenhauer, a right tackle, was a 24-year-old rookie who had not yet caught on with a professional team, until his big brother arranged for a tryout with the Broncos. Between his time as a college player for the College of Emporia (Kansas) and Pittsburg State (Kansas), Eldon was a military policeman for the US Army.

After passing the audition his brother arranged, Eldon became the Broncos starting right tackle through their first six seasons, making two AFL All-Star teams.

Bill? He was traded after the fourth game of the 1960 season to the Boston Patriots. A year later, in 1961, he was coaching Adams City High School in the Denver area. Thanks for finding us your brother, Bill. Now off you go.

Eldon was considered monstrous in his era at 6-foot-5, 235 pounds. His career was cut short when he broke his arm while pushing a stalled car up an icy hill in January 1966. During training camp that year he broke his arm again and decided to retire.

Having worked for the Coors Brewery in Golden, Colorado, during his off-seasons, Eldon wound up running a Coors distributorship in Topeka, Kansas, for 25 years following his playing days. He and his wife then became co-owners of The Red Lion restaurant in Vail. Eldon passed away in June 2021 at the age of 85.

Bill Danenhauer, by the way, had a nice second career as a coach—first, for nine years through the 1960s as a high school coach, and then for eight years, through the 1970s, as a college assistant and head coach at the University of Nebraska Omaha.

MIKE CURRENT (1967–1975)
A third-round draft choice out of Ohio State in 1967, after his rookie training camp, Current was traded by idiosyncratic Broncos head coach Lou Saban to Miami, where he played in two games, then was traded back to Denver, where he spent time on the taxi squad. Beginning in 1968, Current started 105

consecutive games, mostly at right tackle, until he suffered a season-ending injury midway through the 1975 season.

An AFL All-Star in 1968, Current played four more NFL seasons—as a right tackle starter for Tampa Bay in their 0-14 inaugural season of 1976, then three seasons from 1977 to 1979 for Don Shula's Miami Dolphins.

After his playing career, Current ran into financial and criminal problems and took his own life in 2012, one day before he was to enter a plea on charges of sexually assaulting three underage victims.

KEN LANIER (1981–1994)

Do you realize Ken Lanier started more games for the Broncos than did Rod Smith, Champ Bailey, Karl Mecklenburg, Shannon Sharpe, Steve Atwater, Louis Wright, Terrell Davis, Randy Gradishar, and so many other Broncos greats? Lanier's 165 starts are the seventh most in Broncos history, and only two players—Billy Thompson and Simon Fletcher—started more consecutive games than Lanier's 131.

His favorite one?

"My first start against Cleveland," Lanier said in November 2022. "I knew it was going to be broadcast on TV back in Ohio. I got the game ball and everything. That was my rookie year. I started that game. Somebody was hurt. [It was] 1981, midseason. And they found out I could play and they started piecing me in. And in '82 they started me."

It was left tackle Claudie Minor and center Billy Bryan who were hurt going into that 1981 game against the Browns, causing first-year head coach Dan Reeves to shuffle his offensive linemen. The Broncos won 23–20 in overtime that day.

The son of an accomplished musician who grew up in Columbus, Ohio, Lanier never made a Pro Bowl in his 13-plus seasons, but he sure did block off a bunch of them who rushed from the left side. The Raiders' Howie Long and

Greg Townsend, the Chiefs' Derrick Thomas and Art Still, and Seattle's Jacob Green were chief among the group, which also included the likes of Mark Gastineau, Andre Tippett, Chip Banks, Lee Williams, and on and on.

Another game Lanier started: The 1986-season AFC Championship Game at Cleveland. Otherwise remembered for The Drive that was quarterback John Elway's coming-out moment.

"It was, like, we had to get it done," said Lanier of the 98-yard march that led to a game-tying touchdown late in regulation. Again, the Broncos would beat the Browns, 23–20, in overtime. "It was for all the marbles. We got it down the field and John took care of the rest of it."

Through most of his career, Lanier blocked for Elway, whose athleticism was unique among quarterbacks in that era.

"You had to get used to it at first," Lanier said. "Because you never knew where he was going to be. He was such a scrambler. You had to make sure that if the defensive linemen all the sudden stopped, you knew John was on the loose. He threw that ball so hard, you could hear the laces go by your head."

Lanier started in three Super Bowl games. Even if the Broncos didn't win any of them, he got there. Lanier still lives in the Denver area, where he has been married to Arlene for more than 20 years. He has mostly worked as a manager of a self-storage company.

Starter
Ken Lanier. If it's true that greatness is mostly about showing up every day, no other right tackle was close to being as good as Lanier.

Others

Matt Lepsis (1999–2003)
A tight end in college at Colorado, Lepsis went undrafted in 1997 when he spent his rookie season on injured reserve with a

knee injury. He primarily played special teams in all 19 games, including Super Bowl XXXIII, in his second season of 1998, then began a five-year run as a starting right tackle in 1999.

He then switched to left tackle in 2004, where he started for four seasons. It was a solid career that unfortunately was known for inadvertently blowing out the knee of star running back Terrell Davis in game 4 of the 1999 season while making a tackle on an interception return.

Ryan Harris (2008–2010)

If not for a bad back, which first began to give him problems his senior year at Notre Dame, Harris may have become one of the NFL's best offensive tackles. As it was, Harris played 10 years, including 5 over two stints with the Broncos, the team that selected him in the third round of the 2007 draft.

He started three seasons at right tackle from 2008 to 2010 for the Broncos, and for the first three games of 2015, before he switched to the left tackle position. Harris wound up starting at left tackle for the Broncos' Super Bowl 50 team.

Orlando Franklin (2011–2013)

A second-round pick out of Miami in John Elway's first draft as Broncos general manager, Franklin started all but one game at right tackle through his first three seasons. He was switched to left guard for his fourth season, then became a free agent, where he signed a nice contract with the rival Chargers as a left guard.

Franklin handled the right edge for Peyton Manning's record-setting season in 2013 when the quarterback threw for 55 touchdowns and 5,477 yards—marks that still hold two years into the league's expanded 17-game seasons.

RUNNING BACKS

For all the success and influence the Broncos' renowned zone-blocking, one-cut running system had on the NFL, the Denver franchise is not overflowing with great running backs.

There are their two Hall of Famers, Terrell Davis and Floyd Little. They were great. Immortalized with bronze busts in Canton, Ohio. There were two other backs who had a chance to be great in Bobby Humphrey and Clinton Portis. But both got caught up in their contracts and wound up as two-year wonders with the Broncos.

In more recent times, the Broncos have moved to a two-man tailback rotation, and while this has been productive for the team, it hasn't generated the volume of rushing attempts for any one back to keep Fantasy League participants happy.

Through the 2022 season, there were but 15 Broncos running backs who had 1,000-yard rushing seasons. Floyd Little was the first in the 14-game season of 1971. Phillip Lindsay was the most recent, as he went back-to-back in 2018–2019, his first two years in the league.

Six of those 15 Bronco backs had multiple 1,000-yard seasons—Lindsay, Mike Anderson, Portis, Davis, Humphrey, and Otis Armstrong. Davis did it four years in a row, from 1995 to 1998, his first four years in the league. He also recorded the only 2,000-yard rushing season in Broncos history when he remarkably gained 178 yards in the final regular-season game of 1998 to finish with 2,008. At the time, Davis was only the fourth running back in NFL history to achieve a 2,000-yard season, following O.J. Simpson, Eric Dickerson, and Barry Sanders. Only four more running backs have done it since—Jamal Lewis, Chris Johnson, Adrian Peterson, and Derrick Henry.

Among the Broncos' rushing notables who just once enjoyed a 1,000-yard season were two of the Broncos' all-time best running backs, Little and Sammy Winder.

Winder wasn't a great running back. A solid, dependable, steady, and durable back. A running back who had five consecutive seasons of at least 700 yards, but only once did he surpass 800—in 1984, when he churned for 1,154 yards on 3.9 yards per carry.

The Broncos also had some fine fullbacks over the years. During Denver's Orange Crush era in the late 1970s, fullback Jon Keyworth was often the team's leading rusher as tailback star Otis Armstrong battled injuries.

But for this project, it hardly seemed fair to pick one starting tailback from a franchise that had both Terrell Davis and Floyd Little at the position. And so there are two starting running back positions listed on *The Denver Broncos All-Time All-Stars*.

As for the running back position, there was Terrell Davis and Floyd Little, and there was the rest. Here's a look at the two starting tailbacks, followed by the rest who deserve mention.

THE CANDIDATES

Terrell Davis
Floyd Little

TERRELL DAVIS (1995–2001)

Almost all football stars overcame adversity on their way to the top, some more than others. Davis endured more than others. The youngest of six boys born to Joe and Kateree Davis, Terrell grew up poor in a dangerous neighborhood of San Diego with a father who made the boys their lunches and dinners before he would come home often drunk and mean. Dad died of lupus at 41, just before Terrell turned 13.

At Long Beach State, Davis figured his hopes of developing into an NFL prospect were dashed by the unexpected death of his head coach, George Allen. After transferring to Georgia, Davis played behind Garrison Hearst as a sophomore, then split carries with Hines Ward as a senior. A concerning medical check of Davis's knee dropped him to the sixth round of the 1995 NFL Draft, where the Broncos thought they would get a core special teamer who could back up Rod Bernstine at running back.

But a crushing special teams tackle on a kickoff return during a 1995 preseason game in Tokyo earned Davis a promotion.

What followed were four consecutive seasons of 1,117 yards rushing with 7 touchdowns in 1995; 1,538 yards with 13 touchdowns in 1996; 1,750 yards and 15 touchdowns plus a Super Bowl MVP award in 1997; and 2,008 yards with 21 touchdowns to earn the NFL's MVP award in his incredible season of 1998, plus another Super Bowl ring.

Davis also all but single-handedly carried the Broncos over the top from Super Bowl qualifier to Super Bowl champion. After a superb 1996 season in which the Broncos finished with the No. 1 AFC playoff seed, Davis rushed for 91 yards on just 14 carries—6.5 yards per carry—in a shocking upset home AFC playoff loss to upstart Jacksonville in a second-round game. Broncos head coach Mike Shanahan later blamed the crushing defeat on not giving Davis more carries. Running the ball is where teams gain physical superiority over their opponents, in Shanahan's view.

Shanahan learned his lesson. In the next two postseasons, the Broncos played seven games and Davis achieved at least 100 yards rushing in all seven. He was the MVP of Super Bowl XXXII by rushing for 157 yards and 3 touchdowns despite a blinding migraine that caused him to miss a few plays early in the Broncos' upset victory against the Green Bay Packers.

"You can throw those migraines in there, too," Davis said, when the series of obstacles he overcame was mentioned to him. "I've been dealing with these since I was a child. I was actually told by the doctor I shouldn't play football. Because they didn't know what was happening."

Davis then became the NFL's MVP the following regular season after crossing the 2,000-yard barrier.

To be immortalized with a bronze bust in the Pro Football Hall of Fame, one must have attained a level of greatness. Define *great*. There is the Curtis Martin prototype, where one is good for a long time. And there is the Gale Sayers version, where the player was great for a shorter period.

Terrell Davis was great. His streak of seven consecutive 100-yard rushing games in the postseason remains an NFL record. Unfortunately for Davis, he suffered a career-spoiling torn ACL knee injury four games into the 1999 season, when he got rolled up by a teammate while trying to chase down an interception.

"That was it," Davis said. "That was officially, or unofficially, my retirement."

He did return for the 2000 season but only made it to 5 games. He tried again in 2001 and was effective in the 8 games he played, rushing for 701 yards—a pace of 1,402 over a 16-game season.

But the explosion was gone while the pain never really left. Davis retired during the preseason of 2002.

The relative brevity of Davis's career was a difficult barrier when it came to his election into the Pro Football Hall of Fame. He was a top-25 semifinalist each of the 11 years he was eligible for the Hall, but he didn't crack the top 15 finalists until his 9th year. Finally, career comparisons to the great Gale Sayers, plus his record postseason run, generated enough momentum for his induction into football immortality in 2017.

For all he endured, he had overcome.

"The [migraines], [the] death of my dad, dropping the program—I look back on it and, it's not funny, but it's, 'You couldn't make this up,'" Davis said. "Then I go to a college where I didn't have the greatest college career. I wasn't a guy that was highly touted or a guy that was supposed to have any success in the NFL. I guess I got to keep going, don't quit. Live in the moment."

FLOYD LITTLE (1967–1975)

In the late 1960s, NBC carried the American Football League Game of the Week on Sunday afternoons, and while the Broncos usually played the foil to Joe Namath's Jets, Fred Biletnikoff's Raiders, and Len Dawson's Chiefs, Little gained national acclaim as pro football's most versatile offensive player.

"It was Floyd left, Floyd right, and Floyd up the middle," half-joked Billy Thompson, Little's best friend and former teammate.

And until Thompson's rookie season in 1969, Little returned punts and kickoffs, too. "The Franchise" he was called, and not only because he carried an otherwise inept offense—quarterback was always a problem for the early Broncos—to the occasional upset win.

Here's how the moniker came about: From their inception in 1960 through 1966, the Broncos had made some nice selections with their first draft picks, most notably Merlin Olsen, Kermit Alexander, and Bob Brown. Future Hall of Famers Paul Krause and Bob Hayes were selected in the 12th and 14th rounds of the 1964 draft, and Dick Butkus in the second round (first Broncos' selection) of the 1965 draft.

None of them signed with the Broncos, the perennial doormats of the upstart American Football League. All those players opted instead to play in the more established National Football League.

In 1967, the NFL and AFL combined their drafts and with their No. 6 overall selection, the Broncos took Little from the famed Syracuse running back factory.

Once drafted and signed by the Broncos, Little helped generate enough excitement for a local nonprofit group to buy 34,657-seat Bears Stadium for $1.8 million and present it to the city of Denver, which then expanded the capacity to more than 50,000 and renamed it Mile High Stadium in December 1968.

"They were talking about selling the franchise and moving to Atlanta or Alabama, and there was a big push to save the franchise," Little said in 2016 from Syracuse University, where for a time he worked for his alma mater as the special assistant to the athletic director. "That's how I got the name ["The Franchise"] because I went door to door, getting support from the people to get a new stadium. By going out and knocking on doors to raise all that support, they wound up as one of the top NFL franchises."

It was Jim Saccomano, a local radio reporter in the early 1970s, who first called Little "The Franchise." Sacco later became the team's longtime public relations director.

"I remember when John Elway went to the Super Bowl, and won it for the first time," Little said of the Broncos' triumph in Super Bowl XXXII. "He had a golf tournament and I walked in this room to say hello and he got up there and said, thanks for saving our franchise. I tell ya, it brought tears to my eyes when he stood up and said this is the reason why the Denver Broncos just won the Super Bowl. Thanks for saving our franchise. John Elway said that!"

On the morning of his long-overdue induction into the Pro Football Hall of Fame on a hot first Saturday in August in Canton, Ohio, Little and his son Marc had breakfast in a makeshift cafeteria with other Hall of Famers. Little's renewed journey toward Hall of Fame election began in 2006 when his memoir, *Floyd Little's Tales from the Broncos' Sidelines*, was written by an ardent fan-turned-close-friend, Tom Mackie.

Little's primary inspiration behind the book project was to recall so many of the forgotten players from the Broncos' early seasons. The Broncos as a team may have been down-and-outers through the first 13 seasons, but they had some excellent players. They just didn't have enough of them.

The book also reminded the football world that Little somehow had not yet been elected into the Hall of Fame, and sparked momentum for his eventual induction four years later. There were two pieces of statistical data that should have made Little a no-brainer HOF selection soon after the mandatory five-year wait from his retirement following the 1975 season.

One, he was the seventh all-time leading rusher at the time of his retirement, and the six ranked ahead of him—Jim Brown, O.J. Simpson, Joe Perry, Jim Taylor, Leroy Kelly, and John Henry Johnson—were all elected into the Hall of Fame by 1994.

And two, in the six-season period from 1968 through 1973, Little led all NFL players in yards from scrimmage—rushing and receiving—with 6,940, or 1,157 yards per 14-game season.

Yet, by the time Little was eligible for the Hall, the NFL had expanded its season from 14 games to 16. Little's numbers during the 14-game era didn't seem as impressive next to what players were compiling over 16 games. His remarkable career had fallen into a forgotten abyss.

His book in 2006—31 years after his retirement—reignited awareness, and he started getting Hall of Fame consideration from the seniors' committee in 2007 and 2008, only to fall short of receiving a nomination. Finally, in 2009, Little and former Lions cornerback Dick LeBeau were the two senior nominees.

"It's so surreal when you have grandkids," Little said, when asked if he had considered the magnitude of football immortality.

Little was a Hall of Fame–caliber player, whether a voting bloc recognized it or not. But Floyd was always so gracious. Uncommonly so.

"After he got into the Hall of Fame, he mailed me 44 thank-you notes over a 44-day period," Mackie said. "Floyd is the epitome of a role model and football hero. I picked a good one."

Befitting his larger-than-life persona, Floyd Douglas Little was born in 1942 on the Fourth of July, the grandest of America's 365 days, in New Haven, Connecticut. Little was so extremely well-spoken in private and such a moving and eloquent public orator when the opportunity presented, it's difficult to believe he struggled academically as a child.

"I remember being a strong but angry young man in school," Little said in his Hall of Fame speech at Fawcett Stadium in Canton. "After being kicked out of school, I reached an impasse in my life. . . . With the help of those who saw good in me, I was re-enrolled back in school with determination."

Still, his grades weren't good enough at Hillhouse High School to receive any scholarship offers. He attended Bordentown Military Academy where for two years he flourished both in the classroom and on the football field. The result was 47 scholarship offers. Syracuse running back great Ernie Davis personally recruited Little. Not wanting to hurt Davis's feelings, and wanting to get back to his dinner, Little committed to Syracuse.

In truth, Little was more interested in going to Army or Notre Dame, but when he learned Davis had died in May 1963, he remembered he had given his word. Little chose Syracuse, where he was given the famed No. 44 previously worn by Jim Brown and Davis.

Little partnered with fullbacks Jim Nance in his sophomore year, and Larry Csonka as a junior and senior. All three became AFL/NFL greats.

With the Broncos, Little wasn't just a great player. He was a highly popular player. Whenever the Broncos would bring back their alumni—whether for a Ring of Fame ceremony or reunion of some kind—and introduced them to the crowd before a game or at halftime, Little always got the loudest ovation.

Two games represented his popularity. One was "Floyd Little Day" in 1972 and the other was his final home game at Mile High Stadium in 1975.

From the mid-1960s to mid-1970s—a time when athletes didn't draw multimillion-dollar contracts—one of the more popular marketing promotions was for a team to give its star player his own day. Testimonies and gifts would be showered upon the guest of honor.

On October 29, 1972, the Broncos' game against the Cleveland Browns was declared "Floyd Little Day" by team owner Gerald H. Phipps. While such celebrations were not uncommon for active players in Major League Baseball at the time, it was the first—and last—of its kind by the Broncos. It was Little's rushing title with 1,133 yards in the 14-game season of 1971 that inspired the day in his honor.

Little got letters acclaiming him from Governor John Love and Denver mayor William McNichols. A Chevy Blazer was among his gifts.

Fittingly, Floyd Little Day turned out like so many other days in the honoree's career—he played extremely well, but the Broncos lost.

Little was that game's top rusher with 79 yards on just 14 carries. His 5.6-yard average suggested Little should have gotten the ball more. Little also turned a short pass from quarterback Charley Johnson into a 19-yard touchdown, and he added a 23-yard punt return.

To this day, Little is the most versatile offensive player in Broncos history.

Yet, the Broncos lost to the Browns, 27–20. Inside the 2-minute warning, Little came through with a 25-yard run to the Cleveland 18, but Johnson was picked off with 1:12 remaining.

A fitting conclusion to Floyd Little Day?

Indeed it was. After nine seasons, all with the Broncos, Little was not only the NFL's seventh-leading career rusher with 6,323 yards, he added another 2,418 yards off 215 receptions and 3,416 yards on punt and kickoff returns.

Little's 12,157 all-purpose yards held as a Broncos record for 30 years and remain second in team history to Rod Smith's 12,488. But to reiterate Little's versatility, Smith got 91 percent of his total yards as a receiver; Little got just 52 percent of his yards as a rusher.

Yet, in Little's nine seasons, the Broncos' average yearly record was 5-8-1. If it's unfathomable to think any player on such dreary teams could be so popular, understand that prior to Little's arrival, the Broncos' average record was 4-10 through their first seven seasons, from 1960 to 1966.

"It was a time when the Broncos were going through those growing pains," Thompson said.

As NBC brought AFL games to America's households in the late 1960s, Little nearly single-handedly brought pride and relevance to Colorado's major city near the Rocky Mountains.

Make no mistake: Little's biggest disappointment was playing on so many losing teams. It used to bother him that two years after he retired, the Broncos with many of his former teammates played in their first Super Bowl. But Little felt like a champion when the Broncos fans carried him off the Mile High Stadium field following his final home game in 1975.

"That's a memory that resonates with me," Little said for the book, *Mile High Magic: The 25 Greatest Moments in Denver Broncos History.* "It's still a little bit emotional."

Little was going to retire after the 1974 season, but coach John Ralston asked him to stay on for one more year to continue mentoring a talented young running back named Otis Armstrong. Little agreed, and began his final season content with returning kickoffs. Through the first four games, he had just 15 carries for 53 yards.

"My mind was winding down," he said. "I wanted to be a guy that motivated the club and inspired my teammates, as a captain. Lo and behold, four games into the season, Otis goes down."

Armstrong suffered a season-ending knee injury in game 4 against the Pittsburgh Steelers. The next week, game 5 against the Cleveland Browns, Little had 6 carries for minus-2 yards.

"It took me a couple games to get back in playing condition," Little said. "It took a couple games because I had mentally checked out."

But then Little got in a nice running groove over the next six games, rushing for 318 yards on 4.1 yards per carry. Once again, the Broncos were a disappointing 5-7 entering their final home game of the season.

Everyone knew it would be Little's last game in front of the great Broncos fans. Broncomania was still a year or two off. But there was long-held love and gratitude for Little.

He rushed for 56 yards against the Eagles. He caught a screen pass from Steve Ramsey and took it for a 66-yard touchdown to break a 10–10 tie late in the third quarter. The 33-year-old Little was running like he was 23.

"It was emotion," Little said. "The emotions really took over. One of the greatest things about that game was [Eagles linebacker] Bill Bergey and the big, tall wide receiver—Harold Carmichael—and these guys, who I didn't really know, came over to me and said, 'We're going to miss you. You've been a helluva player and helluva ambassador. We wish you all the best.' It was incredible for me."

As the clock ticked down to 20 seconds, Little broke down and wept on the sidelines.

"I was just a mess," Little said. "It was all over. And then the fans picked me up and carried me off. My teammates had already run off to the locker room. The fans came down and swarmed me. They hoisted me up, and carried me off. It was incredible."

The Broncos retired Little's No. 44 and inducted him into their Ring of Fame in their inaugural class of 1984. After a much too long wait, Little was inducted into the Pro Football Hall of Fame in 2010.

After the Broncos on the strength of their season-best running game defeated the Miami Dolphins, 20–13, on November 22, 2020, head coach Vic Fangio awarded one of the game balls to Little.

It had been revealed a few months earlier that Little was battling neuroendocrine tumors (NET), a rare cell cancer. The cancer had metastasized, meaning it had spread through his body.

Little sought treatment at the Mayo Clinic in Phoenix, but on the morning of the Broncos–Dolphins game, Little's wife DeBorah confirmed on her Facebook page that the treatment had been discontinued and her husband had been placed in hospice care.

Broncos' public relations chief Patrick Smyth arranged to have Little's game ball signed by Elway, Fangio, and running backs Phillip Lindsay and Melvin Gordon—who combined for 166 of the team's 189 rushing yards against the Dolphins—then had it delivered overnight to Little's home in Henderson, Nevada.

As he was living out his final days, it was worth recalling how Little had borrowed some profound words to finish up his Hall of Fame enshrinement speech that August night in 2010 on a stage in Canton, Ohio.

"The great writer James Baldwin said, 'Naked I came into this world and naked I shall leave,'" Little said. "We are bound to leave everything we accomplished in this lifetime behind, passing it on. So leave a legacy that you and your family can be proud [of]. I've given you the best that I've got."

Little took his last breath on January 1, 2021. Born on the Fourth of July. Died on New Year's Day. A life worth celebrating.

STARTERS

Again, with zero suspense but major fanfare, the starting running backs on *The Denver Broncos All-Time All-Stars* Terrell Davis and Floyd Little.

Floyd Little © DICK BURNELL / PHOTO ASSOCIATES

OTHERS

The best of the rest of the Broncos running backs were Portis and Humphrey, followed by Winder, Armstrong, Anderson, and Lindsay.

Clinton Portis (2002–2003)

Portis was on his way to becoming an all-time great, but his pursuit of riches got him, first, traded, and then, years after his career ended, imprisoned.

Selected by the Broncos in the second round out of Miami in 2002, Portis was ideally suited for the Mike Shanahan/Gary Kubiak /Alex Gibbs / Bobby Turner–coached one-cut off the zone-blocking system. Portis rushed for back-to-back 1,500-yard seasons to begin his career, scoring 29 touchdowns while averaging 5.5 yards per carry.

When he let it be known he wanted to become the NFL's highest-paid running back before his third season of 2004, Portis instead was traded to Washington in exchange for cornerback Champ Bailey and a second-round draft pick that turned out to be running back Tatum Bell. The Broncos clearly got the better of that deal, as Bailey had 10 good-to-great seasons for the Broncos to become a first-ballot Pro Football Hall of Famer. Bell added a 1,000-yard season in 2006.

Portis did become the NFL's highest-paid running back for Washington in 2004, and he was good, rushing for at least 1,260 yards in four seasons there. But he averaged a pedestrian 4.1 yards per carry during his seven seasons in Washington and 6.5 touchdowns a season.

Portis filed for bankruptcy in 2015, and in early 2022 was sentenced to six months in prison and six months of home confinement for his part in a fraud ring against the NFL's healthcare plan.

Bobby Humphrey (1989–1991)

Money also got the better of Humphrey, who after rushing for 1,151 and 1,202 yards in his first two seasons of 1989 and 1990 held out for a new contract prior to his third season. Broncos head coach and vice president of football operations Dan Reeves didn't budge, and Humphrey didn't end his holdout until mid-October. By then Gaston Green was on his way to a 1,000-yard season and Humphrey wound up with only 33 yards rushing in 1991 before moving on to have one more uninspiring season with the Miami Dolphins. He gained just 504 more rushing yards in his career after his holdout.

Sammy Winder (1982–1990)

Winder is No. 3 on the Broncos' all-time rushing list, with 5,427 rushing yards—nearly 1,000 more than fourth-place Otis Armstrong—which he accumulated over nine seasons at a mere 3.6 yards per carry. John Elway's first starting halfback, Winder is also third on the team with 39 career rushing touchdowns—behind only Davis and Little—and he scored another 9 touchdowns receiving.

Whenever he scored, Winder, who grew up on a farm in the unincorporated town of Pocahontas, Mississippi, would break out his "Mississippi Mud" dance in celebration.

Winder was a Pro Bowler in 1984, when he rushed for a career-best 1,153 yards, and again in 1986 when he scored 14 touchdowns rushing and receiving combined.

Winder was also responsible for the first four plays of the famous "Drive" that Elway orchestrated to tie up the Browns late in the 1986-season AFC Championship Game. It started when Winder caught a 5-yard pass from Elway, moving the ball out from the Broncos' own 2-yard line to the 7. Winder then gained 3 yards and then barely 2 yards on third-and-2 to pick up the first down.

It was so typical of Winder's career—three plays for only 10 yards, but a first down. Move the chains. Winder then gained 3 yards on first and 10 and left the rest of "The Drive" for Elway.

Otis Armstrong (1973–1980)

Armstrong was a sensational multi-threat running back and returner at Purdue, where he followed the great Leroy Keyes to set the school's all-time rushing record. Still, it was surprising when the Broncos made Armstrong their first-round draft pick in 1973 because the team still had Little. Although Little held off Armstrong as the Broncos' primary ball carrier for a season, Armstrong captured the NFL's rushing crown in 1974, with 1,407 yards. Armstrong also had 38 catches for another 405 yards, and he had 12 touchdowns rushing and receiving combined in what was the best single season by a Broncos running back until Terrell Davis's second season of 1996.

But from there Armstrong's career was plagued by injuries for all but one season—1976, when he again rushed for 1,000 yards in a 14-game season. He passed away in October 2021 at 70 years old.

Mike Anderson (2000–2005)

Now this is a wonderful story that cannot go unmentioned. After high school in Fawn Grove, Pennsylvania, Anderson spent four years in the US Marines. He then spent two years at a junior college before playing two more productive years at the University of Utah. He was drafted in the sixth round by the Broncos in 2000.

With Terrell Davis unable to make it back as hoped from his previous season's ACL injury, Anderson as a 27-year-old rookie rushed for 1,487 yards with 15 touchdowns.

He then took a backseat to Davis's comeback in 2001, and then Portis in 2002–2003 before rebounding for another

1,000-yard season in 2005—at age 32—when the Broncos finished 13-3 and hosted the AFC Championship Game.

Phillip Lindsay (2018–2020)

Another remarkable story of a local kid done great. Growing up in the Denver area as a Broncos fan, the 5-foot-7 Lindsay attended Denver South High School before playing four years for the University of Colorado. Despite rushing for 30 touchdowns and more than 2,700 yards in his final two years for the CU Buffaloes, Lindsay went undrafted.

The Broncos signed him as an undrafted free agent, then gave him the ball. He rushed for 1,037 yards and 9 touchdowns on 5.4 yards per carry to earn a Pro Bowl berth as a rookie in 2018. He followed it up with 1,011 rushing yards and 7 touchdowns in his second year.

But the Broncos wanted a bigger back for their passing game. The signing of Melvin Gordon III reduced Lindsay's role in 2020, and he was traded to Houston after that season.

WIDE RECEIVERS

When a Broncos franchise has five quarterbacks who were deemed worthy of its Ring of Fame—Frank Tripucka, Charley Johnson, Craig Morton, John Elway, and Peyton Manning—it follows that there were also numerous terrific receivers in team history.

For this project, the receiver position was easily the deepest for all-time offensive starter candidates. (Linebacker and safety were the deepest positions on defense.) So deep that several "others" would have been receiver starter candidates for many teams. And there were so many "others," there needed to be a third, honorable mention category.

Here are the receiver candidates for the starting lineup of *The Denver Broncos All-Time All-Stars.*

THE CANDIDATES

Rod Smith
Lionel Taylor
Demaryius Thomas
Haven Moses
Ed McCaffrey
Steve Watson

ROD SMITH (1995–2006)

The quintessential rags-to-riches story, on so many levels. Start with the Texarkana projects where Smith, his mom, and four siblings grew up with governmental aid. An All-State high school quarterback, Smith was bypassed by the big schools, so he went to Division II Missouri Southern to play quarterback.

He sat the bench as a freshman, then received two medical redshirt years because of, first, a torn arch in his foot, and, second, a torn ACL. In the meantime, Smith began his conversion to receiver, at first splitting 50-50 with quarterback, then going full-time as a junior in 1991 when he led the Division II nation with 1,439 receiving yards.

He wound up playing six years in college, which is a big reason why Rod Smith became what he was. He was more mature than other rookies when he went undrafted and signed with the Broncos. He further matured by spending his rookie year on the practice squad. Six years in college helped him earn three degrees—in economics and finance, general business, and marketing and management.

After his rookie year, Smith still didn't have a catch two games into his second season, and 59 minutes and 54 seconds into his third.

Game 3 of the 1995 season, September 17 at old Mile High Stadium, was the first NFL game Smith played in. The Broncos and Washington were tied, 31–31, with just 6 seconds left in regulation. It was fourth-and-10 with the ball at the Washington 43. Head coach Mike Shanahan ignored kicker Jason Elam's plea to attempt a 61-yard field goal attempt, opting instead for the Hail Mary.

Elway didn't throw the ball up in typical Hail Mary arching fashion, but with 43 yards of zip. Smith leaped, snagged it away from Darrell Green, Washington's future Hall of Fame cornerback, came down on his back, and hung on.

Time expired as Smith fell back into the end zone. Bedlam. *Who did you say caught it?*

It was the only football game Elway had ever played in—high school, college, or pro—where he threw a touchdown pass on the final play to win the game. A star was born, and his name was Smith.

Even with this clutch performance, though, it took a while for the Broncos to believe in Smith as a receiver. In a bit of a head-scratcher, Smith didn't have another pass thrown his way until game 12 against Houston. He caught that one, too, for 24 yards. He had just 4 more catches in 1995 and 16 in 1996, when he made his mark as a punt returner. Three years after college, Smith had just 21 career catches.

It wasn't until 1997 that Smith had his breakout season, with 70 receptions for 1,180 yards and a career-best 12 touchdowns.

Smith was 27 at the time—a little old to be breaking out as receivers go—but it would be the first of nine consecutive seasons when he had at least 70 catches. Smith hauled in an 80-yard touchdown reception from Elway in Super Bowl XXXIII that was the biggest play in the Broncos' whipping the Atlanta Falcons, but of all his catches, he said his favorite was the first. Against the great Darrell Green, for the win.

More than 16 years after he played his last down, Smith remains the Broncos' all-time leader in the three most significant categories of receptions (849), receiving yards, (11,389), and touchdowns (68).

Receiver seems to be the one position where it's mostly about stats. And stats don't lie about production. But stats should be at least equal, if not secondary, to how a player helps his team win.

And when it came to winning performance, Smith was the Tom Brady of receivers. Here are the won-loss records in games started for Smith compared to two other Hall of Fame receivers, Terrell Owens and Randy Moss:

Receiver	W-L	Pct.	Playoff starts	Super Bowl rings
Rod Smith	111-59	.653	12	2
Terrell Owens	124-89	.582	12	0
Randy Moss	112-96	.538	15	0

Smith had a better career winning percentage than John Elway (.645). And if you think Smith was beholden to Elway, know this: Smith only started two seasons with Elway. Both years ended with Super Bowl trophies. In the years without Elway, Smith had not only his best statistical seasons, averaging 84 catches and 1,075 yards over eight seasons, he also helped the Broncos to a 77-52 record. A .596 winning percentage sans Elway that still exceeds that of Owens and Moss.

Smith's career was epitomized by the fact he had zero catches in his first Super Bowl win to finish the 1997 season and five catches for 152 yards, including an 80-yard touchdown reception that was the game's biggest play, to win his second Super Bowl in 1998.

Smith was a willing blocker for Terrell Davis in one Super Bowl and the No. 1 receiver in the next. Smith is the Broncos' all-time leading receiver in catches, yards, and touchdowns even though in 11 of his 12 playing seasons, the Broncos had a running back rush for at least 1,000 yards.

Yes, receiving stats should matter to a receiver's candidacy. But it shouldn't stop there.

"True story," said Tom Mills, Smith's longtime agent. "In early 2002, we were negotiating Rod's contract extension. The club wanted him to accept some performance incentives that were triggered by statistical thresholds. You know, catches, yards, those types of things.

"Rod could have reached those incentives without doing anything extraordinary. But he just couldn't get excited about the concept. He was coming off of his best statistical season in 2001 [league-leading 113 catches], but the team only went 8-8."

Smith's contract was adjusted so that his incentives were based on wins, and playoff rounds, not stats.

"The greatest teammate I've ever played with," said Hall of Fame safety John Lynch, who played with the Broncos from 2004 to 2007 and has been the 49ers general manager since 2017. "I don't say that lightly, with some of the other guys I played with. What he did for a team in terms of his selflessness, the way he worked—some people are leaders by virtue of the way they work, some are vocal leaders. Rod was all of the above. He was such a professional with the way he did things. His story, being an undrafted free agent, was inspirational. And then he wasn't afraid to be vocal."

LIONEL TAYLOR (1960–1966)

The Broncos' No. 1 receiver in all categories from the franchise's first season of 1960 until tight end Shannon Sharpe passed him in 1999—a span of 39 years—Taylor still ranks No. 4 in team history, with 543 catches and 6,872 yards, and is tied for fifth, with 44 touchdowns.

Keep in mind that Taylor compiled these numbers in only seven, 14-game seasons.

And he didn't join the Broncos until game 3 of the 1960 season. He still led the AFL with 92 catches that year—in just 12 games—and he then became the first receiver in professional history to have a 100-catch season in 1961.

It's not quite true, as the story has been told, that Taylor went from playing linebacker with the Chicago Bears in 1959 to setting a professional football record with 92 catches as a receiver for the Denver Broncos in 1960.

Here's how it really went: After starting for both the basketball and football teams for tiny New Mexico Highlands

University, Taylor did attend the Bears' training camp as a linebacker in 1958.

"[T]he only way I could get invited to camp was as a linebacker," Taylor said in a phone interview from his New Mexico home for the book, *The 50 Greatest Players in Denver Broncos History.* "I ended up as a wide receiver, which I wanted to be. Because I've got news for you: I never hit anybody in four years in college and three years of high school. So I wasn't going to play no defense."

It was different then. As a college linebacker, Taylor could cover would-be pass receivers extremely well—he was really more of a defensive back—but the tackling he left to others.

Still, the linebacker position gave Taylor a chance to show George "Papa Bear" Halas what he could do. Only the Bears cut Taylor in 1958. He spent the rest of that year in Bakersfield, California, playing receiver on the same semipro team as Tom Flores, the future quarterback and head coach of the Oakland Raiders.

In 1959, Taylor returned to the Bears' training camp, this time as a receiver. He was cut again, but this time re-signed after the Bears' second game. He didn't catch a pass in eight games that year.

Taylor went to a third training camp with the Bears in 1960. Again he was waived, with Halas promising to bring him back after the second game. This time, Taylor was intrigued by the American Football League Denver Broncos. Dean Griffing, the Broncos' first general manager, spotted Taylor playing in Bakersfield.

During his two-week waiting period with the Bears, Taylor decided to visit the Broncos. At the time, the team was out east, opening their inaugural season with a game at Boston and another at Buffalo. Taylor met up with the team at their New Jersey hotel the week the Broncos were to play their third game against the New York Titans.

"I didn't think the league was going to make it," Taylor said. "But I thought if I could come over and make a name for myself, I could go back to the NFL and get a little money, get a better deal."

Taylor's first game was the Broncos' third, against the Sammy Baugh–coached New York Titans (later renamed the Jets) at the famed Polo Grounds. Taylor didn't have a catch in the first quarter, but he wound up with 6 catches for 125 yards, including a 31-yard touchdown reception on a pass thrown by Broncos quarterback Frank Tripucka.

Taylor went on to have one of the most remarkable receiving seasons in American Football League–National Football League history in 1960. In just 12 games, Taylor had 92 catches—an all-time professional record at the time. The previous record, 84 catches by Tom Fears of the Los Angeles Rams in 1950, had stood for 10 years.

Taylor also ranked third in the AFL with 1,235 receiving yards and tied for second with 12 touchdowns.

Given the full 14 games the next year, Taylor in 1961 became the first-ever receiver to record 100 catches in a season. His 1,176 receiving yards ranked second.

The Broncos' media guide said Taylor had "unquestionably the greatest hands in football."

In the six-season period from 1960 to 1965, Taylor led the AFL in receptions five times. He averaged 85 catches for 1,071 yards and 7 touchdowns in that span. Again, in 14-game seasons. With Floyd Little not coming along until 1967, Taylor was the Broncos' first star player.

DEMARYIUS THOMAS (2010–2018)

From 2010, when the 6-foot-3, 225-pound Thomas was selected by the Broncos in the first round of the NFL Draft, until he was traded to the Houston Texans halfway through the 2018 season, Thomas compiled enough production to rank second in team history with 9,055 receiving yards and 60 touchdown catches, while his 665 receptions ranked third.

Rod Smith remains the all-time leader in all three categories (849-11, 389-68), while Shannon Sharpe, a Hall of Fame tight end, finished second in catches (675).

Those two greats, though, would admit only that Thomas possessed the rare athletic combination of height, strength, and take-it-the-house-from-80 speed.

Counting his 10 playoff games with the Broncos, Thomas finished his career with 777 catches for 10,522 yards and 69 touchdowns. Impressive, considering he was a raw receiver from a Georgia Tech program that featured a run-oriented option offense during his three seasons there.

Still, in what may have been Josh McDaniels's best decision in an otherwise turbulent two seasons as the head of Broncos football operations, the young coach saw enough in Thomas to take him with the No. 22 overall draft pick, two spots ahead of where the Dallas Cowboys chose the more heralded receiver Dez Bryant and three selections in front of where the Broncos took quarterback Tim Tebow.

Thomas's career got off to a slow start because of off-season injuries prior to his rookie year of 2010 and second year of 2011, but he had two breakout games late in the magical Tebow season of 2011. The first was game 12 at Minnesota, when Thomas snared four catches for 144 yards and 2 touchdowns—all in the second half—to lead Denver to a come-from-behind, 35–32 win.

Impressive as 36 yards per catch was, Thomas did even better in the Broncos' 2011 first-round playoff game against the heavily favored Pittsburgh Steelers when he had 4 catches for 204 yards—51.0 yards per catch—including an 80-yard catch-and-run walk-off touchdown reception from Tebow on the first play of overtime that gave Denver arguably its most exciting home win since their 1977 AFC Championship Game victory against the rival Raiders.

The 2011 season is also where Thomas began his string of 122 consecutive games played—132 including playoffs— perhaps his most unappreciated accomplishment in a career of many. During the four-year period from 2012 to 2015, when Peyton Manning was the Broncos quarterback, Thomas was unquestionably one of the NFL's top three receivers, along with Antonio Brown and Julio Jones. During that remarkable four-year span, Thomas averaged 101 catches for 1,447 yards and 10 touchdowns, easily the most dominant run in team receiving history.

Thomas also played in two Super Bowls during that stretch, setting a Super Bowl record with 13 catches in a 43–8 loss to Seattle in Super Bowl XLVIII, then having just 1 catch in the Broncos' Super Bowl 50 win against Carolina.

During the Super Bowl–champion reception at the White House in June 2016, Thomas arranged to have a letter delivered to Barack Obama, asking the sitting president to pardon his grandmother from a lengthy prison sentence on drug charges. Two months later, Obama did indeed commute Minnie Pearl Thomas's sentence. A year earlier, Obama had commuted the sentence of D.T.'s mom, Katina Smith.

Tragically, Thomas was found dead in the shower of his Roswell, Georgia, home on December 9, 2021, less than three weeks from his 34th birthday, which was on Christmas Day. An autopsy report revealed D.T. died from complications of a seizure.

Even with his celebration of life service closed to the public, approximately 500 people—including well over 100 Broncos-related supporters—attended the event held 11 days after his death at the basketball arena of his alma mater, Georgia Tech.

HAVEN MOSES (1972–1981)

When Lou Saban became the Broncos coach in 1967, one of his first moves was to discard most of the Broncos established stars like Willie Brown, Lionel Taylor, and Goose Gonsoulin. The reverse was true in 1972, when thanks to Saban, the Broncos wound up with one of their best-ever receivers in Haven Moses.

You see, after Saban resigned under fire from the Broncos in 1971, he returned to the Buffalo Bills, whom he had led to back-to-back AFL championships in 1964 and 1965. The Bills' best receiver was Moses, a first-round draft pick in 1968. But after a fine rookie year, Moses's skills were rendered nearly obsolete in 1969, when Buffalo selected running back O.J. Simpson with the No. 1 overall draft pick.

Saban traded away Moses halfway through the 1972 season in exchange for receiver Dwight Harrison, who was in the Broncos' doghouse for getting into an argument with star defensive end Lyle Alzado.

"I was Buffalo's No. 1 pick in '68 when Joe Collier was their head coach," Moses said for the book, *The 50 Greatest Players in Denver Broncos History.* "He drafted me. When he was let go in Buffalo, he came to Denver to be their defensive coordinator. So when I became available, he knew me, and John Ralston knew me from when I was at San Diego State and he was at Stanford. So they knew what they were getting."

Was the trade the best thing that ever happened to him?

"I'm still here," he said.

After nine and a half seasons with the Broncos, Moses retired as the team's third-leading career receiver to Lionel Taylor and tight end Riley Odoms in catches (302) and yards (5,450), and was tied with Taylor for the all-time team lead in touchdowns (44). Moses' 18.0 yards per catch is also a team record that still stands (90 or more catches).

It was incredible production for a receiver who played for a Denver franchise that operated its offense as a complement to its Orange Crush defense. Run the ball. Run it again. And on third down try to pick up the first.

Moses' best season statistically was 1979, when he had 54 catches for 943 yards and 6 touchdowns, and served as a mentor to an undrafted rookie named Steve Watson.

The most memorable game of Moses's career was the 1977 AFC Championship against the Raiders. Simply put, Moses put the Broncos on his back that day and carried the franchise to its first-ever Super Bowl appearance.

In what was then the most monumental game in the Broncos' 18-season history, Moses helped his team relax by catching a Craig Morton pass after running a route from left to right, then racing into the end zone for a 74-yard touchdown and a 7–3 lead against the rival Oakland Raiders.

Later in the fourth quarter, Moses made a diving, 12-yard catch in the end zone for a touchdown that gave Denver a 20–10 lead. It was the winning score, as Denver held on for a 20–17 win.

"That game was the epitome of what I had put into it, showing my talents on a major stage," Moses said. "We were evolving in the '60s with the AFL. In my 14 years, I went through quarterbacks every two years. I never had an offensive coach that gave me the opportunity to do more things as these guys are now.

"However, my numbers—however small they might look now—if you look at them, they were impactful."

Most notably in averaging 18.0 yards per catch.

ED MCCAFFREY (1995–2003)

If not the best receiver in Broncos history, McCaffrey was the most popular. Why? He was unselfish for one. Receivers can be divas, but McCaffrey was arguably the NFL's best blocking receiver in the six-season period from 1995 to 2000—although

Rod Smith would argue with him. McCaffrey and Smith used to have "de-cleater" contests as they were both trying to break into the starting lineup in the mid-1990s through blocking for Terrell Davis. Some of those blocks might draw a penalty flag now. But it was a different time.

Fans also appreciated McCaffrey's fearlessness. At 6-foot-5, 215 pounds, he was a tall, relatively slender target who would never cower from routes across the middle to catch John Elway or Brian Griese passes—even though McCaffrey would often get pulverized by hard-hitting linebackers and safeties who loved to pop the airborne, defenseless receiver. It was a different time. McCaffrey would get up and catch the ball over the middle again.

Twenty years after McCaffrey played his last game for the Broncos, he still ranks No. 5 among Broncos with 462 catches and 6,200 yards, and he's No. 4 with 46 touchdown catches.

For all his accomplishments, Broncos and NFL fans often link McCaffrey with the opening of Denver's new football stadium on September 10, 2001, the eve of 9/11. It was a Monday night and McCaffrey was having a terrific opener against his former New York Giants teammates, catching six passes for 94 yards. On that sixth catch, McCaffrey snagged a 19-yard pass from Griese and pivoted to run up field when his lead leg inadvertently kicked safety Shaun Williams. McCaffrey's leg hit Williams so hard, his leg snapped.

"It was a bad day. And an even worse tomorrow," McCaffrey said in the *50 Greatest Broncos* book.

Just after midnight of September 11, McCaffrey underwent surgery to repair his leg. He woke up the next morning with a morphine drip attached through an IV and the television showing our country under attack. After terrorists had flown the first plane into the World Trade Center's North Tower, McCaffrey was lying in his hospital bed watching live when the second plane crashed into the South Tower.

"It felt like the world was coming to an end," he said.

After months of pain, sweat, work, and intense rehab, McCaffrey returned for the 2002 season and had 69 catches for 903 yards. His first catch in his first game back was a 23-yard touchdown in the fourth quarter that beat St. Louis.

McCaffrey is also known for his immediate and nuclear families.

Ed was the oldest of five children born and raised Catholics by Edward and Elizabeth McCaffrey. Ed was born in Waynesboro, Virginia, but the family moved when he was four to Wilmington, North Carolina, where he played pickup basketball at Empie Park. Five years earlier, Empie Park was the same stomping grounds for a young hoops player named Michael Jordan.

McCaffrey's father was a systems analyst who got moved around, and he brought the McCaffreys to Allentown, Pennsylvania, when Ed was in seventh grade. His Allentown Central Catholic High School basketball team won two state championships while his football team went 0-11 his junior year.

He went on to Stanford to play both football and basketball, but soon committed to the gridiron because he was devoted to the Cardinals head coach, Jack Elway, John's dad.

Ed's sister, Monica, was a four-year letterman basketball player at Georgetown (1988–1991). His brother Bill played for Duke, where he was the Blue Devils' third-leading scorer on their national championship team that upset UNLV in the 1991 Final Four and Kansas in the championship game. Bill then transferred to Vanderbilt and became the co-SEC Player of the Year with Kentucky's Jamal Mashburn in 1993. Mike McCaffrey was a four-year basketball starter at NAIA Hasson College. Youngest sister Meghan was into dance.

Ed and Lisa have four sons—Max, Christian, Dylan, and Lucas. All enjoyed football glory at one time in their lives. Max had 117 catches, 12 touchdowns, and more than 1,300 yards receiving at Duke, plus he played in six NFL games.

Christian, the superstar of the family, had 2,019 yards rushing, 645 yards receiving, 1,200 return yards, and 39 yards passing—3,903 yards and 17 touchdowns total—in 2015 alone for Stanford to nearly win the Heisman Trophy. In 2019 with the Carolina Panthers, Christian joined Roger Craig and Marshall Faulk as the only three players in NFL history to have 1,000 yards rushing and 1,000 yards receiving in the same season. He is now with the San Francisco 49ers.

Dylan McCaffrey played quarterback for Michigan and coach Jim Harbaugh before transferring to Northern Colorado to play for his dad and brother Max, who served as Ed's offensive coordinator.

Luke was so good at everything that he perhaps was hurt by versatility, as he spent his first three college years playing quarterback before converting full-time to receiver at Rice in 2022, when he had 58 catches for 723 yards and 6 touchdowns.

Max, Christian, Dylan, and Luke had helped Valor win 8 of 10 state football championships. Ed was the head coach for Valor's state championship in 2018 with Luke as his quarterback before moving on to take over the Northern Colorado program. It didn't work out for Ed there, but that experience only proved he's human.

Shoppers can still buy Ed McCaffrey's mustard and horseradish at King Soopers. And in 2022 he was inducted into the Colorado Sports Hall of Fame.

STEVE WATSON (1979–1987)

Unquestionably the most underrated receiver in Broncos history. "Blade," as coach Red Miller first called Watson, because of his tall, skinny build, was an undrafted rookie receiver out of Temple in 1979. He not only became the Broncos' No. 1 receiver, he was one of the NFL's best during a five-year run from 1981 to 1985 in which he compiled 5,017 receiving yards that ranked No. 3 in the league in that span, trailing only future Hall of Famers James Lofton (5,804 yards) and Steve Largent (5,242).

Deceptively fast, Watson's trademark became the 50-50 ball thrown high down the sideline by quarterback Craig Morton. "Craig would be in the huddle and he would just say, 'Hey, I'm coming up,'" Watson said. Watson could outmaneuver any defensive back for the lofted pass and had the hands to finish.

Morton was Watson's quarterback in 1981, Steve DeBerg and Morton during the strike season of 1982, DeBerg and a rookie named John Elway in 1983, and Elway from 1984 to 1987.

Watson retired as the Broncos second-leading receiver to Lionel Taylor, with 353 catches (Watson now ranks eighth) and 6,112 yards (now sixth). His career 17.3 yards per catch remains second to Haven Moses' 18.0 among Broncos, with at least 100 catches.

STARTERS

Luckily the NFL has gone to where teams use three-receiver sets more than they use two running backs. The three receivers picked for the starting lineup in *The Denver Broncos All-Time All-Stars:* Rod Smith, Demaryius Thomas, and Lionel Taylor.

Taylor was dominant in the 1960s; Thomas was one of the league's best receivers in the 2010s; and Smith was consistently good from the mid-1990s through the mid-2000s.

Lionel Taylor © DICK BURNELL / PHOTO ASSOCIATES

OTHERS

Emmanuel Sanders (2014–2019)

Sanders ranks No. 7 all-time on the team receptions list with 404, even though he only played five and a half seasons in Denver. That was long enough for him to officially retire as a Bronco when he called it a career following the 2021 season, after playing 12 seasons with the Steelers, Broncos, 49ers, Saints, and Bills.

In a four-season period from 2014 to 2017 with the Broncos, Sanders joined the late Demaryius Thomas to form one of the league's best receiving duos. In the postseason, Sanders's best was during the Broncos' run to Super Bowl 50 in 2015, when in three games he had 16 catches for 230 yards. His 6 catches for 83 yards against the Carolina Panthers in the Super Bowl helped set up field goals on the first possession of each half in the Broncos' 24–10 victory.

Sanders and Thomas each had 100-catch seasons for a combined 3,000-plus yards in 2014. It was the first of three consecutive 1,000-yard receiving seasons for Sanders.

Vance Johnson (1985–1993, 1995)

During phase one of Elway's career—the phase where the Broncos reached three Super Bowls only to get whipped in all three—Johnson was his favorite Amigo. Johnson's best year was 1989, when he had 76 catches for 1,095 yards and 7 touchdowns. He retired as the Broncos' second-leading receiver (to Lionel Taylor) with 415 receptions, and still ranked No. 6 in catches through the 2022 season. Johnson also ranks No. 8 in both yards (5,695) and touchdowns (37) on the Broncos' all-time receiving list through 2022.

Later in life, Johnson publicly admitted he was abusive to his ex-wife and other woman. He also admitted to alcohol and pill addiction, but later became a rehabilitation ambassador and an inspiring example of redemption.

Al Denson (1964–1970)

Denson succeeded Taylor as the Broncos' No. 1 receiver in the late 1960s, and had monster seasons in 1967 and '69, when he was top 10 in catches and yards each season. He led the AFL with 11 touchdown catches in 1967 and was No. 3 behind the famed Raiders duo of Warren Wells and Fred Biletnikoff in 1969, with 10. Denson was selected to the AFL All-Star teams those two seasons.

Tall and slender at 6-foot-2, 210 pounds, Denson played tight end in 1966 when he had 36 catches for 725 yards. Lou Saban then wisely shifted him to flanker for the 1967 season.

Denson sat No. 2 in team history for a decade in the top categories of catches (250), yards (4,150), and touchdowns (32), and he still ranks in the top 14 in all three.

Brandon Marshall (2006–2009)

Marshall only played four seasons in Denver after he was a fourth-round selection in 2006. After playing behind Javon Walker and Rod Smith as a rookie, he was the Broncos' top receiver from 2007 to 2009, when he had three consecutive 100-catch, 1,100-yard seasons. He set a single-game record with 21 catches (for 200 yards) in a 2009 loss at Indianapolis, a record he still holds more than 13 years later.

Behavioral issues in Marshall's youth caused high-strung head coach Josh McDaniels to trade his star receiver away after the 2009 season. To Marshall's credit, he became a better pro as he matured, and he continued to put up 1,000-yard seasons for the Dolphins, Bears, and Jets before his lengthy career ended in 2018, with 970 receptions, 12,351 yards, and 83 touchdowns—but not one playoff appearance—in 13 seasons.

Mark Jackson (1986–1992)

The most underrated of the Three Amigos, but also the most charismatic, Jackson made his mark by catching the two most important John Elway passes during the famed Drive—a 20-yard reception to convert a third-and-18, and a forward-falling, 5-yard touchdown snag of an Elway bullet that completed the 15-play, 98-yard drive.

Jackson never produced less than 436 yards in his seven Broncos seasons, with 926 yards off 57 catches in 1990 his best. He ranks 12th all-time with 276 catches, 11th with 4,746 yards, and tied for 14th with 24 touchdowns. His 17.2 yards per catch is eclipsed only by Moses' 18.0 and Watson's 17.3 among Broncos receivers with at least 170 catches.

Courtland Sutton (2018–2022)

A second-round draft pick out of SMU, Sutton was meant to help ease the Broncos' transition from their aging dynamic duo of Demaryius Thomas and Emmanuel Sanders, and for a while, Sutton was fulfilling that promise.

Sutton finished his rookie season with 42 receptions for 704 yards and 4 touchdowns. He then took off in his second season of 2019 when, despite working with three different starting quarterbacks, he had 72 catches for 1,112 yards and 6 touchdowns. His forte became the 50-50 catch—the ball in the air, well-covered by a defensive back—which Sutton seemingly turned into a 70-30 percentage in his favor thanks to his big body, strength, and leaping ability.

Unfortunately for Sutton, injuries hindered his promising career. As of this writing, Sutton has been unable to repeat his 2019 season. Days before the 2020 season-opener, Sutton leaped to make a catch in an early pass-and-catch drill against air, and landed awkwardly on his shoulder, spraining the joint. That forced him to miss the first game, and he probably should have missed one more.

For in game 2, his shoulder harnessed in such a way that he couldn't raise his hands above his helmet, Sutton dropped a pass thrown at his head, and the ball ricocheted into an interception. Angry at himself, Sutton chased down the interceptor, made the tackle—and came away with a torn ACL.

Sutton was never quite the same after that, although he did make an impressive comeback. He had 58 catches for 776 yards with 2 touchdowns in his comeback season of 2021, and 64 catches for 829 yards and 2 touchdowns in 2022.

Without the same explosiveness he had before the ACL injury, Sutton couldn't separate from defenders as he used to, and the 50-50 ball truly became 50-50.

Honorable mention: Rick Upchurch, Eric Decker, Bob Scarpitto, Eddie Royal.

TIGHT END

Tight end is perhaps the most unappreciated position in football—until it's third-and-6. If the key to every football game were third down—with either punt or move the chains at stake—and a medium distance to go, tight ends would get all the commercials. When it's third-and-6, there is no greater mismatch that favors the offense than a tight end against a linebacker.

Speaking of which . . .

It was the 1997-season AFC Championship Game at Pittsburgh's Three Rivers Stadium. The Broncos were up 24–14 at halftime, but the offense did nothing in the second half, while Steelers quarterback Kordell Stewart threw a touchdown pass with 2:46 remaining in the fourth quarter to draw within 24–21.

The yellow Terrible Towels were waving. The fans were stomping and screaming. At the 2-minute warning, the Broncos were backed up to their own 15-yard line.

Third-and-6.

Fail to convert, and a Broncos punt would give the Steelers the ball no worse than their own 40 with plenty of time to at least tie the game with a field goal. At the 2-minute warning, Broncos head coach Mike Shanahan called "All pivot," which meant everybody would run a hook pattern, out of the "Cinco" formation, which meant empty backfield.

"Mike [Shanahan] was the type of coach that if he put a play in during training camp and you ran it, at any point during the season he felt we should be able to re-call that play whether it was five weeks ago or 10 weeks ago or whatever it was," Shannon Sharpe said in the book, *The 50 Greatest Players in Denver Broncos History*, and verbatim again in late October during the Broncos' Super Bowl XXXII reunion. "I'm looking at John [Elway] and going, 'That's not in the game plan. What do you want me to do?' And he said, 'Go get open.' That was the first time he told me I could ad-lib."

The Steelers surprisingly dropped their 3-4 pass-rushing linebacker, Jason Gildon, into coverage. Gildon was terrific going forward, as he would have 54 sacks in the following five seasons as an edge-rusher. But on this play he wound up back-pedaling to cover Sharpe.

"All he had to do, if he would have just stuck his hand out, instead of try to swipe the ball, it would have hit the back of his hand and hit the dirt," Sharpe said.

Gildon's swipe came up empty and Sharpe caught it, turned, and picked up 18 yards. First down. You should have heard the silence. The Broncos ran out the clock. On to Super Bowl XXXII.

"I had great numbers," Sharpe said. "I had been an All-Pro. But I hadn't really had that signature moment. John was great but he had The Drive. [Joe] Montana, he had John Candy and John Taylor.

"For a player, you must have a signature moment. You have to have a signature play. Up until that point, I had big games, multiple touchdown games, but I really hadn't had a signature play. And it's funny how that signature play happened because we didn't practice that play."

It was perhaps the biggest play ever by a Broncos tight end, if one of many third-and-mediums Sharpe had converted during his record-breaking, 14-year career, 12 of which were with the Broncos.

Sharpe's production and outsized personality aside—he went on to become a leading national sports commentator—the tight end has the second-lowest franchise-tag salary among all positions to running back. But at least the running back gets the ball on running plays. The tight end has to block. Yes, the running back has to sometimes block blitzing linebackers. But so does the tight end, who is often asked to either stay in and block on passing downs, or chip an edge-rusher on his way out to a pattern. And the running back receives far more endorsements and fan popularity.

Even offensive guards have a higher franchise-tag number than tight ends because they get lumped in with left tackles.

It's the blocking portion of the job description that makes the tight end one of the least understood and least appreciated positions. Fantasy leaguers want catches. Many of the best tight ends might catch one or two passes a game, but a greater priority is to serve as a third offensive tackle in the run game.

The Broncos have had a nice mix of blockers and receivers at the tight end position over the years. The position produced some incredible pass catchers, none more so than Sharpe, who in 2011 became the fourth Broncos player to be inducted into the Pro Football Hall of Fame—after Elway, left tackle Gary Zimmerman, and running back Floyd Little. But there were some other large, pass-catching freaks who wore orange and blue, like Julius Thomas, Tony Scheffler, and Noah Fant.

Perhaps the best two-way tight end in Broncos history—receiving and blocking—was Riley Odoms from the Orange Crush era. Odoms is one of the greatest omissions from the Broncos' own Ring of Fame.

There was never a better blocking tight end than Clarence Kay—which was evident by the fact that although he repeatedly had problems with drugs, alcohol, and arrests, he still lasted nine seasons with the Broncos, from 1984 to 1992, and missed just nine games. Head coach Dan Reeves may have seemed like a taskmaster, but he would occasionally look away from Kay's misdeeds. His blocking was simply invaluable.

There really isn't much doubt as to the best tight end in Broncos history, but the careers of Odoms and Kay are worth examining, along with Sharpe's.

THE CANDIDATES

Shannon Sharpe
Riley Odoms
Clarence Kay

SHANNON SHARPE (1990–1999, 2002–2003)

When he called it a career after 14 seasons in the spring of 2004, Sharpe was the all-time leader among NFL tight ends in the Holy Trinity statistical categories of catches (815), receiving yards (10,060), and touchdowns (62). No. 1, No. 1, and No. 1.

Tony Gonzales, Jason Witten, and Antonio Gates eventually passed him in each of those categories, but those three tight ends had three less Super Bowl rings combined than the three Sharpe had earned—two with the Broncos in 1997 and 1998, and another with the 2000 Baltimore Ravens.

It took until his third year of eligibility, or two years too long, but Sharpe has the right to annex the letters "HOF" to his autograph.

"Before it was three-time Super Bowl winner," Sharpe said. "Now it's Hall of Fame. It's funny how those three little letters, how much cachet they carry. They look at you in a different light. Because there are [more than 25,000] men who have played this game, and at the time I went in, there were only 258 who could say they were Hall of Famers. And I think there were only 150 who were living. So it's very, very elite company.

"It's still hard for me to absorb that I'm in the same building as Jim Brown, or Mean Joe Greene. I grew up watching Mean Joe. And some of the guys I played against, I played against

Reggie White and Derrick Thomas. Some of the all-time great, greats. Deion Sanders and I are in the same building.

"It's still hard for me to believe that a kid who wasn't drafted until the seventh round and started out on special teams, and they found a position for him. At the time only three teams had an H-back position—the Broncos, the Chargers, and [Washington]. So I went to one of the three teams that had an H-back position."

Talk about a guy born for the position. Sharpe was too athletic and fast for linebackers to cover—he once scored 52 points in a high school basketball game for Glennville High School—and at 6-foot-2, 235 pounds, was too big and strong for defensive backs. He was the prototype mismatch.

"I was drafted as a receiver, but it's funny how it happened—every tight end got hurt," Sharpe said about his rookie 1990 season when he converted from receiver to tight end in-season. "Clarence Kay got hurt, Orson Mobley got hurt, Chris Voorheis, he was hurt. I was the biggest wide receiver. They didn't bring guys in during the season like they do now."

Sharpe started dedicating himself to the weight room—a habit he never lost the next 20 years after his retirement. He made his first Pro Bowl in 1992, his third year in the league, first as a full-time starting tight end. When Wade Phillips succeeded Dan Reeves as the new head coach in 1993, Jim Fassel was brought in as offensive coordinator. Sharpe's career took off. He had 81 and 87 catches in 1993 and 1994, for 1,101 and 995 yards.

Incredible NFL success given where he came from.

Sharpe, his older sister Libby, and older brother Sterling grew up so poor in a cinder-block house in rural Georgia that featured a tin roof and cement floors, he once joked that when his house was robbed, "We robbed the robber." From the time he was 3 months old until he was 15, Shannon shared a bed with his grandma, Mary, who raised the Sharpe children, while Sterling shared a bed with Grandpa Barney.

From these humble, meager beginnings, the Sharpe brothers worked the chicken coop, cut tobacco, tended to hogs—and played football, basketball, whatever and whenever they could. Shannon "played up" with his brother's friends. They both grew up to be Hall of Fame football players. Only problem was, Sterling had a medical issue that stopped him from finishing off what had been an illustrious career. Sterling had a little more speed than Shannon—one reason why Green Bay selected Sterling with the No. 7 overall selection out of South Carolina in the 1988 NFL Draft, while Shannon wasn't selected until the seventh round in 1990 by the Broncos.

You thought Shannon was great? Sterling was sensational from the jump with the Packers, averaging 85 catches, 1,162 yards, and 9 touchdowns over seven seasons.

Jerry Rice, who would later set every significant NFL receiving record by wide margins, averaged 75 catches in his first seven seasons.

Had an abnormality between his top two neck vertebrae not brought a premature end to Sterling's career, granny Mary would have raised two Pro Football Hall of Famers in that tiny cinder-block house with the cement floors and tin roof. Shannon Sharpe was initially given the No. 1 jersey when he joined the Broncos, then No. 81. When receiver Ricky Nattiel was traded to Tampa Bay in January 1992, Sharpe took his No. 84—Sterling's number in Green Bay.

"I never felt the pressure of wearing my brother's number," Sharpe said. "Because I always felt he really wanted me to do well. He got greater satisfaction in seeing me succeed than in his own joy. When I was in high school and he was in college, he would come back and watch me run track or watch me play basketball. I always had my best games when he was there. So when I got to the NFL, he had already led the league in catches, he was All-Pro [in 1989, with 90 catches], and people were like, 'You're Sterling's little brother and you're playing special teams?' And all the sudden, everybody got hurt and Dan put me in there [at tight end]. But once I got that number 84, I was, like, 'Okay, now I'll really show 'em.'"

Sharpe had at least 61 catches and 756 yards in 10 seasons. He had added 62 more catches and 814 yards in 18 playoff games. No other tight end in Broncos history came close to his receiving totals.

RILEY ODOMS (1972–1983)

Tight end is perhaps the most unappreciated position in football—until it's second-and-8 in the AFC Championship Game.

Riley Odoms recalled the setup to the favorite play of his 12-year NFL career, all with the Broncos. It was early in the third quarter and the Broncos were leading the hated Raiders, 7–3, in the 1977 AFC Championship Game played at frigid Mile High Stadium. Denver had just recovered a fumble by Raiders running back Clarence Davis and were just 17 yards away from taking a commanding lead. After a short run by Jon Keyworth, Broncos quarterback Craig Morton hit Odoms for a 13-yard pass play to set up first-and-goal at the 2.

It set up the most famous non-fumble in Broncos history. Rob Lytle was crushed by Raiders' safety Jack Tatum. The ball came loose and the Raiders recovered—BUT! The officials said the play was blown dead because Lytle's forward momentum had been stopped. Replays showed the Raiders got robbed, but no one felt sorry for the silver and black in those days, at least not anyone in Broncos Country. The Broncos scored on the next play for the 14–3 lead. Denver eventually won, 20–17, to reach its first Super Bowl.

Odoms had 37 catches in that championship 1977 season before having a career-best 54 receptions for 829 yards and 6 touchdowns in '78.

"Our offense was never highly rated—it was just the Orange Crush defense that everybody recognized," Odoms said in *The 50 Greatest Broncos*. "It wasn't until we crossed the 50 when they let us go. Even though we had Otis Armstrong and Haven Moses, our offense was set up so we would not make a mistake on this side of the 50 because we knew teams couldn't go 80 yards against our great defense. So we never wanted to leave our defense with a short field. But once we got across the 50-yard line, we had a very explosive offense. Once we crossed the 50, then we'd start throwing the ball around a little bit.

"But I don't complain. Our era just started to throw to the tight end. I watched John Mackey growing up as a kid. And I would go, 'Whoa, this Mackey can catch the ball.' But then he'd go back to blocking."

A joke that ain't funny is that Riley Odoms is not in the Broncos Ring of Fame.

Odoms was the Broncos' incredibly strong and athletic tight end during the Orange Crush era. He played in the same era as the Raiders' Dave Casper and the Lions' Charlie Sanders, who are in the Pro Football Hall of Fame. Look at how Odoms stacked up next to those two HOFers:

Riley Odoms: 1972–1983 (12 years): 396 catches, 5,755 yards, 41 touchdowns

Dave Casper: 1974–1984 (11 years): 378 catches, 5,216 yards, 52 touchdowns

Charlie Sanders: 1968–1977 (10 years): 336 catches, 4,817 yards, 31 touchdowns

Odoms whipped Sanders in every category and beat out Casper in all but touchdown receptions. And do you remember the Broncos offense during their Orange Crush years? It was a conservative, play-to-its-great-defense offense. Odoms blocked far more than he went out on pass patterns.

Odoms was a four-time Pro Bowler and back-to-back, first-team All-Pro in 1974 and 1975. First-team All-Pro. The best, at a time when some of the other NFL tight ends were Charlie Young, Jerry Smith, Rich Caster, Bob Tucker, Raymond Chester, and Sanders.

There are athletic freaks and there is Riley Odoms. In high school, he was a 6-foot-10 high jumper—while using the scissor-cut style. He hurdled 6-10, in other words. He played football and basketball his freshman year at the University of Houston, where football made him a third-team All-American his senior year.

In 1972 Odoms became what was then the highest draft pick in Broncos history when he was taken with the No. 5 overall selection.

He was the best tight end in Broncos history until Sharpe was converted from receiver in 1990.

"I don't spend my life thinking about the Ring of Fame," Odoms said in July 2022 from his home in Missouri City, a suburb of Houston. "At my age [73] I'm just happy every single day I get to enjoy life. It would be nice to be recognized, but there's always someone else when you played on a good team."

CLARENCE KAY (1984–1992)

Clarence Kay made it to game day; got to give him that. He may have missed a practice or several dozen as he battled addictions and wound up with a fairly lengthy arrest record between 1984 and 2000. But in his nine seasons with the Broncos, the oft-in-trouble Kay only missed nine games. That means he played in 146 of a possible 155 games, counting playoffs.

The 6-foot-2, 237-pound Kay—big for an NFL tight end in those days—was considered one of the best, if not *the* best, blocking tight ends in the NFL during the late 1980s. His hands softened as he moved to the middle part of his career, as he had 34 catches for 352 yards and 4 touchdown receptions in 1988.

Kay helped open up running lanes for 1,000-yard rushers Sammy Winder, Bobby Humphrey, and Gaston Green while also protecting John Elway in the passing game. When Dan Reeves was fired as head coach following the 1992 season, that was it for Kay, with the Broncos and the NFL. Reeves would give Kay some tough love, suspending him here and there for his off-field misdeeds, but he never gave up on him.

STARTER

While the Broncos had several talented tight ends with a variety of skill sets—receiver types like Sharpe, blockers like Kay,

Shannon Sharpe © ERIC LARS BAKKE

and an All-Pro two-way tight end like Odoms—there really wasn't much of a contest for the starter on *The Denver Broncos All-Time All-Stars*. Let the Hall of Fame break all ties. It's Shannon Sharpe.

OTHERS

Gene Prebola (1961–1963)

It wasn't easy getting noticed on a Broncos team that featured Lionel Taylor in its early years, but in 1962 Prebola led all American Football League tight ends with 41 catches. It's just that his receiver teammate Taylor led the entire AFL with 77 catches.

In his three seasons with the Broncos, Prebola had 100 catches for 1,419 yards. Growing up in West New York, New Jersey, Prebola attended Memorial High School, which never lost a game in his four years. At Boston University, he was a two-way starter and also lettered for two seasons on BU's basketball team. After his final season with the Broncos—in the early years of the AFL, players made about as much money as the guy next door—Prebola became a teacher and coach in New Jersey, where he and Patricia, his wife of 56 years, raised four children.

Dwayne Carswell (1994–2005)

Carswell took the "blocking" requirement of the tight end position to another level, as he was so good at it, he finished his career as an offensive tackle. Undrafted out of Liberty University in 1994, Carswell spent most of his rookie season on the Broncos practice squad, then played mostly special teams in his second season. He broke out in the 2000 season with 49 catches for 495 yards, and the following year he made the Pro Bowl team with 34 catches and 4 touchdowns.

He was a better receiver than Kay, but just as good a blocker and similarly durable. In the nine-year stretch from the end of 1995 through the first half of 2004, Carswell played in 153 consecutive games, counting the postseason. Carswell's career was halted midway through 2005 when he was involved in a multi-car crash that left him with broken ribs and a ruptured diaphragm.

Julius Thomas (2011–2014)

Thanks to the likes of Tony Gonzalez and Antonio Gates, college basketball power forwards converting to professional tight ends became a thing in the NFL in the 2000s. The Broncos made their move by taking Thomas in the fourth round of the 2011 draft. Thomas was a four-year basketball player at Portland State, helping the program to two NCAA tournament appearances and leaving as the school's all-time leader in games (121) and field-goal percentage (.663).

Although his unique athleticism was immediately evident on the football field, a troublesome high ankle sprain that eventually required surgery drastically curtailed his first two NFL seasons. But in the 2013 Season of Peyton, Thomas took off, catching 65 passes for 788 yards and 12 touchdown passes, the latter of which was a Broncos' single-season record among tight ends. Manning threw for 5,477 yards and 55 touchdowns that season for NFL single-season records that still stand.

Thomas was having an even better season in 2014, with 38 catches and a whopping 12 touchdowns through only nine games. But another ankle injury in game 9 all but shut down Thomas's season, and he wound up leaving for free agency and a five-year, $46 million contract with Jacksonville.

Tony Scheffler (2006–2009)

The second-round pick in the Broncos' great 2006 draft class that also included quarterback Jay Cutler in the first round, receiver Brandon Marshall and pass-rusher Elvis Dumervil in the fourth round, and guard Chris Kuper in the fifth, Scheffler fell a tad short of expectations but still had nearly 1,900 yards receiving and 14 touchdowns in his four seasons in Denver.

Like Cutler and Marshall, Scheffler got sideways with new head coach Josh McDaniels and was traded to his hometown Detroit Lions prior to the 2010 season.

Noah Fant (2020–2022)

A first-round draft pick (No. 20 overall) out of Iowa in 2020, no Broncos tight end has come close to matching Fant's first three-year production of 170 catches for 1,905 yards and 10 touchdowns with the team. Compare those numbers to Shannon Sharpe, who had 82 catches after his first three seasons for 1,061 yards and 4 touchdowns. While Sharpe posted big numbers in 9 of his next 10 seasons, the Broncos couldn't wait to see how Fant developed, as he became a key piece in the trade package that brought star quarterback Russell Wilson from Seattle prior to the 2022 season.

FULLBACK

And the regressively least position shall be the most difficult decision.

Long ago NFL history is considerably more kind to fullbacks than the modern era has been.

The great Jim Brown was a fullback. Joe Perry and Jim Taylor, who followed Brown as the NFL's three all-time leading rushers through the 1960s and halfway through the 1970s, were fullbacks. Franco Harris and John Riggins were pretty much the last of the fullbacks who were Hall of Fame ball carriers.

Once the West Coast offense started taking over the NFL in the 1980s, the fullback began to gradually evolve—or is that devolve?—into a lead-blocker position.

The Broncos have their own significant slice of NFL history—and the modern era. They also went through two types of fullbacks—the ball-carrying type in the 1960s and '70s, and the battering ram who could slip out and occasionally catch a pass in the flat from the 1980s on.

"It has been interesting to see how that has become two different positions," said Howard Griffith, the blocking-type fullback for the Broncos in the late 1990s. "Even from when I played in the West Coast offense, it continued to evolve."

Selecting the starting fullback for *The Denver Broncos All-Time All-Stars* came down to two choices—Jon Keyworth, a fine ball carrier in the 1970s, and Griffith, a terrific lead blocker for Terrell Davis and others during a short, but decorated, four-year stint in the late 1990s.

THE CANDIDATES

Howard Griffith
Jon Keyworth

HOWARD GRIFFITH (1997–2000)

After bouncing between the Colts, Rams, and Carolina Panthers through the first four seasons of his NFL career, Griffith became somewhat of a missing piece when he signed as a free agent with the Broncos prior to the 1997 season.

In Griffith's first two seasons in Denver, the Broncos won back-to-back Super Bowls.

A terrific lead blocker, the Broncos in Griffith's four seasons had four 1,000-yard rushers—Terrell Davis in 1997 and 1998, when he rushed for 2,008 yards; Olandis Gary in 1999; and Mike Anderson in 2000. What was it like to exist in a world where you did the dirty work and your partners T.D., Gary, and Anderson got the write-ups, accolades, and spotlight?

"To have a career in the National Football League, I realized I needed to make a transition to a position that was self-less," Griffith said in December 2022. "I knew I wasn't going to get the ball a lot. I've always been a team guy. It probably bothered family members more than it bothered me. Because for me it was, 'This is what I do.' I'd get the ball maybe once a month. But the thing is, you had to deliver.

"Ultimately it was realizing my job was just as important as everybody else's job. That may not be the perception. But if I don't do my job, things break down. It's like any other position, you're 1/11th of what's out there. So I was always driven by that. The fear of not being able to deliver for my teammates. I never wanted to let them down."

As for his ability as a playmaker, Griffith was a more productive receiver (77 catches, 551 yards, 8 TDs, counting playoffs) than rusher (137 yards, 3 touchdowns) in his four years with the Broncos, but he always had a nose for the goal line. This became obvious during a college game for the University of Illinois when Griffith scored an astounding 8 touchdowns in one game against Southern Illinois.

His playmaking skills were never more on display than in the 1997 AFC Championship Game at Pittsburgh.

Not only did he help Davis rush for 139 yards and a touchdown in that game, Griffith came through with less than 2 minutes remaining in the first half. With the Broncos down, 14–10, Griffith reached back for an Elway pass thrown behind him and made a one-handed snag before turning and moving into the end zone for a 16-yard touchdown that put the Broncos up for good.

"That's probably the play I think about the most," Griffith said. "Because we started rolling after that."

He also rushed for two short-yardage touchdowns in the Broncos' 34–19 victory against the Atlanta Falcons in Super Bowl XXXIII.

"The second [Super Bowl] was so rewarding," Griffith said. "The first one was easy to win, relatively. After the first one, guys couldn't wait to put on their suits, go out, talk to the media. You're excited about what happened. You go look at the guys doing media after the second one, guys didn't even think about putting on their suits. Guys went back to the hotel in shorts and sweats. Because it was that exhausting. It was a relief. Glad the season is over. We accomplished it. The second one was so stressful. And so rewarding."

A neck injury suffered in a training camp drill in 2001 was initially diagnosed as nothing serious. But the pain and discomfort persisted, and the next report was Griffith would be sidelined six weeks. He wound up missing the entire season, and finally the neck injury caused him to retire in 2002 after having not played since a 2000-season playoff loss to Baltimore.

"It was frustrating," he said. "Because I wanted to play, I wanted to be out there, but something just wasn't right. It never did subside. There was an opportunity for surgery, but it was only 50-50, if I remember correctly, that it would correct the issue. Neck surgery with no assurances you could play is not where you want to be.

"The other part of it, too, was, I didn't know how much I had left. I knew I could play another year. But I didn't know how long I could keep playing at the rate of doing what I was doing."

Griffith is healthy and happy working as an analyst for the Big Ten Football Network, where he finished up his 16th season in 2022.

JON KEYWORTH (1974–1980)

At the University of Colorado, Keyworth played eight positions and on both sides of the ball—quarterback, split end, wing-back, tight end, tailback, and fullback on offense; linebacker and defensive back on defense. Washington drafted him as a sixth-round tight end in 1974, but his rights were traded to the Broncos in exchange for two draft choices before the start of training camp.

The Broncos played Keyworth at fullback where as a rookie he tied for seventh in the NFL with 10 touchdown runs. The next year, 1975, he rushed for 725 yards and had 42 catches—impressive production in what was then a 14-game regular season.

Keyworth was not only one of the Broncos' most popular players during their iconic 1977 Super Bowl season, he wrote and sang a hit song about the team called "Make Those Miracles Happen." He later recorded an album, *Keys*, and played in establishments all over the state of Colorado and the Rocky

Mountain region during his playing days (Friday nights during the season; sometimes five nights a week in the off-season).

As a father, Keyworth has endured more than his share of tragedy. The Broncos' 1980 media guide listed Keyworth as having three sons: Jonathan (11/29/76), Jared (4/30/79), and Scott (2/26/80). One week into the 1980 training camp, son Scott died of sudden infant death syndrome. In October 2021, son Jared, an army veteran who had escorted the riderless horse in President Reagan's funeral procession, was killed in a vehicular crash while in the line of duty for the US Marshals Service.

Keyworth retired just prior to reporting to training camp in 1981. At the time, Keyworth was the Broncos' No. 3 all-time rushing leader with 2,653 yards, trailing only Floyd Little and Otis Armstrong. More than 30 years later, Keyworth is still ranked No. 10—and tops among fullbacks. Rick Parros, who was Keyworth's successor in 1981, is a distant second among Broncos fullbacks, with 1,330 rushing yards.

STARTER

Can't call it. It's a tie between Keyworth and Griffith. Essentially, fullback is football's only position that split into two positions and required two distinctly different skill sets.

Keyworth was one of the Broncos' best rushers, period, and came up with a song about the team during its magical Orange Crush season of 1977.

Griffith is one of the all-time best blocking fullbacks in NFL history, much less the Broncos. And he instantly helped the Broncos win back-to-back Super Bowls.

OTHERS

Billy Joe (1963–1964)

Billy Joe only played two seasons for the Broncos before finishing his seven-year career with the Bills, Dolphins, and Jets.

But in those two seasons in Denver, Joe rushed for a combined 1,061 yards and 6 touchdowns while adding another 27 combined catches for 106 yards and another TD. He was the UPI and AP AFL Rookie of the Year in 1963. He was traded to the Buffalo Bills prior to the 1965 season in exchange for another fullback, Cookie Gilchrist.

Cookie Gilchrist (1965, 1967)

This mercurial star was the AFL's Jim Brown. He had three terrific seasons with the Buffalo Bills, becoming the AFL's first 1,000-yard rusher in 1962 when he was named the league's MVP, before he was traded to the Broncos in 1965. He led the AFL in his first season with the Broncos with 252 carries and 6 touchdowns while finishing second with 954 rushing yards (the Chargers' Paul Lowe won the rushing title that year with 1,121 yards). Gilchrist also had 18 catches for another 154 yards and a touchdown and was named to his fourth consecutive AFL All-Star team.

In 1966, Gilchrist refused to report to training camp at the Colorado School of Mines in Golden, Colorado, claiming the Broncos owed him $59,000. He was traded to Miami in the middle of that 1966 season, but only rushed for 252 yards in eight games. Gilchrist was traded back to the Broncos in 1967, where he would reunite with former Bills head coach Lou Saban, but knee problems limited him to just one game—the final game of his career.

Wendell Hayes (1966–1967)

Hayes was Cookie Gilchrist's halfback partner in 1965 when Hayes rushed for 526 yards and 5 touchdowns. After Gilchrist left, Hayes took over the fullback position for the next two years and rushed for a combined 677 yards. Trader Lou Saban sent Hayes to the Kansas City Chiefs where he had his best years blocking for, and sharing carries with, tailbacks Mike Garrett, Robert Holmes, and Warren McVea.

Fran Lynch (1967–1975)
Lynch was never really called a fullback, but it was a fullback role he played for nine years as Floyd Little's lead blocker, backup running back, and roommate. Lynch only averaged 140 yards rushing a year in his career, but the fact he lasted nine seasons speaks to how well he did at other aspects of the job.

Jim Jensen (1977–1980)
Jensen replaced Keyworth as the starting fullback the second half of 1979 and all of 1980, rushing for 876 yards combined those two seasons.

Rick Parros (1981–1984)
A fourth-round draft pick in 1980, Parros missed his entire rookie season because of a training-camp knee injury, but then rivaled Keyworth's 1975 as the best rushing season ever by a Broncos fullback when in 1981, Parros led the team with 749 yards rushing and 37 receptions. Parros fell off in the strike-shortened, nine-game season of 1982, then missed much of 1983 with a shoulder injury—although earlier that year, Parros had the distinction of catching John Elway's first-ever NFL touchdown pass, a 33-yarder against the Eagles.

Parros became the No. 3 halfback behind Sammy Winder and Gerald Willhite in 1984, then spent three more seasons with the Seattle Seahawks.

Aaron Craver (1995–1996)
Craver was Terrell Davis's lead blocker the first half of T.D.'s remarkable four-year run that led to Canton, Ohio, and the

Hall of Fame. Craver not only rushed for 565 yards and 7 touchdowns those two seasons, he also combined for 82 catches and 666 receiving yards and another 2 touchdowns.

Craver started three more years for the Chargers and Saints—in all, an eight-year career.

Andy Janovich (2016–2019)
A sixth-round draft pick out of Nebraska, Jano didn't touch the ball much, but there was a year or two when he was the NFL's top lead-blocking fullback.

DEFENSE

CORNERBACKS

For a good chunk of the Broncos' initial success from the late 1970s through the late 1980s, their cornerback position was a way station to a second career at safety.

Billy Thompson, Steve Foley, Tyrone Braxton, and Mike Harden were Broncos starting cornerbacks first, before finishing out their careers as safeties. Even Dennis Smith, one of the best safeties—if not *the* best in Broncos history—started his career playing slot corner.

The transition from corner to safety was a core belief in the defensive philosophy of Joe Collier, the architect of Denver's strong defenses for exactly 20 seasons, from 1969 to 1988. The switch from corner to safety made sense for two reasons. One, players aren't quite as quick or fast as they get older, making cornerback a more difficult position to play for those who don't quite have the same leg burst. Two, safety is a position of wisdom, a read-and-react-and-cover the entire field. And these skills are better refined if you understand the cornerback position and those players who cover receivers one-on-one.

The conversion from corner to safety didn't completely go away following the Collier era. Kareem Jackson was a nine-year Houston Texans corner from 2010 to 2018 before the Broncos signed him to play safety for four seasons, from 2019 to 2022. Jackson was an exception, though, not the rule, as the NFL increasingly became more specialized beginning with the advent of free agency in the mid-1990s.

Through their long history, the Broncos had two cornerbacks who stood out way above the rest—Champ Bailey and Louis Wright. There was no converting to safety late in the careers of Wright and Bailey. They were too good at cornerback for a long time to allow them to leave one of the top-four premier positions on a team. (Quarterback, left tackle, and edgerusher are the others. All are related to the passing game.)

Wright and Bailey spanned different eras. Wright was the Broncos' first-round draft pick out of San Jose State in 1975. He played 12 seasons, all with the Broncos, before retiring following "The Drive" season of 1986.

Bailey was Washington's first-round draft pick out of Georgia in 1999. He played five seasons for Washington, then was traded—along with a second-round draft pick that turned out to be running back Tatum Bell—to the Broncos prior to the 2004 season, in exchange for star running back Clinton Portis.

Bailey played 10 seasons for the Broncos and wound up as a first-ballot inductee in the Pro Football Hall of Fame Class of 2019. Both Bailey and Wright went into the Broncos Ring of Fame in short order after they retired.

Wright and Bailey were similar in that they were pure cover corners. Collier didn't mess with converting Wright to safety. He was a cornerback through and through. Wright and Bailey often shadowed the opponents' No. 1 receivers. Both were good tacklers—great by cornerback standards.

There were other fine cornerbacks in Broncos history, and it appears Pat Surtain II, a first-round draft pick in 2021, is on his way to joining the Bailey–Wright pantheon of greats. But there were two, and only two, serious candidates for the two starting cornerback positions on *The Denver Broncos All-Time All-Stars*: Bailey and Wright.

"I'm honored to receive such a distinction," Wright said. "But it won't be long before Pat Surtain bumps me down to second team. He is excellent. His technique is so above anyone I've seen in a long time. A lot of these cornerbacks, they don't have the footwork technique they should have. But this Surtain kid, he comes out of a break at full speed. And he's so big [6-foot-2]. I haven't seen another one like him in a long, long time."

Leave it to Louis to deflect flattery for himself upon another.

The Candidates

Louis Wright
Champ Bailey

Louis Wright (1975–1986)

Once inside linebacker Randy Gradishar finally gets into the Pro Football Hall of Fame—he's been a near-miss finalist multiple times, and again in 2022—the voters can start looking at the case for Wright.

This was a 6-foot-2 shutdown cornerback for 12 seasons before Deion Sanders came along to inspire the term "cover corner."

"Ahead of his time," former Broncos linebacker Tom Jackson said of Wright. "Ahead of his time not only in his skill set, but his size, his speed, his ability to cover. As complicated as the Orange Crush was, we went into a game with, 'You 10 guys have to be totally coordinated with everything you do—Louis, you take their best receiver. You take Lynn Swann, you take Steve Largent, John Jefferson, and you shut him down and we'll win.'"

Wright made five Pro Bowls in his career with back-to-back All-Pro distinctions in 1977 and 1978. He played in every game in 8 of his 12 seasons, 166 total, and helped the Broncos reach two Super Bowls (1977; and he started in The Drive game at Cleveland in the 1986-season AFC Championship).

Louis Donnell Wright lived one day of his youth in Texas and the rest in Bakersfield, California. The one day in Texas was his first day, in his parents' hometown of Gilmer.

"They were living in California and in the 1950s, you know, Black people couldn't just walk into any hospital and have a baby," Wright said. "So my mom went back home where she knew the doctor and had all three of her children. I have another brother and sister. We were all born there, but we never lived there."

Back in Bakersfield, where the summer days could reach suffocating temperatures, Wright and his brother Fred grew up with a father-instilled work ethic. Glover C. Wright had moved from Gilmer, Texas, to Bakersfield to take a job delivering mail for the US Post Office.

"When he got off work, he was a gardener," Wright said. "He'd go cut people's yards. He was a workaholic. So as soon as we'd get out of school, he'd load us in the truck and we'd cut yards till the sun went down. I think I was in third grade when he first started taking me."

Glover was a fair man. He would pay his kids. He kept a log in his truck.

"Every day you had to go to work except Sundays," Wright said. "Unless you had a school activity. That's the only thing that could get you out of work. Naturally, I was in student council. I was in sports. I was in everything. 'Sorry, Dad, I have a track meet today.' 'Okay.' Whatever activity I could get in, I was there."

Wright played receiver and defensive end, believe it or not, in high school, and wound up attending Arizona State on a football scholarship for coach Frank Kush. The same Frank Kush who John Elway didn't want to play for when he was drafted No. 1 overall by the Baltimore Colts in 1983.

Maybe after being raised by Glover C. Wright, Frank Kush was a pushover. After his freshman year, though, Wright transferred back home to Bakersfield Junior College.

Where he sat on the bench his entire sophomore year.

"I think I wound up playing six or seven plays," Wright said. "The whole year. Bakersfield Junior College I sat on the bench. I rode it out and went out for track. And I did really good at track, so I got a track scholarship to San Jose State. I had given up on football."

Luckily for Wright and the Broncos, San Jose State's defensive backs coach Jim Colbert happened by track practice one day. Colbert convinced Wright to try out for the San Jose State football team that fall. It was Colbert's only year of coaching at San Jose State. Talk about serendipity.

Wright eventually played well enough to earn a spot in the Senior Bowl. The North team's coaches were the Denver Broncos staff led by John Ralston and Joe Collier.

Still, when Wright was the Broncos' first-round selection, No. 17 overall, in the 1975 draft—one spot behind New England tight end Russ Francis and one spot ahead of Dallas linebacker Thomas "Hollywood" Henderson—he was surprised.

"I was like, 'What?'" Wright said. "They never said a word to me the whole week. They never gave an inkling they even knew who I was."

He was still playing at a high level late in his career, recording five interceptions in 1985 and three more in 1986 for a combined total of 100 return yards. But he decided to retire around training camp, 1987.

"I thought about it, and you know what, there is no perfect time to leave the NFL," Wright said. "Or any sport. Whether you're Muhammad Ali or Michael Jordan. It's almost impossible to retire at the exact perfect time. Either you retire too early or you retire too late.

"I said, I'd rather retire too early than too late. I just made that decision. I didn't want the coaching staff to call me into the office and say, 'Hey, you're not doing it and we're going to have to cut you.' And I didn't want to have to say, 'Those jerks, they cut me.' I didn't want any friction on either side. Thank you for 12 years. What [else] can a guy ask for?"

He went back to San Jose State to finish his degree, then got into the geology field for one and a half years, an occupation that paid well but too often took him away from home to desolate places. He wound up teaching and coaching in the Aurora and Denver school systems.

What was he doing in the fall of 2022 at 69 years old? Still teaching physical education at Aurora Gateway High School. He was there when he turned 70 on January 31, 2023, an age when just about everyone else is collecting social security. Proving the work ethic instilled by Glover C. Wright never waned.

"A lot of my friends and family at my age are retired," Wright said. "But I just love doing what I'm doing. I'm probably going to retire, but health-wise, I'm blessed. I've got a good job, I've got good kids. I say a prayer every day. I don't know what else I could ask for."

How about a nomination from the seniors' committee for the Pro Football Hall of Fame?

"It would be an incredible honor if it was to happen," Wright said. "The people that are in there, I have utmost respect [for them], because you have to do a lot to even be considered to get in there. Some of the people that have been elected, especially in the defensive back category, I think—I'm not better than them, but I think I was as good as them.

"But I think the biggest enjoyment and satisfaction I have is my teammates and my coaches and people I was with for 12 years. I really think—and I could be wrong—but I really think they could depend on me. They [could] look at me in the face and know this was my assignment and this was my job to win the game, and I would come through. I felt I did everything I could for my teammates."

CHAMP BAILEY (2004–2013)

In the great history of the NFL, only two defensive players had more Pro Bowl appearances than Bailey. Rams defensive tackle Merlin Olsen had 14. Eagles and Packers defensive end Reggie White had 13. All were elected in their first year of HOF eligibility.

Bailey had 12 Pro Bowls, tied with the defensive likes of Junior Seau, Ray Lewis, Ken Houston, and Randall McDaniel. Bailey rightly was a first-ballot inductee as well for the Hall of Fame Class of 2019.

"I really look at two guys when I think about first-ballot corners: Darrell Green and Deion Sanders," Bailey said. "Two mentors early in my career, first and second year in the league, I got a chance to play with both these guys. And to continue to follow in their footsteps in that way means everything."

A three-time first-team All-Pro, only tight end Shannon Sharpe among Broncos had more than Bailey, with four.

There was no single moment that made Bailey a Hall of Famer, although there were his back-to-back seasons of 2005 and 2006 that put him over the top. He combined for 19 interceptions, 301 return yards, and call it 4 touchdowns (let's give him that last yard on his end-to-end interception return against Tom Brady in an AFC second-round playoff game) in those two seasons.

Although Bailey was known as a preeminent man-to-man corner, it was an injury, and a new strategy by Broncos secondary coach Bob Slowik, that led to those two iconic seasons.

After Bailey tweaked his hamstring during the 2005 preseason, Slowik adjusted by having his top cornerback play off the line of scrimmage. Off-man, they called it. By playing off, Bailey could begin covering his receiver from 5 yards back, a cushion that allowed him to peek in to read the quarterback— and pounce on the thrown ball. It's difficult to pick off an interception while playing man-to-man because a cornerback often winds up running with his back to the quarterback.

"I always felt like I was a better press corner," Bailey said. "Fortunately for me, I really started doing that [playing off] because of my hamstring. Because when you're playing bump-and-run you're always full speed. Because that guy can run past you at any second.

"But if I'm off, I can slow play everything. So the hamstring kind of enabled that. I just utilized it a lot more because I thought, playing off, I'm actually pretty good at this.

"Slowik's way of thinking was, you read the quarterback. That was the first time a coach told me to read a quarterback. So I took it to heart and I tried to use that even down the line a little bit [in my career]."

The 2005 season was special for Bailey. The Broncos were trounced in their season-opener at Miami, 34–10, then were booed into their halftime locker room by their home crowd as they were down, 14–3, to the San Diego Chargers in game 2. On the first play of the second half, Bailey changed the game—and the Broncos' season—with a 25-yard pick-six off Drew Brees.

The ever-fickle home crowd went bonkers with cheers.

The Broncos carried the momentum from the Bailey pick-six to win 20–17, and went on to a 13-3 record and AFC first-round playoff bye. Hosting New England, which had won three of the previous four Super Bowls, in the second-round playoff game, Bailey's 100-yard interception return against Tom Brady in the second half was a 14-point play swing in the Broncos' 27–13 victory.

It was Bailey's ninth interception of the season. Although he nearly had another pick-six against Ben Roethlisberger and the Pittsburgh Steelers in the AFC Championship Game at Invesco Field, it wasn't the Broncos' day. The Steelers stunned the Broncos at home, then went on to win Super Bowl XL by defeating the Seattle Seahawks in Detroit.

But Bailey was even better in 2006 when his 10 interceptions nearly garnered him NFL Defensive Player of the Year. He finished second to Dolphins defensive end Jason Taylor, who not only had 13.5 sacks, but two pick-sixes. Taylor received 22 votes to Bailey's 16.

Since Bailey's 10-interception season in 2006, there have only been three other double-digit pick seasons—the next year, in 2007, by Antonio Cromartie, who otherwise never had more than 4 picks in a season; Xavier Howard's 10 in 2020; and Trevon Diggs's 11 in 2021.

But no cornerback since Everson Walls in 1981–1982 has surpassed Bailey's two-year production of 19 interceptions in 2005–2006. (New England's Asante Samuel also had 19 picks, counting the postseason, in 2006–2007.)

"I think rule changes," Bailey said when asked to explain why the 10-interception season had become all but obsolete. "I think the new rules really put a lot of pressure on the defense.

"And then one thing I noticed with my last two coordinators [Dennis Allen and Jack Del Rio], they were trying to be more conservative and just make sure—don't give up the big ball. So I think guys are not taking as many chances as they used to."

It wasn't just interceptions that made Bailey a Hall of Famer. Unlike two other premier cover corners that sandwiched his career—Deion Sanders and Darrelle Revis—Bailey was a strong tackler.

Which brings up another injury that didn't stop Bailey from having his tremendous season in 2005.

In the opener in Miami that year, Bailey separated his shoulder early in the second half. He played the rest of the season in a shoulder harness.

First game with his new constraint, he made the season-altering pick off Drew Brees.

"Even that played a role in it," Bailey said of his harness. "It was tough. It was challenging. It was my left shoulder, so my right one now feels worse than my left."

With the left shoulder protected, the right shoulder was alone in its physical punishment.

"I had to tackle with something," Bailey said. "Fortunately with me, I was able to use my right shoulder and be effective with it."

He practiced that same week. Champ laughed at the memory.

"I thought I was a tough guy," he said, with his patented Hall of Fame chuckle.

He wound up with Gold Jacket No. 319 and—after an impassioned 30-minute, 30-second induction speech on the stage in Canton, Ohio—his bust in the Hall of Fame museum on the very first ballot.

STARTERS

Champ Bailey and Louis Wright
Really, the only two choices—at least until, as Wright said, Surtain stacks on a few more All-Pro years.

OTHERS

Aqib Talib (2014–2017)
A naturally vibrant personality who had off-field issues, Talib made four Pro Bowls in his four years with the Broncos, from 2014 to 2017. He was part of the Broncos' tremendous defense that carried Denver to its Super Bowl 50 title, the third Lombardi Trophy in franchise history. Remarkably, 6 of Talib's 11 interceptions during his four seasons in Denver were returned

Louis Wright © ROD HANNA

for touchdowns. For his career, Talib had 10 touchdowns off interceptions, ranking him fourth all-time, and just two behind the all-time leader, Rod Woodson.

Chris Harris Jr. (2011–2019)

Unlike Talib, who was signed to a lucrative contract as an unrestricted free agent, Harris was undrafted in 2011 out of Kansas and wound up with the Broncos on a $2,000 signing bonus. He eventually got his paychecks, though, thanks to four Pro

Bowl seasons with an All-Pro honor in 2016. A willing and sure tackler, there was a three- or four-year period when the scrappy Harris was considered the best nickel defensive back in the NFL. He played in 139 games in nine seasons with the Broncos before continuing his career with the Chargers for two seasons and the New Orleans Saints for one.

Willie Brown (1963–1966)

When Lou Saban was hired to much fanfare as the new Broncos head coach in 1967, one of his first moves was to discard nearly every star player he had inherited. Even Willie Brown, who later became a first-ballot Hall of Famer primarily as an Oakland Raider.

But first, Brown was an AFL All-Pro for the Broncos in 1964, when he made a career-best 9 interceptions with 140 return yards. He also made two AFL Pro Bowls during his four seasons in Denver.

With the Raiders, though, Brown played 12 more seasons and made six more All-Pro teams and seven more Pro Bowls. He had a 75-yard touchdown interception return off Fran Tarkenton to clinch Super Bowl XI.

Ray Crockett (1994–2000)

The starting left cornerback on the Broncos' back-to-back Super Bowl championship teams in 1997 and 1998, Crockett was a seven-year starter for the Broncos, missing just six games. He played his first five seasons for the Detroit Lions, the last three and a half as a starter.

He was part of the NFL's second unrestricted free agent class in 1994, signing a then-eyebrow-raising contract of four years, $6.4 million, to join the Broncos. He played in 117 games for the Broncos (counting 11 in the postseason), with 115 starts,

18 interceptions, and 2 pick-sixes. He also averaged better than 65 tackles a year.

He finished his career with two more seasons for the rival Kansas City Chiefs. Not many cornerback careers last for 14 seasons, so Crockett was among the league's most underrated.

Mike Harden (1980–1987)

As Louis Wright was getting up there in the mid-1980s, Harden was "the other" corner who in a five-season stretch from 1983 to 1987 led the Broncos with 25 interceptions and an astounding 570 return yards (114 per season) and 4 pick-sixes. He switched to safety part-time in 1987 and full-time in 1988 before finishing his career in Oakland for two seasons. Played nine seasons for the Broncos, seven as a starter.

Darrent Williams (2005–2006)

The first of three cornerback picks in the 2005 draft, Williams had a superb rookie season as he started opposite Champ Bailey and had his own 80-yard interception return for a touchdown. He was also the team's punt and kickoff returner, bringing one punt back 52 yards.

Although the 5-foot-8, 188-pound Williams was nicked up in his second season, he had four interceptions with another pick-six, and again was an effective punt returner.

Tragically, Williams was killed in a drive-by shooting hours after the Broncos' final regular-season game in 2006. Since his passing, Broncos media issues the Darrent Williams Good Guy Award to the player who each year exemplifies Williams's enthusiasm, cooperation, and honesty.

Pat Surtain II (2021–present)

He became new general manager George Paton's first draft pick in 2021, when Surtain was taken out of Alabama with the No. 9 overall selection. The son of a 10-year NFL cornerback, PS2 made the NFL's all-rookie defensive team and was a first alternate Pro Bowler. He had a 70-yard pick-six against Chargers quarterback Justin Herbert in game 11 of his rookie season, and four interceptions total in 2021.

In his second season of 2022, Surtain became the only Bronco selected as a starter on the AFC Pro Bowl team and first-team All-Pro. Early signs point toward greatness, but Surtain will have to do it over 10 years if he is to join the company of Bailey and Wright.

DEFENSIVE TACKLES

Nobody dreams of growing up to become a defensive tackle. Millions of kids may dream of becoming an NFL player. But not a defensive tackle.

Not even Trevor Pryce, who figured out in eighth grade that his size and speed made him unique among boys, to the point where he would one day play in the National Football League. But defensive tackle, where every snap is a close-range collision with not one but two or three 285-pound (the beginning of Pryce's career) to 330-pound (the end of Pryce's career) offensive linemen?

"I came out as a defensive end out of college," Pryce said. "I worked out at the combine as a linebacker as well. I got to Denver and they told me I was a defensive tackle. I was like, what? What's that? They asked me to play the 3 technique. I was like, where do I go?"

For *The Denver Broncos All-Time All-Stars*, picking two starting defensive tackles mirrored the difficulty of deciding on two defensive ends and one fullback, as there are two different types of players at the positions: There is the leading rusher or blocker at fullback; the 3-4 defensive end who is really more of a defensive tackle; and the 4-3 defensive end who is more similar to a pass-rushing outside linebacker.

As for the pure defensive tackle position, there is the gap-plugging, nose tackle who plays over the center in the 3-4 and the more traditional defensive tackle who plays in the narrow spaces between center and guard, or guard and tackle, in the

4-3. In the increasingly specialized NFL, there are body types and skill sets for each gap placement, or "technique."

"To me what makes the defensive tackle unique is that [it's] the closest position to the quarterback," Pryce said. "That's what makes it unique."

And for the Denver Broncos, who perhaps utilized a higher percentage of 3-4 defense than any other NFL team over the years, selecting two, and only two, defensive tackles adds another layer of complexity. Furthermore, the Broncos were not lacking for quality defensive tackle candidates.

THE CANDIDATES

Trevor Pryce
Bud McFadin
Dave Costa
Rubin Carter
Paul Smith
Greg Kragen

TREVOR PRYCE (1997–2005)

He was not only the most talented defensive tackle in Broncos history, but the most productive. Even though it's been 17 years since he played his last game with the Broncos, Pryce still ranks No. 7 on the team's all-time sack list, and No. 1 among pure defensive tackles, with 64.0 in 121 games. Second place among Broncos defensive tackles was Paul Smith, with 55.0 sacks in 133 games.

Pryce could have put up even greater numbers in a Broncos uniform had head coach Mike Shanahan let him be, for what he was. Shanahan, like all coaches, loved players dedicated to the craft. He struggled with players like quarterback Jake

Plummer and Pryce, who had other interests once they left team headquarters.

"When you have a young person who's never had that kind of money before—I grew up where if you went to the mall to buy something it was a big deal," Pryce said. "So when you're a young person going to a city like Denver, you buy a house, buy some cars, and then you get to the off-season, what do you think that kid does?

"To me it became very apparent I had to fill my time with something else or trouble was going to find me. So music became my outlet. I began to compartmentalize my job. I knew from the time I was in eighth grade I was going to be a professional football player. I knew I was different from everybody else. I had this sinking feeling that being my size and that fast was special. But when does trouble happen? Trouble happens in the off-season. I knew very early this could go sideways. I watched it go sideways with a lot of my teammates.

"So those questions, whether you love football or not, [are]: I have a job, and I looked at it as a job. People don't bring their jobs home. It's no different to me than being a policeman. The job for NFL players is combat. You can't take that [stuff] home. You just can't. You have to find a way to turn that off. I can talk about it now and process it at my age."

Joining a Broncos team in 1997 that had a roster so stacked it was about to win back-to-back Super Bowls, Pryce was inactive for the first eight games. At 6-foot-5, 285 pounds, Pryce was uniquely built as defensive tackles go. Most players his height play defensive end. His play sped up in his second season of 1998 and then he became almost unblockable beginning in his third season of 1999, when he was selected first-team All-Pro after registering 13.0 sacks. He came back with a 12.0-sack encore in 2000—unheard-of sack totals for a defensive tackle at the time—while drawing the first two of four consecutive Pro Bowls.

But after that 2000 season, Shanahan fired defensive coordinator Greg Robinson. Pryce's next two defensive coordinators, Ray Rhodes and Larry Coyer, devised schemes that were not suited for the defensive tackle's pass-rush abilities. The new scheme for Pryce was to gather blockers and let the linebackers clean up the quarterback and ball carriers.

That's great for the fire hydrant–built defensive tackles. But it wasted Pryce's interior pass-rush skills. The Broncos prematurely released him following the 2005 season for salary-cap reasons. Premature because Pryce matched his career-best with 13.0 sacks in his first season with the Baltimore Ravens in 2006.

The renaissance quality within Pryce may have irritated his controlling coaches but it helped him adjust in a major way upon his retirement as a player following his 14th season in 2010. Pryce wrote a trilogy book series, *An Army of Frogs*, that was animated for Netflix for two seasons before it was picked up by Hulu for a third season, starting production in December 2023. According to the Netflix synopsis, the animated streaming series *Kulipari: An Army of Frogs* is a tale about fearless frogs going to war against sinister scorpions and spiders that have teamed up to conquer the amphibians. Season three is set for release in the summer of 2024. Pryce is the creator, writer, and producer of the series, working from his Baltimore-area studio.

Trevor Pryce. The gift that keeps on giving.

BUD MCFADIN (1960–1963)

An original Bronco, McFadin was the franchise's first defensive leader he made the All-AFL team his first three seasons, then was named an AFL All-Star in 1963. Four out of four ain't bad.

He was a two-way lineman at the University of Texas, then a first-round draft pick, No. 11 overall, as a guard in 1951 by the

NFL Los Angeles Rams. McFadin missed his rookie year for the most honorable of reasons—to serve in the US Air Force during the Korean War.

He then played five seasons for the NFL Los Angeles Rams from 1952 to 1956, switching from guard to defensive tackle in 1955, and was a two-time Pro Bowler his last two seasons there. He retired after the 1956 season following a hunting shooting accident, then came out of retirement when the AFL was established in 1960.

McFadin scored three touchdowns off fumble recoveries (two with the Broncos) and also kicked two field goals, from 41 and 45 yards, with the Rams. He passed away in 2006 at age 77.

DAVE COSTA (1967–1971)

Lou Saban made several regrettable trades during his time as Broncos boss—most notably sending Hall of Famers Willie Brown to Oakland and Curley Culp to Kansas City—but one he got right was when he acquired Costa from the Buffalo Bills in exchange for a draft pick prior to the 1967 season.

Costa was a five-year captain for the Broncos where he started 70 of a possible 70 games. He was an AFL All-Star selection each of his first three seasons with Denver. He had 20.5 sacks combined in the two seasons of 1969 and 1970, remarkable production from the inside pass-rush position.

And that was before Saban stated, "We could use about a dozen more Costas," in the Broncos 1968 media guide.

Costa attended Northeastern Junior College in Sterling, Colorado, for a year, then transferred to the University of Utah, from where the Oakland Raiders drafted him in 1963 in the seventh round. Costa was runner-up AFL Rookie of the Year in 1963 to Broncos fullback Billy Joe.

During his time with the Broncos, Costa was in charge of a 17-player Broncos basketball team that played in the Denver area during the off-season. The team was named the Dave Costa All-Stars, as Saban didn't want the group attached to the Broncos name. Costa was also a banker in the off-season.

Costa died in 2013 at age 71.

Rubin Carter (1975–1986)

Rubin Carter was made with two games left in the 1976 season. Denver's star defensive end Lyle Alzado blew out his knee on the first defensive play of that year and missed the entire 14-game season. Through adversity, defensive coordinator Joe Collier discovered a boon. Absent Alzado, Collier experimented with the switch from the 4-3 defense to a 3-4 alignment. It was Carter who would play the nose whenever Collier got his 3-4 itch. But always before the next game the Broncos would switch back to the 4-3.

Finally, with the Broncos officially eliminated from the postseason with their 7-5 record, and at least a dozen players grumbling about their head coach John Ralston, Collier went exclusively with the 3-4 defense for the final two games.

The Broncos beat the Chiefs, 17–16, at old Mile High Stadium and the Bears, 28–14, at Chicago's Soldier Field. Kansas City was held to 59 yards rushing on 29 carries, or a meager 2.0 yards per carry. Chicago quarterback Bob Avellini completed 2 of 17 passes. That's right, 2 of 17. Carter had 3 tackles and an assist in each game.

The 3-4 alignment could stop the run, and thwart the pass. The 3-4 was here to stay.

"We became the Orange Crush—this gets a little bit technical—there is nothing more important than the nose," said Broncos star linebacker Tom Jackson. "Because you have to stop the run with limited people up front."

One after another, the testimonials came in. Rubin Carter was seldom honored by anyone, except for every one of his teammates. He never was named to a Pro Bowl. All he did was make history.

"Rubin Carter was the anchor," said Broncos receiver Haven Moses. "He was the anchor of the Orange Crush. I remember getting him from [the University of] Miami. When he came in he said he was 6 foot, but I think he was shorter than that. But boy, there was no one tougher. They had to double-team him. Which really made Lyle more than anybody. Because Rubin and Barney [Chavous, the Broncos left end in their three-man front] would tie up the offensive lines and Lyle would pretty much freelance.

"And then Rubin really helped make our linebackers. We had it up front, we had it in the middle, and we had it in the back. But Rubin Carter was the key to making that defense."

"He was the nose guard of the decade, Rubin Carter," said Broncos cornerback Steve Foley. "Rubin, you could not move him. He was 6-foot, 260. Stretch like a ballerina. Was the softest-spoken player, but we had the best run defense in the league for a few years running. And Rubin and Barney, you could not move.

"He may not have made as many plays, but he allowed everyone else to make them. Because you had to double-team him. That was the whole essence of our defense, is let the linebackers come free and they can handle their gaps. We were a gap-control defense and we were excellent at it. You didn't see holes."

Carter was underappreciated in many respects, but he had the respect and admiration of his peers. What else is there?

"I've always said a nose tackle was like a manhole cover: You don't miss them till they're gone," Carter said.

Nose tackle may be the toughest of the 22 positions lined up on a football field. But from what Carter saw and lived through as a youth, playing the nose position in the 3-4 was easy money.

His parents, Charlie and Susie Carter, were migrant workers. They worked up and down the Eastern Seaboard, picking fruits and vegetables, riding a bus from town to town. Rubin was the eighth of their eight children. He was born in Pompano Beach, Florida, only because that's where the migrant workers' bus stopped when Susie Carter was ready to deliver.

"I was born in Pompano Beach, but we wound up all the way up to Salisbury, Maryland," Carter said. "And they were touring the bus and that's the way we traveled, so I learned hard work early in my life. Because as a migrant worker, what you pick is what you're paid for. If you don't produce, you don't get paid."

Carter did not always toil in obscurity. On October 17, 1977—exactly one year after the 3-4 Orange Crush defense was born—a close-up photo of the helmet-wearing Carter filled the cover of *Sports Illustrated*. It wasn't a menacing look Carter was wearing, but a serious, businesslike, "Snap-the-ball, let's-go" stare.

The accompanying article was entitled, "Say Hello to the Fearsome Threesome." It was Carter's face that was picked to represent the Orange Crush.

"I was shocked that they wanted me on the cover," Carter said 40 years later for the book, *The 50 Greatest Players in Denver Broncos History*. "I told them, 'Are you sure you've got the right guy? Tommy's making a lot of plays and Randy [Gradishar's] making a lot.' And they said, 'Well, you cause those guys to be free. You're clogging up things in the middle.'

"It was quite an honor. Going on the cover of *Sports Illustrated* was one of the better things that happened to me. It was recognition from people throughout the league and also from opponents I was playing against. That's the highest form of flattery as a nose tackle."

Perhaps one reason why Carter didn't earn any Pro Bowls is a 3-4 nose tackle wasn't up for a vote. He had more than 1,036 tackles in his 12-year career with the Broncos and 33 sacks—unheard-of statistics for modern-era nose tackles. Had the NFL appreciated the position like it does today, Carter's 6.0 sacks in 1977 and 6.5 sacks in 1978 from the nose tackle position would have been worth a contract between $10 million and $15 million per year.

He wasn't the first NFL nose guard. That distinction belonged to Curley Culp, who was the Broncos' first player taken in the 1968 draft, but who was discarded before playing his first game by coach Lou Saban.

Culp wound up becoming a Pro Football Hall of Fame defensive lineman for the Kansas City Chiefs.

"Growing up I watched him a lot when he was with Kansas City and I was in high school," Carter said. "I would notice some of the action he had, and certainly he was the strength of that defense, because he would get double- and triple-teamed. He had the strength and ability to play with natural leverage, and just the quickness he had to be able to beat blocks, and pursue down the line of scrimmage and make plays. A lot of that I tried to implement into my game and what he'd done."

Carter was a quick study. He wound up playing more games at nose tackle (152) than any other player in NFL history. For the longest time, the journey to Super Bowl XII was the highlight of the Broncos franchise. The game was a drag, although Carter shined with six tackles and two sacks.

"Rubin was very . . . he was good. He was very good," said Chavous, Carter's longtime defensive line mate and friend. "He was the epitome of a nose tackle. No one center could block Rubin. He was very physical. That's something we took pride in. Rubin was very good at getting people off him to get to the ball. People had to double-team Rubin because they couldn't leave the nose one-on-one with the center. When they put two on him that meant the linebackers would be free."

While finishing his playing career on injured reserve in 1986, Carter served as an unofficial player-coach to the likes of Greg Kragen, Andre Townsend, and Rulon Jones.

Carter was so good at it that he coached football for the next 29 years. He coached for the college programs of Howard, San Jose State, Maryland, Temple, Florida A&M (where he was head coach), New Mexico, Towson, and Purdue. He coached in the NFL for Washington and the New York Jets. He coached at a Miami high school and was most recently a volunteer coach for high school kids in the Tallahassee, Florida, area, where he and his wife Karen have otherwise retired.

Carter's son, Andre Carter, had a nice 13-year, NFL career, registering 80.5 sacks. Better believe Andre played 13 because dad played 12.

Paul Smith (1968–1978)

There was a four-season stretch from 1970 to 1973 when Smith was the most underrated interior pass-rusher in the NFL as he compiled 45.0 sacks. How unsung was Smith? In 1971, Minnesota defensive tackle Alan Page had 9.0 sacks while becoming the first defensive player ever to be voted the NFL's MVP award. That same year, Smith had 12.0 sacks from his defensive tackle position—3.0 more than Page—yet his only honor was honorable mention All-AFC.

Smith, who passed away at the too-young age of 54 in 2000, was considered a large man in the 1970s at 6-foot-3, 256 pounds. What he may have lacked in agility—"Tombstone" Jackson used to tease Smith about his struggles with the rope ladders—he made up for with incredible quickness.

Those four terrific seasons—which included Pro Bowl berths in 1972 and '73, plus the fact he became the first 10-year player with the club—is why Smith was part of the third class of 1986 to be inducted into the Broncos Ring of Fame.

At one time, Broncos head coach John Ralston called Smith "the finest defensive tackle in football." Which was saying something, when NFL defensive tackles of that era included Page, "Bubba" Smith, "Mean" Joe Greene, Bob Lilly, and Merlin Olsen.

After a ruptured Achilles in the second game of the 1974 season put a crimp on Smith's terrific career, he still managed to contribute in the following seasons of 1975 (4.5 sacks) and 1976 (3.0 sacks).

In 1977, when Broncos defensive coordinator Joe Collier went full-time with the 3-4 system, he alternated a second-string front three of Smith, John Grant, and Brison Manor every third series. The starting three of Chavous, Carter, and Alzado played two out of three series.

"One of the most wonderful influences for me was Paul Smith," Chavous said. "When I came in as a rookie, Paul was a [second-team] All-Pro defensive tackle. Paul made me feel so comfortable. He gave me confidence. Everyone on the team felt confident when he was around."

Smith gave back to the younger players, just as Tombstone Jackson gave to him.

"An All-American guy," Jackson said. "Very humble. He paid attention to details. He had all the tools to play and he was eager to learn. You could see when he came in he paid attention. You could tell that. Sometimes you try to help guys but you can see they're not coachable. But Paul, you didn't have to tell him more than once. He just took off. We got to the point where we told each other: 'Let's develop our thing where we'll have our meeting at the quarterback.'"

Ralston once said that during the 1972 season Smith was so good Oakland Raiders owner Al Davis offered to trade his backup quarterback Kenny Stabler straight up for the Broncos defensive tackle. Ralston declined, and while hindsight says the Broncos should have taken a Pro Football Hall of Fame quarterback in exchange for a Ring of Fame defensive tackle, at the time the trade offer was made, it would have been considered a lopsided trade in the Raiders' favor.

Remember, Smith may have gone down as one of the best defensive tackles in NFL history if not for his torn Achilles early in 1974.

"I did call Ken Stabler's college coach at Alabama, Paul Bryant, and he was adamant that Ken would be a great player," Ralston once said in an interview with the *Denver Post*. "He said, 'If you can get him for any cost, do it.' But it wasn't worth it. I also had polled all of our coaches who had been with the Broncos, and I even called Lou Saban. They said you never give up a Paul Smith.

"Of course everybody will say I should have listened to 'Bear' more than the NFL people. But I felt that strongly about Paul. He was an amazing player. He could overpower you or run right by you."

After his 11th season with the Broncos—a franchise record in service time during that era—Smith played two more years with Washington before retiring. He was credited with 55.5 sacks with the Broncos—which still ranks ninth on the team's all-time list entering the 2023 season—and 57.0 in his career.

Paul Smith had a son, Paul Smith Jr., and three grandchildren. At his funeral, held at New Hope Baptist Church in Denver in April 2000, former Broncos head coach Red Miller said of Smith: "A lot of guys you have to talk into playing football. He would have played in the parking lot. It didn't take much to start his engine. His engine was going."

Greg Kragen (1985–1993)

If there was ever a book on the Denver Broncos All-Time Overachievers, Kragen would be somewhere in the top five. Undrafted out of Utah State in 1984, Kragen was cut as a rookie and wasn't invited back to the Broncos until the next season, 1985. A 263-pound nose tackle who was as gritty and scrappy as they come, Kragen was also much stronger than interior blockers credited him for—until they discovered otherwise.

A starter on three Broncos' AFC Championship teams, Kragen was a first-team, All-AFC nose tackle as selected by the Pro Football Writers in 1989. UPI gave him the same honor in 1991. And in 1992 he was named second-team All-Pro after he recorded a career-most 5.5 sacks. He had an astounding 140 tackles in 1988 and four fumble recoveries, one for a touchdown in 1989 when he was named to his only Pro Bowl.

Broncos Ring of Famer Karl Mecklenburg said he got all those tackles as an inside linebacker thanks to Kragen holding up blockers in front of him, freeing him to make the stop.

In an 18-season stretch from 1976—when the Broncos first went to the 3-4 alignment—through 1993, Denver's D had just two nose tackles—Rubin Carter (1976–1986) and Kragen (1985–1993).

After nine seasons in Denver, Kragen finished his career with one season in Kansas City and three more in Carolina. Kragen's son Kyle was an outside linebacker out of Cal who was with the Broncos briefly in 2016.

STARTERS

Trevor Pryce and Rubin Carter get the nod. Neither player is a Ring of Famer, which is almost perfect for this position. Pryce was the best inside pass-rusher among Denver's defensive tackles, while Carter was the best blocker-eating nose tackle who made history as the centerpiece in the Broncos' famed 3-4 Orange Crush defense.

Paul Smith was third, and had it not been for an Achilles injury, he may have gone as the best of all time.

OTHERS

Keith Traylor (1991–1992, 1997–2000)

Few players have ever reinvented themselves in the midst of an NFL career as Traylor did. A 260-pound linebacker when he was drafted by the Broncos in the third round out of Central State (Oklahoma) in 1991, Traylor played two years in Denver, moved on to Green Bay and Kansas City, then returned to the Mile High City in 1997 as a 304-pound defensive tackle—who could still dunk a basketball.

Traylor wound up playing 16 seasons in the NFL. By the time he finished playing in 2007 with Miami, Traylor was listed at 337 pounds.

He not only started all 20 games (regular-season and post-season) in the Broncos' first Super Bowl–winning season of 1997, he had a 61-yard interception return for a touchdown.

He started all but one game for the Broncos in their second Super Bowl season of 1998.

Sylvester Williams (2013–2016, 2020)

The Broncos' first-round selection, No. 28 overall, in the 2013 NFL Draft, Williams took a while to break in, as he was inactive through the first three games of his rookie season, but he eventually became a starter by season's end. He was a starter the next three years and anchored the nose tackle position for Denver's iconic Super Bowl 50 defense.

Allowed to leave for free agency in 2017, Williams played for four teams over three years before he was brought back to the Broncos for the second half of the 2020 COVID-19 season.

Kevin Vickerson (2010–2013)

Some players take a minute. Vickerson was a seventh-round pick of the Miami Dolphins in 2005 but never played for them, as he suffered a knee injury in a preseason game as a rookie and missed his entire first season. In his second season of 2006, he was inactive for all 16 games, then was among the final cuts in his third season of 2007.

Vickerson was assigned to NFL Europe's Cologne Centurions, where he played for two months, then was signed to Tennessee's practice squad. He finally made his NFL debut for the Titans in December 2007.

A part-time player who was Tennessee's No. 6 defensive lineman in 2008, Vickerson finally broke through as a rotational player in 2009, then became a full-time, four-year starter for the Broncos starting in 2010. He was playing at his best in 2013 when he suffered a season-ending dislocated hip in game 11.

He played one more season for the Chiefs to conclude his 10-year career.

Mike Purcell (2019–present)

A local man does good by living the adage: If at first you don't succeed, try, try again. (Difficult to refer to a 6-foot-3, 328-pound nose tackle as a local "kid.") Purcell was a second-team All-State defensive lineman for Highlands Ranch High School in 2008 before he played four years at the University of Wyoming. Undrafted in 2013, he signed as a free agent with the San Francisco 49ers and defensive coordinator Vic Fangio.

Purcell then began a journey where he was cut 10 times by six teams before he finally caught on with the Broncos in 2019, when Fangio became Denver's head coach. Purcell became a four-year starting run-stuffer for a Denver defense that consistently ranked among the league's top 10 all four years he was there.

He had one more year left on his contract at the time of this writing, in February 2023.

Malik Jackson (2012–2015)

One of John Elway's most astute draft picks, as Jackson was taken in the fifth round of the same 2012 draft where the Broncos took Derek Wolfe in the second round. It took Jackson three years to develop into a full-time starter, but he found his home as a 3-4 defensive end opposite Wolfe in 2015. Jackson was dominant that season, registering 6.5 sacks during the regular season and recovering a fumble in the end zone for the first score in the Broncos' Super Bowl 50 win against Carolina.

Jackson and Wolfe were both offered the same four-year, $36.75 million contract extension after the 2015 season. Wolfe took it, while Jackson became a free agent and received a larger contract with Jacksonville. Both Wolfe and Jackson had 10-year careers. The difference was that Jackson bounced around, playing with four teams, while Wolfe played 8 of his 10 seasons with the Broncos.

DEFENSIVE ENDS

Easily the most difficult position to rank players because of the most fundamental of reasons: Given the history of Denver's defensive alignments, who exactly was a defensive end?

The Broncos were at the forefront of the 3-4 defense (three defensive linemen; four linebackers) with defensive coordinator Joe Collier making the then-innovative move about midway through the 1976 season. And 3-4 defensive ends would be defensive tackles in the more traditional 4-3 alignment.

As passing picked up in the 1980s, the defense countered by having a 4-3 defensive end evolve into a pass-rushing outside linebacker in the 3-4.

Then there were versatile players like Karl Mecklenburg, who played inside linebacker on first down and defensive end or outside linebacker on third down. He made his Pro Bowls as an inside linebacker, but most of his 79.0 career sacks came from the outside.

For this project, we placed Mecklenburg among the linebacker candidates, although we did so without complete confidence this was his best position. When you're the ultimate hybrid defender, all positions work.

Still, we must pick two defensive end starters for *The Denver Broncos All-Time All-Stars.*

THE CANDIDATES

Barney Chavous
Rich "Tombstone" Jackson
Lyle Alzado
Rulon Jones
Derek Wolfe

BARNEY CHAVOUS (1973–1985)

There is consistency and there is Barney Chavous. In 1973, as a 22-year-old rookie, Chavous had 6.0 sacks while starting all 14 games for the Broncos as a left defensive end in Joe Collier's 4-3 defense. In 1985, the last of his 13 NFL seasons, a 34-year-old Chavous had 6.0 sacks while starting 15 games at left defensive end in Collier's 3-4 defense.

The NFL changed from 14- to 16-game seasons during the Chavous playing era. Collier changed from a 4-3 to 3-4 defensive system during Chavous' playing career. Only Barney Chavous' steady production never changed.

He still ranks No. 4 on the team's all-time sack list, with 75.0. And that was during a time when defensive ends were evaluated first on stopping the run. Sacks weren't the be-all, end-all, ka-ching, ka-ching until the league started changing the rules to make it a pass-happy league. The increased significance and value of the sack started gradually with Lawrence Taylor in the mid-1980s.

Barney Lewis Chavous grew up in Aiken, South Carolina, the son of Barney Oscar Chavous and Mary Bell.

"My mom's family came from slavery," Chavous said for the book *50 Greatest Broncos*. "My dad's family was a free family. So, it was a good balance for us growing up. We understood both sides.

"My dad, he was so special. He used to lay brick, he built houses. He was an auto mechanic. I got bits and pieces of him. Anything he could put his mind to do, he could do it. He was very gifted, especially with his hands."

Chavous became a certified mechanic before he attended his first class in college. Which only followed his work career as he started driving a school bus, before and after school, before he earned his high school diploma. Chavous, you see, started driving a school bus when he was 16 years old. He got his sunup to sundown driver's license at 14, then two years later drove a school bus for one job and added some financial stability by working at his uncle's automatic transmission shop.

A high school coach approached him and said he could get Chavous a college scholarship if he tried out for the football team. Chavous cut back on his auto mechanic hours, quit driving a school bus, and played football. His high school coach was William Clyburn Sr., who at the time of this writing was in his 28th year as a member of the South Carolina State House of Representatives.

Chavous played so well at South Carolina State that he was the Broncos' second-round draft pick in 1973. In the first 40 seasons of the Broncos franchise, Chavous was employed for 25 of them—13 as a player, 12 as an assistant coach—which makes him one of the more troubling omissions from the team's Ring of Fame.

The highlight of his career?

"It's hard to pick just one highlight, but I can give you two: the Super Bowls, when [I] played in it as a player and won it as a coach," Chavous said for the book *The 50 Greatest Players in Denver Broncos History*. "That first Super Bowl that we won [against Green Bay, to cap the 1997 season], that's your dream and goal as a player and a coach.

"And then when we went to the Super Bowl in '77, that was a highlight from the standpoint that when I first came to Denver, they had never had a winning season. And then our first winning season in '73 was my rookie year. I started that year. It was great to be a part of that. The Broncos tradition started then and it's been going on ever since."

RICH "TOMBSTONE" JACKSON (1967–1972)

A charter member of the Broncos Ring of Fame when he was inducted with the inaugural class of 1984, Jackson was on his way to the Pro Football Hall of Fame until he suffered a serious knee injury at a time when surgical repairs weren't nearly as advanced as they are today.

Jackson had 31 sacks in the three-year span from 1968 to 1970: 10 in 1968, 11 in 1969, and 10 in 1970, when he became the first Bronco named to the NFL All-Pro team. Remember, those double-digit sack totals were in 14-game seasons.

Jackson not only started on both the offensive and defensive lines in high school, he first began going both ways for his high school team when he was in eighth grade. He also ran the 100- and 200-yard dashes and anchored the 440 and 880 relay teams in track, and he was a state champion shot-putter.

It was in high school that his rare athletic blend of size, track speed, and strength brought on the nickname "Tombstone." He couldn't be blocked. A ball carrier couldn't run away from him. And no one could outsmart him.

"The termination of life. The symbol of death. The end of the road," Jackson said. "That's what 'Tombstone' means."

Perhaps, a more glowing tribute came from *Sports Illustrated*'s Paul Zimmerman, who placed Tombstone on his NFL All-Time Team. Zimmerman picked three defensive ends for his starting defense—Reggie White, Deacon Jones, and Rich "Tombstone" Jackson. Tombstone was the most surprising

THE DENVER BRONCOS ALL-TIME ALL-STARS

choice on Dr. Z's team and generated the most discussion. This was at a time when the Internet was just starting to sputter through phone-line hookups and well before the creation of Twitter, Facebook, and Instagram.

Zimmerman once wrote of Jackson, "In his prime, he was the very best run-pass defensive end the game has seen."

Al Davis, the renegade Oakland Raiders owner, signed Jackson out of Southern University in 1966. But after playing Jackson sparingly as a linebacker in his rookie season, Davis traded his find to the Broncos in exchange for two of the best players in Denver history, receiver Lionel Taylor and center Jerry Sturm.

Several years later, Davis lamented trading Jackson away, saying, "He was the best player they ever had."

LYLE ALZADO (1971–1978)

One of the most iconic, and arguably the most popular, NFL defenses among its fan base was the 1977 Orange Crush. The Denver Broncos had primarily been AFL/NFL doormats from their inception in 1960 until taking positive steps forward in the mid-1970s, with Broncomania at its absolute zenith in 1977, when the Broncos finally smoked the Raiders (2-24-2 in 14 previous seasons), finished 12-2 to capture home-field advantage in the AFC playoffs, and won the AFC Championship.

The best player on that 1977 Orange Crush defense? Right defensive end Lyle Alzado finished fourth in the NFL MVP voting that year, and narrowly missed getting elected as NFL Defensive Player of the Year to Dallas's Harvey Martin (27 votes to 25). Alzado was named the AFC Defensive Player of the Year in votes by United Press International and the Kansas City 101 Club, and was also named to the Associated Press's first-team All-Pro that year.

Alzado was a 4-3 defensive end until he suffered a season-ending injury in the 1976 opener. Without Alzado anchoring the

174

right side, Collier reasoned he had more good players at the line-backer position than up front. To get his 11 best defensive players on the field, Collier played 4 linebackers and 3 defensive linemen.

When Alzado returned from injury in 1977, he was a 3-4 defensive end. His injury-marred 1976 season aside, Alzado had between 7.0 and 13.0 sacks in each of his seven healthy seasons with the Broncos. And he was better against the run, at least according to his defensive line coach Stan Jones, who was later elected into the Pro Football Hall of Fame for his two-way play as an offensive guard and defensive tackle from 1953 to 1965 with the Chicago Bears.

Alas, Alzado was an admitted steroid user. He was hardly the only professional player using artificial enhancements in that era, but he may have been the poster child for steroid use because of his menacing approach both during the play and after the whistle. Moreover, Alzado was not just a steroid user but an abusive addict for 20-plus years, starting with 1969 for Yankton (South Dakota) College, two years before the Broncos drafted him in the fourth round.

His habit, according to the first-person account he gave to *Sports Illustrated*, published 10 months before he died in 1992 at age 43 due to complications from brain cancer, began with 50 milligrams of Dianabol a day. Then he moved on to the stronger stuff, like Bolasterone and Quinolone. He never cycled off the recommended length. He would mix the 'roids and increase the doses. Then came human growth hormone.

"Lyle, he wanted to be great," said Rich "Tombstone" Jackson. "He would hang around and he would work out in the gym afterwards. We had a small group of guys who would work out—they knew the importance of being physically prepared and ready. He worked out hard. I think his attitude of being great is what, like a lot of guys, led to him feeling like he needed some enhancements."

In a sense Alzado's 'roid rage helped him become one of the NFL's most popular players in his time. His maniacal motor and violent temper were viewed as passion by many fans and teammates alike. No one ever questioned his effort. Fans love that in a player. A contract dispute precipitated Alzado's trade from Denver to Cleveland after the 1978 season, and three years later he was traded again to the Raiders.

He was ranked No. 9 all-time with 112.0 career sacks at the time of his first retirement in 1985, with 64.5 coming in his seven healthy seasons with the Broncos.

Rulon Jones (1980–1988)

Growing up in Liberty, Utah, a town so small that it didn't have a school, Jones and his two brothers and sister attended elementary school and junior high in one neighboring town and high school in another. He didn't put on football pads until his sophomore year in high school. Then he suffered a broken arm early that year, so he didn't really start playing football until his junior year.

He played long enough to get a football scholarship to Utah State, where in a serendipitous moment he came across a graduate assistant coach named Rod Marinelli, who went on to become one of the NFL's top defensive assistant coaches.

"I had no coaching up until that point," Jones said for the book, *The 50 Greatest Players in Denver Broncos History*. "I was just real skinny and he got me in the weight room and put some weight on me and gave me discipline. I was lucky. Then I got with Stan Jones there in Denver and Stan was a great coach, too."

Selected in the second round by the Broncos, No. 42 overall, the 6-foot-6, 260-pound Jones got off to an explosive start as a rookie, registering 11.5 sacks in 1980, and was named to the NFL's All-Rookie Team by the Pro Football Writers Association. He had 9 sacks in 1981.

The year before Jones arrived, the Broncos had just 19 sacks in 1979 as they struggled to generate a pass rush after trading away Lyle Alzado. But after drafting Jones in the second round and signing Greg Boyd, the Broncos more than doubled their sack total in 1980, with 39.

Jones seemed to be on his way to becoming an all-time great, but his third and fourth seasons with the Broncos were impeded by the players' strike / owners' lockout in 1982 and an injured knee ligament in 1983.

He bounced back to have 11 sacks in 1984, 10 sacks in 1985, and 13.5—for 152 yards in losses—in 1986. He added another 3 sacks in the 1986 postseason, including a sack safety of New England quarterback Tony Eason late in a back-and-forth, second-round AFC playoff game. The Broncos had just taken a 20–17 lead when Jones's safety made it 22–17, which held as the final score.

There are some longtime Broncos observers that swear old Mile High Stadium never shook more from the rafters than during the moment of Jones's safety.

"It was hard to enjoy it because the second after it happened, my teammates tackled me," Jones said. "They had a big pile there in the end zone. It was fun. I went home, my kids weren't at the game, they were real young then. They put a big banner up on my garage and I think the score was 22–17 or whatever, and they had an arrow pointing to the 2 and saying that belonged to Dad."

The next week came The Drive in Cleveland. The 1986 season is also known as the year New York Giant Lawrence Taylor changed the game as an unstoppable pass-rushing outside linebacker. Taylor became the second defensive player in history (after Alan Page in 1971) to be named the NFL's MVP. But Jones was recognized by UPI as the AFC Defensive Player of the Year.

Jones was on top of the football world. But then came another work stoppage in 1987 when NFL owners used replacement players for three games and contracted a fourth, leaving Jones and the regular players with just 12 games to play that season. It was a tough deal for players of the 1980s. They sacrificed their career stats—many surrendered their careers, period—so players of today could enjoy great fruits. There has been no work stoppage that caused the cancellation of games played since the 1987 season. Astronomical salaries started coming in the mid-1990s when the advent of free agency coincided with the explosion of network TV deals.

Jones had 7.0 sacks in 12 games in 1987, plus two more in three postseason games, including one of Washington quarterback Doug Williams in the Super Bowl.

The 1988 season brought on another right knee injury that eventually forced Jones to retire. He was just 30 years old when he played his last game. A case can be made for Jones being the best defensive player who is not in the Broncos Ring of Fame. (Riley Odoms would be the best offensive player who was not yet an ROFer as of early 2023.)

Jones, his wife Kathy, and their children moved back to Utah where he opened two guided hunting ranches that are now run by two of his sons, and they later added a third ranch in Mexico, near Monterrey. Rulon and Kathy aren't working while living halfway down Mexico along the Pacific Coast.

DEREK WOLFE (2012–2019)

Wolfe had his share of ups and downs during his eight seasons with the Broncos, but he was healthy and dominant during Denver's 2015 ride to the Super Bowl 50 championship.

Wolfe was the Broncos' first draft pick in 2012, although it didn't come until the No. 36 overall selection in the second round. He started all 17 games—counting the excruciating playoff loss to Baltimore—as a rookie, and had 6.0 sacks that remained his career-best until his final season of 2019 with the Broncos, when he had 7.0 sacks before suffering a season-ending dislocated elbow in game 12.

In between, Wolfe had a scary moment in 2013 when he suffered seizures as the team was about to bus to the airport for a trip to play the Kansas City Chiefs. Wolfe said his heartbeat got down to 12 to 15 beats a minute and that doctors had to induce a coma. He missed the final five games, plus three more in the postseason, including Super Bowl XLVIII.

"It was almost all taken away from me," Wolfe said. "I wasn't in a place financially where I was going to be taken care of [for] the rest of my life if that happened. It would have been a miserable existence for me and [filled with] regret, living with that. But I was able to battle back from that and show some resolve."

He returned in 2014 to start all 16 games, plus one more in the postseason, then teamed with fellow 3-4 defensive end Malik Jackson to produce the kind of consistent inside push up front that allowed outside linebackers Von Miller and DeMarcus Ware to create a devastating pass rush from the edge in 2015. With star quarterback Peyton Manning playing on his proverbial last legs, it was the Denver D that carried the Broncos to a 12-4 record—10 wins coming by a one-score margin—and the No. 1 AFC playoff seed.

In the postseason, defense was again the difference in hard-fought home wins against Pittsburgh and New England before Miller delivered an MVP performance in a 24–10 thumping of favored Carolina in Super Bowl 50. What made that defense so special?

"I would say the camaraderie," Wolfe said. "And you can't overlook the talent, right? We had so much talent. When you take all that talent and put the egos aside and put it towards one goal, it's so difficult to do. Because we had a lot of guys going into contract years. And a lot of guys could have been, 'Forget about the team, I'm worried about myself.' That didn't happen. We were all focused on winning that Super Bowl. And we did it. And they can't take that away from us."

Wolfe got a nice four-year, $36.7 million contract extension just before the 2015 postseason, and when it expired after 2019, he became a free agent and signed with Baltimore. Wolfe had a solid, if injury-plagued, season with the Ravens in 2020, then missed all of 2021 with injuries to both hips that required off-season surgeries.

He officially retired as a Bronco prior to the 2022 season. He and his wife Abigail and two daughters, Tatum and Roxie, continue to live in the Denver area, where Wolfe began his post-playing career as a sports talk radio co-host on 104.3 The Fan.

"I don't miss the physicality of the game," Wolfe said. "I do miss being around the guys."

STARTERS

Rich "Tombstone" Jackson and Rulon Jones
Jackson is the only Ring of Famer among the defensive end candidates, and he was the Terrell Davis of Denver defenders in that he was great for a relatively short time. Jones barely edged Barney Chavous for the second starting position. Chavous had a longer career and was more consistent, but Jones was the more impactful player who made two All-Pro teams and was the UPI AFC Defensive Player of the Year in 1986.

OTHERS

Alfred Williams (1995–1998)
Easily the most popular defensive end in Broncos history—even though he only played four seasons for the team, and was

Rich "Tombstone" Jackson © DICK BURNELL / PHOTO ASSOCIATES

healthy in just one of those, which resulted in the best individual year of his career.

Williams first began to earn local-legend status during his days as a first-team All-American and Butkus Award winner as a defensive end/outside linebacker at the University of Colorado during a time when the Buffaloes played in back-to-back national championship games in 1989 and 1990. A first-round draft pick of the Cincinnati Bengals in 1991, Williams eventually signed a five-year, $9 million contract with the Broncos as a free agent in 1996.

He rewarded the Broncos and then some in his first season when he posted a career-best 13.0 sacks in the regular season—after just 12 games as coach Mike Shanahan began to rest his regulars down the stretch after the team clinched the No. 1 playoff seed—and had one more sack in the team's shocking playoff loss to Jacksonville.

Williams was named first-team All-Pro that season and finished third in the NFL Defensive Player of the Year voting to future Hall of Famers Bruce Smith and Kevin Greene.

The next year Williams suffered a torn left triceps in a 1997 preseason game against Miami, and then he tore his right triceps in a regular-season game against San Diego, but still managed to finish with 8.5 sacks, plus 2.0 more in the postseason when the Broncos finished off their first Super Bowl championship.

That's 24.5 sacks in his first two seasons with the Broncos.

Surgeries to repair those two torn triceps after the 1997 season forced Williams to miss the first six games of 1998. He returned to play in third-down packages in his final 10 games, registering another 3.0 sacks.

Healthy at the start of 1999, Williams had 4.0 sacks in seven games, but then blew out his Achilles, which essentially ended his career.

Soon after his playing career ended, Williams became "Big Al" as a larger-than-life sports talk radio host who was known for his booming laugh, outsized, enthusiastic personality, and deep knowledge of the game, although he did occasionally present an out-of-left-field opinion. He was going on 19 years as a sports talk radio host as of early 2023.

Chuck Gavin (1960–1963)

After two years in the Canadian Football League, Gavin joined the new American Football League in 1960 and became an inaugural member of the Denver Broncos. A four-year starting defensive end, Gavin was considered one of the league's top pass-rushers in 1962–1963, although he was only credited with 7.5 sacks. A knee injury forced his retirement in 1964. He worked as a juvenile probation officer before becoming the longtime director of the Gilliam Youth Center. He died just shy of his 78th birthday in 2012, and a day after his 57th Christmas Day wedding anniversary with his wife Earnestine.

Neil Smith (1997–1999)
A five-time Pro Bowler in his first nine NFL seasons with the Kansas City Chiefs, Smith signed a make-good, one-year, $1.5 million contract with the Broncos and immediately helped push the franchise over the top. Smith had 8.5 sacks in his first season of 1997 in Denver and added 3.0 more in the postseason, helping Denver win its first-ever Super Bowl. He was named to the Pro Bowl and All-Pro second team that year.

That earned Smith a new four-year, $13.5 million extension, and he helped the Broncos go back-to-back in 1998 with another Super Bowl title. Smith finished with 104.5 career sacks with 19.0 coming in his three seasons with Denver.

Pete Duranko (1967–1974)
A first-team All-American defensive end on Notre Dame's 1966 national championship team, Duranko was selected by the Broncos in the second round of the 1966 AFL Redshirt Draft. A part-time fullback in his freshman year at Notre Dame, the 6-foot-2, 250-pound Duranko began his pro career with the Broncos as a linebacker, but he switched to the defensive line by the end of his 1967 rookie season.

In the five-season stretch from 1968 through 1973, the Broncos' first winning season, Duranko had 30.5 sacks, an average of more than 6.0 sacks a year (he missed the entire 1973 season from a preseason knee injury).

Duranko was diagnosed with Lou Gehrig's disease (ALS) in 2000 and fought a courageous battle for a decade before passing away in 2011 at age 67.

Andre Townsend (1984–1990)

A second-round draft pick in 1984 out of Mississippi, Townsend had 5.0 sacks as a defensive end backup each of his first two seasons, then started all 16 games at defensive end in 1986, the season of the Broncos' second Super Bowl appearance. Listed at 6-foot-3, 265 pounds, Townsend mixed in at defensive tackle. He was moved full-time to nose tackle in 1990, then suffered a torn elbow ligament in the training camp of 1991, which led to his release among the Broncos' final roster cuts.

INSIDE LINEBACKERS

One of professional football's most evolving positions, there has nevertheless been one constant with inside linebackers, from the no-facemask 1920s to the no-helmet-launching 2020s: tackling.

Inside linebackers by and large are the leading tacklers on any defense, game to game, season to season.

They may not be the Menacing Monsters of the Midway like Butkus, or wild, eccentric showmen like Wahoo McDaniel. They may be built more along the lines of sleek, premium sports cars fueled by high-energy drinks. But the inside linebacker is still asked to shuffle up and fill gaps, hustle from sideline to sideline, and accept more high-speed body collisions than any other.

Like so many other seven-man positions, inside linebackers are not easily quantified by placing a skill set and characteristics in a box. In a 4-3 defense, the only inside linebacker is the middle linebacker. The outside linebackers in a 4-3 aren't pass-rushers on the edge but athletic hybrids who can run with a running back or tight end on a pass pattern, yet still push off a 300-pound pulling guard to take on a fullback.

The inside linebackers in a 3-4 defense, conversely, are like two middle linebackers paired side by side. Instincts and awareness are more important than speed, but the difference between good and All-Pros comes down to instincts, awareness, and speed.

The Broncos played as much 3-4 defense—thanks to coach Joe Collier's innovative ways starting in the late 1970s—as the 4-3 alignment over the team's nearly 65-year history. So there were many fine inside linebackers to choose from, with no two alike.

Here are the inside linebacker candidates for placement on *The Denver Broncos All-Time All-Stars*:

THE CANDIDATES

Karl Mecklenburg
D.J. Williams
Al Wilson
Randy Gradishar
Bill Romanowski

KARL MECKLENBURG (1983–1994)

Versatility—the flexibility to play multiple positions and do various things—is a magnanimous virtue in everything except apparently receiving Hall of Fame consideration.

Wade Phillips, the longtime great defensive coordinator, had it right when he was asked in 2016 whether Broncos' defensive great Karl Mecklenburg was worthy of football immortality.

"Karl Mecklenburg, he's a Hall of Famer because I've never seen a guy, and I've never heard of one, that's in the Hall of Fame that could play inside and rush the passer," Phillips said. "It's just a combination that nobody else had. He was a tremendous pass-rusher. I've never been around anybody that played inside backer as well as he did. He was great at it.

"And then on third down, you'd put him outside and let him rush. He could have been a defensive end all the time. His stats would have gone up where his sacks are concerned, but he made so many tackles you had to play him inside at an inside backer."

For this project, we let Mecklenburg pick his position. It was a no-brainer that he would be a starter on *The Denver Broncos All-Time All-Stars*. But where? He played, at one time or the other, all four positions along the defensive line and all three linebacker positions.

Primarily he played inside linebacker on first and second down and outside linebacker or defensive end on passing downs. "I was an inside linebacker 75 percent of the time," Mecklenburg said. "All my Pro Bowls I was selected as an inside linebacker."

So there you go. Mecklenburg wasn't drafted until the 12th round, No. 310 overall—309 spots after where John Elway was selected in the same 1983 draft. A wonderful connection, because for nine consecutive seasons of Elway's career (1985–1993), Mecklenburg was the Broncos' second-best player.

Together, Elway and Mecklenburg led the Broncos to three Super Bowls. Didn't win any of them, but they got there.

While Elway was the most highly touted draft prospect in the 56-year history of the common NFL Draft, Mecklenburg was a classic tweener who kept falling further and further behind on NFL draft boards. Here was a 240-pound nose tackle out of Minnesota who was a biology major and an accomplished guitarist. He was raised in Edina, Minnesota, by a father who was a physician in the Washington, DC, area and a mom who was undersecretary of the Department of Health, Education, and Welfare.

Mecklenburg in so many ways was overqualified for the NFL.

The Broncos didn't know what to do with him. They had one scout say he was too slow to be a linebacker; maybe he could be a defensive lineman. Another scout reported he was too small to be a defensive lineman; maybe he could be a linebacker.

They were both right.

In 1985, his first season as a starter, Mecklenburg had 13.0 sacks, 4 pass deflections, 5 forced fumbles, and 65 tackles. The next year, The Drive season of 1986—when the Broncos went to the first of Elway's five Super Bowls—Mecklenburg was second on the team with 127 tackles and added 9.5 sacks, an almost unheard-of near triple-double.

In 1989, Mecklenburg registered a team-high 143 tackles and 7.5 sacks.

There was an eight-season stretch when Mecklenburg had no fewer than 97 tackles, and six times had at least 102 tackles. He also had eight seasons of at least 7.0 sacks.

He finished his career with 1,145 tackles and 79.0 sacks. That puts him No. 3 all-time on the Broncos' sack list (behind only Von Miller and Simon Fletcher) and No. 2 in tackles (behind only Dennis Smith).

Name another player who has compiled that kind of tackle-sack combination stats? There isn't one. Yet, Mecklenburg was never a top-15 modern-era finalist for the Pro Football Hall of Fame. Maybe the HOF seniors' committee will one day make the correction.

"The problem is, I played all those positions," Mecklenburg said. "If you call me a middle linebacker, then I don't have as many tackles and interceptions as I should have. If you call me a pass-rusher, I don't have as many sacks as I would have if I was rushing the passer all the time. You want to define players, and unfortunately for something like this, a lot more players were defined more than I was."

D.J. WILLIAMS (2004–2012)

The NFL is full of players who were high school stars. Then there was D.J. Williams. A three-year starting running back and linebacker at the football factory of De La Salle High School, his school went 36-0 with three state championships in his three varsity seasons. He was so good, John Madden—the Hall of Fame former coach of the Raiders who became the highly popular NFL color analyst—said at De La Salle's sports banquet that Williams—the *USA Today* high school defensive player of the year—was ready to play in the NFL right now.

Williams went to the college football factory that was the University of Miami first, where he was a fullback as a freshman, then a three-year starting linebacker. The Hurricanes went 46-4 in his four seasons there that included the 2001 national championship.

A first-round selection, No. 17 overall, by the Broncos in the 2004 draft, Williams was an eight-year starter at four linebacking positions—weakside (39), inside (31), strongside (29), and middle (16). He led the Broncos in tackles as a rookie in 2004 (114), then again in 2007 (170), 2009 (122), 2010 (119), and 2011 (90). He was twice suspended in his ninth and final season with the Broncos in 2012, missing nine games and starting just one.

Williams never made a Pro Bowl, though, as he played at a time when Baltimore's Ray Lewis was an automatic at his position. Williams came on as a blitzer in the four-year stretch from 2008 to 2011, when he made 16.5 of his 22.5 career sacks.

AL WILSON (1999–2006)

Fresh off back-to-back Super Bowl titles, the Broncos used their first-round pick in the 1999 NFL Draft to select Wilson out of Tennessee, where he had helped guide the Vols to an undefeated 1998 season and the national championship. Wilson was a five-time, Pro Bowl selection and perennial team captain for the Broncos until a neck injury suffered late in the 2006 season brought a premature end to his career.

Although Wilson was a first-team All-Pro in 2005, his season for the ages was 2002, when he had a career-most 132 tackles and 5.0 sacks.

The neck injury became a point of contention as Wilson filed a $7.5 million medical grievance against a neurosurgeon affiliated with the Broncos, only to have an independent arbitrator rule in the doctor's favor.

Among players eligible, but not in the team's Ring of Fame, none have more Pro Bowl nods than Wilson's five. His name has come up in recent Ring of Fame committee meetings and it appears it's a matter of when—not if—he is elected.

It took 12 years before the relationship between the Broncos and Wilson began to thaw. Prior to a 2018 home game against the Cleveland Browns, Wilson was invited by Broncos public relations boss Patrick Smyth to come out for a practice, tour the team's considerably upgraded facilities, and serve as the team's honorary captain for the pregame coin toss. During the game, Wilson was recognized on the stadium's jumbo screen as their "Broncos Legend."

After the practice Wilson attended, he was called out to the team's breakdown by head coach Vance Joseph, who recited many of the former linebacker's accomplishments, then asked Wilson to break the huddle.

Broncos on three. Here's to Al Wilson.

RANDY GRADISHAR (1974–1983)

After the Broncos made him their first-round draft pick in 1974, No. 14 overall, out of Ohio State—where Woody Hayes called him the "best defensive player I ever coached"—Gradishar made seven Pro Bowls in his 10 seasons with the Broncos.

He has called the win against rival Oakland Raiders in the 1977 AFC Championship Game at old Mile High Stadium the greatest single moment of his career. The next year he was named the NFL's Defensive Player of the Year—an honor not even first-ballot Hall of Famer Champ Bailey or future Hall of Famer Von Miller ever won.

Gradishar is the only Bronco to ever capture the NFL Defensive Player of the Year Award. He was also the leading tackler and defensive play caller of the Broncos' famed Orange Crush defense that also included Louis Wright, Lyle Alzado, Billy Thompson, Tom Jackson, Steve Foley, Rubin Carter, and Barney Chavous. Those superb defensive players on one of the NFL's most famed defenses allowed just 10.6 points a game in their Super Bowl–appearing season of 1977.

It's not just Gradishar who keeps getting bypassed for the Pro Football Hall of Fame, outrageous as his snub may be. Just as preposterous is the fact that not one member of Denver's iconic Orange Crush defense is represented in Canton.

The Steel Curtain from the 1970s has five defensive players in the Hall of Fame: Mel Blount, Joe Greene, Jack Ham, Jack Lambert, and Donnie Shell. Granted, the Steelers won four Super Bowls in the '70s, but they also had five Hall of Fame offensive players in Terry Bradshaw, Mike Webster, John Stallworth, Lynn Swann, and Franco Harris.

The other dominant AFC team from the 1970s, the Raiders, have two defenders with bronze busts: Willie Brown and Ted Hendricks.

The 1977 Broncos, who beat both the Steelers and the Raiders in the 1977 AFC playoffs, have none.

With apologies to Jack Lambert, Gradishar was the NFL's best middle linebacker in the seven-year period from 1975 to 1981. Lambert played at 225 pounds, spread over a 6-foot-4 frame. Gradishar was 6-3, 240. Who would you rather get hit by?

"As good as there ever was," Tom Jackson, who played on the outside right of Gradishar in the Orange Crush's four linebacker set, said in *The 50 Greatest Players in Denver Broncos History*. "And I don't say that lightly. His competitive spirit, his ability to tackle—I don't think there's anything more important in football. He also collected, out of a '30' defense, 20 interceptions. Over 100 tackles every single year of his life."

The Orange Crush wasn't a defense, it was a movement. It was the beginning of Broncomania. Even new Broncos owner Condoleezza Rice talked about growing up in that special time during the new Denver ownership group's introductory press conference in August 2022.

"I'm a part of the 'Orange Crush' generation where you'd go into any grocery store or any restaurant and there were all of those Orange Crush cans piled up with [cutouts of] Rubin Carter or Louis Wright peering over them," Rice said.

Louis Wright is the next Orange Crush defender worthy of the Hall of Fame, followed by Billy Thompson and Tom Jackson. But Gradishar was the leader of the Orange Crush and has always had the first chance from that famed unit to attain football immortality.

"I've been a finalist a few times, and you get excited and hope for the best," Gradishar said.

As of this writing, Gradishar has yet to receive the Hall of Fame nod. He played 10 seasons, all for the Broncos, from 1974, when he was a first-round pick out of Ohio State, through 1983, John Elway's rookie season. Besides his 20 interceptions, Gradishar had 19.5 sacks and 13 fumble recoveries.

He has been eligible for Hall of Fame election since 1989—34 years ago. He was twice a finalist on the modern-era ballot and was among the finalists for the 2020 Hall of Fame Centennial Class, but was surprisingly not among the 10 seniors elected. He was a senior finalist again in 2022, but once again was bypassed.

BILL ROMANOWSKI (1996–2001)

Bill Romanowski received the invitation and knew he was going to accept, even if his feelings were slightly mixed.

The invitation was for the 25th anniversary reunion of the Broncos' first Super Bowl title team from 1997. The gathering was held in mid-October 2022 at the team's stadium now known as Empower Field at Mile High.

"I was excited," said Romanowski, a starting rightside linebacker in the Broncos' 4-3 defense for their 1997 and 1998 Super Bowl titles, but also a starting leftside linebacker in other seasons. "I couldn't believe that it's been 25 years. Went by like that [snaps his fingers]. But to get reunited with all my buddies that we won two Super Bowls back-to-back with? Priceless."

Romo helped epitomize those Broncos' back-to-back Super Bowl championship teams, at least on defense.

"We weren't the most talented, but we were the best team in the National Football League," Romanowski said. "And because we gave it up for one another week in and week out, that was the difference. We weren't going to be denied."

There was supreme talent on the Broncos offensive side of the ball with future Hall of Famers John Elway, Terrell Davis, Shannon Sharpe, and Gary Zimmerman, plus a dynamic receiver duo in Rod Smith and Ed McCaffrey. But the Denver D was a bunch of blue-collar overachievers led by the hyper-intense Romanowski.

After six seasons with the San Francisco 49ers, where he was part of two more Super Bowl champion teams, and two with the Philadelphia Eagles, Romanowski became a free agent following the 1995 season and picked the Broncos over the Chargers.

"The Denver Broncos were great on offense," Romanowski said, explaining his decision. "They needed a leader on defense and they didn't have it. I don't mean this in an egotistical way. I just knew what I could bring and felt like if I went there I really believed we would win a Super Bowl.

"I truly believed Mike Shanahan, coming from the 49ers, he was going to bring coaching-wise what it takes to win a Super Bowl. And I thought I could bring the leadership on defense. They had what they needed on offense and we could get this done. Sure enough, I made the right decision."

Not immediately. With Romanowski playing strongside linebacker, the Broncos started 12-1 in 1996, clinching the No. 1 AFC playoff seed and first-round playoff bye with three games remaining in the regular season.

But in a second-round playoff game, the Broncos were stunned by the upstart Jacksonville Jaguars. We'll never know—because they didn't finish—but many Broncos observers would say the 1996 team was better than the ones that won back-to-back Super Bowls the next two years.

"That was a damn good team," Romanowski said of the '96 Broncos. "One of the problems was, we clinched a little too early. And by doing that I felt like we let our guard down a little bit. We still practiced hard. We prepared hard. We just lost our edge a little bit."

Romanowski wasn't just an inspirational leader for the Broncos. He also was a playmaking, tackling machine, registering career bests with 128 stops and 12 pass deflections in 1996, while adding 3 interceptions and 3 sacks to earn his first Pro Bowl trip. In 1998, he had 95 tackles with a career-best 7.5 sacks with 2 picks, 3 forced fumbles, and 3 fumble recoveries to make his second Pro Bowl team.

His stellar period with the Broncos was also remembered for spitting on J.J. Stokes and breaking the jaw of Carolina quarterback Kerry Collins while coming in on a blitz.

"I hold myself accountable for all my actions," Romanowski said. "But, yeah, I would do some things differently."

Romanowski also became a one-man marketing liaison between the Broncos and Golden-based EAS fitness products.

Romo had two lockers, one filled with EAS products that he distributed at no cost to his teammates upon request.

He estimates he spent $1 million on supplements, training machines, and personal trainers and therapists during his career, for himself and his teams.

What does he remember most from his six Broncos seasons? "The people," he said. "The fans. I love the fans in Denver."

STARTERS

Karl Mecklenburg, Randy Gradishar, and Al Wilson
Mecklenburg and Gradishar are Broncos Ring of Famers and should be Pro Football Hall of Famers. Wilson had a relatively short career but packed in five Pro Bowls. This book is about the all-time greats, and one day Wilson will be elected into the team's Ring of Fame.

Hated to leave out Romanowski and D.J. Williams, who were excellent inside linebackers over a combined 15-year period.

Karl Mecklenburg © ERIC LARS BAKKE

OTHERS

Josey Jewell (2018–present)

A fourth-round pick out of Iowa in the 2018 draft, Jewell was a starter midway through his rookie season. Not the fastest or the biggest, but few linebackers are smarter or tougher. Jewell only stayed healthy through one of his first five seasons—in 2020, when he finished second on the team to Alexander Johnson, with 113 tackles. He also played in 13 of 17 games in 2022 when he had a career-most 128 tackles, which was again second on the team, this time to Alex Singleton.

He is the leader of the defense who wears the "green dot" as the player who relays the plays after getting the call from the defensive coordinator.

Brandon Marshall (2013–2018)

No, not that Brandon Marshall. The linebacker Brandon Marshall. A Las Vegas native who played his college ball at Nevada, Marshall was a fifth-round draft pick by the lowly Jacksonville Jaguars in 2012, yet was cut three times before the start of his second season. After his third cut, Marshall decided against returning to the Jacksonville practice squad to sign instead with the Broncos practice squad, where he stayed throughout the 2013 season until Christmas Eve, when he was promoted to the 53-man varsity.

"I didn't imagine it would go this well," Marshall said. "I will tell you a story. In training camp that year [2013], before I got cut, my grandfather called me, God rest his soul, and he called me and said, 'Brandon, I had a dream that you were in the Super Bowl.'

"I was excited. And then I hung up the phone and realized, 'I'm still in Jacksonville.'"

It was Peyton Manning who helped push Marshall for a promotion. Manning set all the passing records that season with 55 touchdown passes and 5,477 passing yards while guiding the Broncos to a record 606 points (37.9 points per game). But one of Manning's toughest opponents all season was Marshall during practice. Manning told head coach John Fox that Marshall was a good player, and before he was through, Marshall the linebacker made the Hall of Fame quarterback look like a genius (for the couple hundredth time).

"[Offensive coordinator] Adam Gase told me Peyton Manning was the one who started noticing me," Marshall said. "'Who's this '54' kid?' So, then Adam Gase started coming up to me weekly and was like, 'Man, you're doing a helluva job. I'm going to try to get you up on the roster.'

"And then he started coming up to me, [saying] 'I got something for you today,' almost like they were game-planning against me."

Von Miller suffered a torn ACL in the Broncos' 15th game of the 2013 season at Houston, and Marshall got the call up to the 53-man roster for the season finale against the Oakland Raiders. Just in time to play in the postseason, including Super Bowl XLVIII in New York.

That game against Seattle was a nightmare, but Grandpa's dream had come true. The Broncos would return to the Super Bowl two years later, and with Marshall relaying calls from defensive coordinator Wade Phillips to his teammates, the Denver defense dominated in the postseason, frustrating first Ben Roethlisberger and the Steelers, then Tom Brady and the Patriots in the AFC Championship Game, and finally NFL MVP Cam Newton and the Carolina Panthers for the world championship in Super Bowl 50.

Marshall had three 100-tackle seasons for the Broncos.

"I didn't imagine it would go this well," Marshall said.

Among the lasting legacies from Marshall's six-year run with the Broncos was as the guy who took a knee during the playing of the National Anthem. It was in the 2016 season-opener, the first game as defending Super Bowl champions, the first game of the NFL season before a prime-time audience.

"Or they're going to think I'm the receiver," Marshall said with a smile about the Broncos' former star receiver with the same name.

He knows his decision to kneel during the National Anthem before a national television audience in the NFL's 2016 season-opener, followed by similar demonstrations against social injustice over the next two seasons, created an overpowering image.

"I'm fine with it, because I think every man, every individual, has to make decisions throughout their lives on what they believe in, or what they feel strongly about, what they're convicted in," Marshall said. "And that whole year I was able to go home and sleep peacefully knowing the decisions I made and the risks that I could potentially take on."

Not all Broncos fans were happy when Marshall took a knee during the National Anthem. But for a guy who was cut three times by a terrible Jaguars team, Marshall's playing career in Denver was worth celebrating.

Michael Brooks (1987–1992)

Growing up in Ruston, Louisiana, as the youngest of 13 children, Brooks was a third-round draft pick out of LSU by the Broncos. Primarily a special teamer his first two years, Brooks then compiled 123 and 175 tackles in his first two seasons as a starter at right outside linebacker opposite Simon Fletcher in 1989 and 1990, then moved to left inside linebacker and registered a whopping 153 and 170 tackles in 1991 and 1992. That's an average of 155 tackles over a four-year period. He was named to his only Pro Bowl following the 1992 season.

Brooks was part of the NFL's first unrestricted free-agent class in 1993 and followed coach Dan Reeves to the New York Giants on a then-impressive three-year, $6 million contract.

Danny Trevathan (2012–2015)

The best Day 3 draft John Elway ever had in his 10 seasons as Broncos general manager was in 2012 when he selected defensive tackle Malik Jackson in the fifth round and Danny Trevathan in the sixth.

Trevathan wasn't the biggest or the fastest—which is why he lasted until the sixth round despite two All-American seasons at Kentucky—but he possessed a linebacker's heart, instincts, and relentless motor that made him a sideline-to-sideline tackler. He only started two seasons for the Broncos, but they were the 2013 and 2015 Super Bowl–appearing years when Trevathan led the Broncos in tackles with 129 in 2013 and 109 in 2015.

Trevathan had a huge interception—the only decent defensive play of the game—off Tony Romo in a 51–48 win at Dallas in a 2013 regular-season contest and recovered two fumbles in the Broncos' Super Bowl 50 win against Carolina that capped the 2015 season.

There were too many good players who needed to get paid after the 2015 season, and Trevathan was reluctantly allowed to hit free agency where he signed a nice, four-year, $28 million contract with the Bears.

He wound up playing 6 seasons in Chicago and 10 overall in the NFL, with his last season in 2021.

John Mobley (1996–2003)

An eight-year starter including during the Broncos' Super Bowl championship seasons of 1997 and 1998, Mobley is often remembered for making what was then the biggest defensive play in team history. It was Super Bowl XXXII against the Packers in San Diego. The Broncos were huge underdogs, but they were leading the Packers, 31–24, with less than 2 minutes remaining.

The Packers behind their great quarterback Brett Favre had quickly moved the ball from their own 30 to the Broncos' 31-yard line, but it became fourth-and-6 with 32 seconds remaining. Favre threw across the middle to tight end Mark Chmura, but Mobley deflected the pass away. Incomplete. Ball game. John Elway kneeled off the final seconds and the Broncos had won their first Super Bowl in franchise history.

Mobley was a first-team All-Pro linebacker that year, as besides leading the team with 132 tackles, he added 4.0 sacks and a 13-yard interception return for a touchdown. Not bad for a first-round draft pick, No. 15 overall, out of Division II Kutztown University in 1996.

Besides his decorated 1997 season, Mobley had two other 100-plus-tackle seasons, but his career was cut short midway through his eighth season of 2003 when he suffered a spinal-cord contusion while colliding with a teammate while making a tackle. That injury ended his season.

He tried to return in 2004, but his preseason physical revealed the contusion was still evident, and he eventually was forced to retire because of his neck injury. He played his last game just two weeks after his 30th birthday.

Wahoo McDaniel (1961–1963)
The greatest middle linebacker names in professional football history—Butkus, Nitschke, Bednarik, and Wahoo McDaniel. Official birth name was Edward Wahoo McDaniel. Yes, McDaniel was of Native American descent, and went by the ringside name "Chief Wahoo" during his long professional wrestling career that began part-time in 1960 while he was

playing in the AFL for the Houston Oilers. He became a full-time champion and popular wrestler after his football career with the Miami Dolphins ended in 1968, and he continued until he had to retire from the ring for health reasons in 1996.

With the Broncos, McDaniel was a three-year starter who had 6 interceptions and 5.5 sacks, while tackles weren't officially recorded by the team in the 1960s.

Tom Graham (1972–1974)

In his two full seasons with the Broncos, Graham was a starting middle linebacker who led the Broncos in tackles each season with 73 (plus 3 sacks and 2 interceptions) as a rookie in 1972, and 95 in 1973.

In 1974, Graham was moved to left linebacker as he began to give way to a first-round draft pick named Randy Gradishar, a middle linebacker from Ohio State. Graham was traded at midseason to Kansas City before becoming a three-year starter for the San Diego Chargers. Ever present in the Bronco community after his playing days, Tom Graham passed away May 30, 2017, after a battle with brain cancer.

His son Daniel Graham starred at Thomas Jefferson High School and the University of Colorado, winning the John Mackey Award as the nation's top tight end during his senior year in 2001.

Daniel Graham became a first-round draft choice of the defending-champion New England Patriots as a tight end in 2002. Daniel had his best seasons with the Patriots before the Broncos made him the highest-paid tight end in NFL history in 2007.

Known as a lethal blocker in the NFL, Daniel Graham had 24, 32, 28, and 18 catches in his four seasons with the Broncos. He wound up playing 11 years in the NFL before retiring after the 2012 season.

Todd Davis (2014–2019)

A classic overachiever, Davis was an undrafted, small college linebacker who was cut three times as a rookie before he became a three-time tackle leader and Super Bowl champion for the Broncos.

It was November 2014 when Broncos director of player personnel Tom Heckert Jr. convinced his boss John Elway to put in a waiver claim on Davis, who had just been cut for the third time by the New Orleans Saints.

Undrafted out of Sacramento State, Davis signed as a college free agent with the Saints. Heckert loved what he saw from the rookie Davis during the 2014 preseason. The third time Davis was cut that season, Heckert, who passed away in 2018, urged a waiver claim. While NFL executives almost never say this about a rookie waiver claim, Heckert told Elway and top personnel assistant Matt Russell that he thought Davis could not only help the Broncos as a special teamer now, but could become a legitimate NFL starting linebacker.

Davis played two years behind Brandon Marshall and Danny Trevathan before becoming a Broncos starter in 2016. In three of the next four seasons, Davis led the Broncos in tackles, topping out with 134 in 2019.

"Super Bowl 50 is definitely high on my list," Davis said when asked about the top highlights of his career. "Winning the Super Bowl is something that not many people can say they have done. But another thing that was really big for me was signing my second contract."

It was for three years and $15 million.

"It wasn't the contract so much as what it represented," Davis said. "I was cut multiple times, came into the league as an undrafted free agent. A guy a lot of people thought would make it no more than one or two years in the league. So to sign that contract, that was huge for me."

While winning the Super Bowl might seem like an obvious highlight, Davis was a backup linebacker then.

"Yeah, but I was an undrafted free agent who was named a captain for the Super Bowl and I got to be out there for the coin toss," Davis said. "And I did play a couple plays on defense, but being named a captain in the Super Bowl, second year in the league—I was the youngest captain out there. It was me, Peyton Manning, and DeMarcus Ware—that right there was the highlight for me."

OUTSIDE LINEBACKERS

Vonnie B'VSean Miller, otherwise known as Von, arrived upon this Earth on March 26, 1989. By then, Tom Jackson, also known as "TJ" or "Tommy," had been retired three years from his long, distinguished career as a player and was coming off the first of his seven Emmys for Outstanding Studio Show as an ESPN NFL analyst.

And yet we are tasked with comparing the two outside linebackers two generations removed. Comparing players over different eras—does anyone look fast or athletic off those grainy, black-and-white films from the 1960s?—was only one challenge for *The Denver Broncos All-Time All-Stars* book. Even if you limit the outside linebacker position to the 3-4 scheme, thus ignoring outside linebackers in the 4-3 alignment, this is still another position where there are two different players.

There used to be 3-4 outside linebackers who lined up next to the two inside linebackers, making it a true 3-4 with four linebackers across.

And there are 3-4 outside linebackers who line up outside the defensive end positions, making it really a 5-2 alignment.

The outside linebackers who lined up along the defensive line were pass-rushers, first.

The outside linebackers who lined up along the second level inside linebackers were run defenders, first.

Big difference. The Broncos over the years had very good players for each type of outside linebacker. There were the four-across linebackers utilized by Joe Collier's 3-4. And there were the two along the defensive front 3-4 that the likes of Wade Phillips, Vance Joseph, and Vic Fangio employed.

To pick two starting outside linebackers for *The Denver Broncos All-Time All-Stars*, we needed to look at outside line-backers from each set.

THE CANDIDATES

Simon Fletcher
Elvis Dumervil
Von Miller
DeMarcus Ware
Tom Jackson

SIMON FLETCHER (1985–1995)

Tall as outside linebackers go at 6-foot-5, 240 pounds, Fletcher broke free from his back-and-forth team sack record with Karl Mecklenburg late in the 1993 season and held it until late in 2018, when Von Miller picked up the 98th sack of his career.

To hold such a team sack record for 25 years is a nice run.

"I don't think it could have happened to a better guy," Fletcher said of Miller after the record transition. "He works hard. He does great things in the community, and he makes everybody who's ever worn that uniform proud to be associated with him."

Fletcher was known for coming on late in the season. In 1992 he had 3.5 sacks through nine games and finished with a career-best 16—12.5 in his final seven games. In 1993, he fell behind Mecklenburg for the team sack record, as Fletcher had 3.0 sacks through nine games. Fletcher finished with 13.5—or 10.5 in his final seven games.

"Simon was basically the Von Miller of his day," Meck-lenburg said. "He was just faster around the corner than the tackle could get back. He would come around the corner and just beat guys.

"The other thing about him was, everyone else would wear down at the end of the game, and that's when he would make his plays. Everyone would wear down at the end of the season—I mean, if you look back at his statistics, I would guess two-thirds of his sacks were in the last third of the season. He was still going full blast while everyone else was nicked up from the season. That's why he didn't make any Pro Bowls. He was kind of middle of the pack in sacks until the end of the year when he would blow by everybody, but it was too late for the Pro Bowl voting."

It was preposterous Fletcher didn't make any Pro Bowls in the five-year period from 1989 to 1993, when he posted, in succession, 12.0, 11.0, 13.5, 16.0, and 13.5 sacks. An average of 13.2 sacks over five years.

The likes of Derrick Thomas, Howie Long, and Rufus Porter got the AFC nod in 1989, even though each had fewer sacks than Fletcher. Greg Townsend, Neil Smith, and Greg Lloyd were chosen ahead of the sack-superior Fletcher in 1991.

In Fletcher's 16.0-sack season of 1992 that held as a Broncos record—until Elvis Dumervil picked up 17.0 in 2009—all but Leslie O'Neal among AFC linebackers and defensive ends had fewer sacks.

Pro Bowl snubs despite impressive sack totals would have never happened today, as sacks have become increasingly valued with the NFL altering its rules to enhance the passing game. That's just it about Fletcher's sack totals: He compiled them in a time when it was still a run-first league.

And don't get the idea Fletcher was a garbage-time sack collector. In the three-year period from 1990 to 1992, Fletcher amassed 30 of his 36.5 sacks in games decided by 7 points or less.

"When it's crunch time you've got to get your stinger out and try to hold on if your offense put you in position to win a game or you're close behind," Fletcher said. "I think in those moments you have to dig to find any extra that you can."

The Broncos only had two losing seasons during Fletcher's 11 years, which were offset by five, 10-win-or-better seasons and five playoff appearances. After a perplexingly long, 21-year wait, Fletcher was finally inducted into the Broncos Ring of Fame in 2016 along with safety John Lynch and kicker Jason Elam.

Fletcher's proudest accomplishment, though, stemmed from his durability. From the time the Broncos selected him with the second of their two second-round draft picks in 1985 until he retired in 1995, Denver played 172 games (not including the three replacement player games in the strike of 1987). Fletcher played in all 172—184 counting the postseason.

"Clearly, the fact that I played in every game, that I never had to close my eyes and put on a blindfold and go to the pay window," Fletcher said, when asked about his proudest moment as a Bronco. "I was paid to play in a set number of games. I showed up to every single one. Being from where I grew up, my grandparents right in the area around me, that is who they are, and . . . they tried to instill the right values in me. It was my job to be there every play."

Elvis Dumervil (2006–2012)

It's almost hard to believe, but in Denver's long lineage of defensive standouts, Elvis Dumervil is the only player in franchise history to have led the NFL in sacks during a single season, which he did with 17.0 in 2009. Von Miller never led the league in sacks. Finished second once, but never first. Simon Fletcher, Rulon Jones, Lyle Alzado, Rich "Tombstone" Jackson—all terrific pass-rushers. None ever finished a season ranked No. 1 in sacks.

Despite only playing six seasons in Denver, Dumervil ranks seventh on the team with 63.5 sacks. His 10.6 sacks per season is better than the six pass-rushers ahead of him on the Broncos' all-time sack list. And his 20 multi-sack games are tied for the most in team history with Fletcher.

Dumervil was named to three Pro Bowls in his six Broncos seasons.

"What I am thankful for is [that] Mike Shanahan drafted me," Dumervil said. "Mike Shanahan gave me a chance to play defensive end in this league. Josh McDaniels came in and gave me a chance to be a linebacker.

"There were always obstacles. There was always a first rounder I had to prove worthy of beating out. Jarvis Moss and Robert Ayers."

Neither Moss nor Ayers could replace Dumervil. Another first-round pass-rusher, Von Miller, became Dumervil's pass-rushing sidekick in 2011–2012.

Dumervil wasn't as highly regarded coming out of college. Although he earned the Bronko Nagurski Trophy as the NCAA's Defensive Player of the Year in his senior season at Louisville—when he posted a remarkable 20 sacks and college-record 10 forced fumbles—he wasn't selected until the Broncos' second pick in the fourth round of the 2006 NFL Draft.

Why? He was considered undersized as a pass-rusher at 5-foot-11, 248-pounds. (Wide receiver Brandon Marshall was the Broncos' initial fourth-round pick in 2006, with returner/receiver Domenik Hixon becoming the third of the Broncos' selections in that round, giving Denver arguably the best single fourth round in NFL Draft history.)

Never mind that Dumervil's relatively short stature included uniquely long arms that helped him gain leverage on lumbering offensive tackles.

"Physically, it's the leverage thing, but I think the biggest thing about Elvis is he plays the game with a little bit of a chip on his shoulder," said Mike Nolan, Dumervil's defensive coordinator during his league-leading 17.0 sack season in 2009. "He is a little shorter and people bring it to his attention, including me, but he overcomes it. He's very competitive."

It was the 3-4 defensive system implemented by Nolan, first-year head coach Josh McDaniels, and linebackers coach Don "Wink" Martindale in 2009 that transformed Dumervil from a "third down" pass-rushing defensive end to one who earned a Pro Bowl berth in the three consecutive seasons he played in 2009, 2011, 2012. (Dumervil suffered a torn pectoral muscle in training camp of 2010 and missed the entire season.)

The new defensive alignment moved Dumervil from a 4-3 defensive end who rushed from a three-point stance to a 3-4 outside linebacker who took off from the standing position.

"They drafted Robert Ayers to be the 3-4 edge-rusher going into my contract year [of 2009]," Dumervil said. "They told me to figure it out and get in there somewhere. I remember [inside linebacker] Andra Davis was an integral part of that season. He was a motivator for me. He sat next to me in the meeting room. Andra Davis was a really cool teammate."

Dumervil's mother, Maria Noel (Dumervil), was 21 when she arrived here from Haiti, while his father, Frank Gachelin, migrated at 25. They met in Miami, and on January 19, 1984, they had a son and named him Elvis Kool Dumervil.

While Elvis was young when his parents separated, he was one of 10 kids who became the family's first generation born in America. Many of their kids, including Elvis, were raised in Miami's transplanted Caribbean culture known as Little Haiti.

Dumervil grew up in a tiny triplex, off a small side street, with his mom and siblings. There is a well-kept school yard down the block, but the street is where Elvis spent day after day playing football.

"You can play tackle football, anywhere," said Curry Burns, Elvis's older half-brother who was an NFL safety from 2003 to 2006. "Street ball, that's where we all started to realize we were pretty good at football. Kool, we thought he was something ever since he was young. We would play Little League, and watching him play running back, he used to run people over."

The breakout game in Dumervil's professional career came in week 2 of the 2009 season when he had four sacks in a 27–6 home win against the Cleveland Browns. Dumervil beat perennial All-Pro left tackle Joe Thomas for one sack and right tackle John St. Clair for the other three.

Unfortunately, Dumervil's exit from Denver was bitter and memorable for the Dumervil Fax Fiasco. It began when the Broncos asked him to take a pay cut from the $14 million he was supposed to draw in 2013. After weeks of contentious negotiations, there was an oral agreement 40 minutes before the free-agent deadline on a reduced $8 million salary for the 2013 season—not enough time, apparently, for the two sides to fax over signed contracts.

When the fax carrying Dumervil's signature didn't arrive as the deadline ticked down, Broncos cap guy Mike Sullivan made the hasty decision to release him. Although the Broncos tried to re-sign Dumervil, the damage was done and he signed with Baltimore.

After playing four seasons with Baltimore and one last season in San Francisco, Dumervil finished his career with 105.5 sacks to officially rank No. 31 all-time.

"The fans there were awesome," Dumervil said. "It was always a pleasure playing in that stadium. It's one of the top environments to play in. I had great teammates. Loved my teammates. Champ. Brandon Marshall. Von. Chris Harris, Derek Wolfe. Nate Jackson. Robert Ayers was cool, too."

VON MILLER (2011–2021)

With apologies to Champ Bailey, a first-ballot Hall of Famer, Von Miller goes down as the best defensive player in Broncos history. It was close and Bailey was every bit the cornerback as Miller was a pass-rusher. But single-handedly winning a Super Bowl puts Miller over the top.

The Broncos' first-round draft pick, No. 2 overall, in 2011, Miller was the first-ever draft selection of then general manager John Elway. Miller won the NFL Defensive Rookie of the Year Award in 2011, then recorded a career-most 18.5 sacks in his second season of 2012.

He encountered self-inflicted adversity in 2013 when he was suspended six games for violating the NFL's drug policy, and later that season he suffered a season-ending torn ACL injury.

He returned to have 14.0 sacks in 2014, then exploded in the postseason of 2015, getting 2.5 sacks on Tom Brady and the New England Patriots in the AFC Championship Game and 2.5 more sacks, with two forced fumbles that led to touchdowns, in the Super Bowl win against Cam Newton and the Carolina Panthers.

Miller was named MVP of Super Bowl 50.

"Always have Super Bowl 50," Miller said November 1, 2021, a couple hours after he was traded to the Los Angeles Rams in exchange for second- and third-round draft picks. "Seen the pictures on my way out. Made me tear up."

His performance in 2015 led to intense, and sometimes acrimonious, contract negotiations between Elway and Miller's agent Joby Branion before cooler minds prevailed and the outside linebacker wound up with a six-year, $114.5 million deal—$19.083 million per year—that made him the NFL's highest-paid defensive player, a distinction Miller held for two consecutive years.

But while Miller lived up to the first three years of that contract with 13.5 sacks in 2016, 10.0 sacks in 2017, and 14.5 sacks in 2018, he never got a chance to repeat as Super Bowl

MVP. As of this writing, the Broncos are mired in a seven-year playoff drought.

Miller fell off to 8.0 sacks in 2019, then missed all of the COVID season of 2020 after suffering a torn ankle tendon in the first practice of the regular season.

The Broncos in March tried to cut his 2021 salary in half from his scheduled $18 million (later bumped to $19.03 million because of the league's added 17th game). Miller wouldn't accept it. Rather than release Miller, the Broncos decided to keep him at his current rate.

Miller had 4.0 sacks through the Broncos' first three games of the 2021 season—all wins—but after recording a half-sack against Baltimore's Lamar Jackson in game 4, he went sackless over his final four games with the Broncos.

After he was traded to the Rams, Miller's sackless skid continued for four more games, but then he exploded for 5.0 sacks in his final four regular-season games, helping the Rams reach the playoffs as a wild card. He had 2.0 more sacks against the Bengals' Joe Burrow in Super Bowl LVI to earn his second Super Bowl ring.

In all, Miller finished with a team-record 110.5 sacks in his 10 and a half seasons with the Broncos. Only cornerback Bailey and possibly Orange Crush linebacker Randy Gradishar are in the conversation with Miller as the greatest defensive player in Broncos history.

"Had a lot of beautiful years here," Miller said. "Had a lot of great memories here, a lot of great teammates. A lot of great coaches, lot of great fans. I'll never forget all those people."

DeMarcus Ware (2014–2016)

The Broncos didn't always get the best of DeMarcus Ware, but they most certainly did once.

It was the 2015-season AFC Championship Game against the New England Patriots, who were favored as visitors.

Overcoming a balky back that had caused him to miss five games that year and limit his effectiveness in many others, Ware may have taken an extra pain shot knowing it would be his best chance of ever playing in a Super Bowl.

"Actually, I didn't [take a painkiller]," Ware said after it was announced February 9, 2023, that he had been elected into the Pro Football Hall of Fame. "I told the guys if I get an opportunity to play in a playoff game, I'm going to play.

"Back was hurting, neck was hurting. I was in a lot of pain. But I didn't think about myself. I was thinking about Broncos Country. I was thinking about the players I was playing with and I was willing to sacrifice that."

It was in his second year of eligibility that Ware received the Pro Football Hall of Fame nod from 49 voting media members.

"It feels good knowing that the sacrifices we went through to be the best, we know [we] can say all those sacrifices will be enshrined forever," Ware said.

Immortality was far more certain for the pass-rushing outside linebacker than a Super Bowl ring as he was winding down his career.

"First of all, DeMarcus should have been a first-ballot Hall of Famer," said Brandon Marshall, the Broncos' play-calling inside linebacker on that iconic 2015 Denver defense. "Top 10 [officially] in sacks. He had an illustrious career. I understand the Hall of Fame is about what you do on the field, but off the field he embodied everything a Hall of Famer should be. He should have been in on the first ballot, but I'm excited to see him finally get enshrined [on the second ballot] and get what he deserved."

A first-round draft pick out of Troy in 2005, Ware had played nine seasons with the Dallas Cowboys, averaging 13.0

sacks a year, including monstrous seasons of 20.0 sacks in 2008 and 19.5 in 2011. The Cowboys' playoff record during his time there, though, was 1-4. Never had he come close to playing in the Big Game, much less winning it.

He also went one-and-done in the playoffs to finish his first season with the Broncos in 2014. But in 2015, the Broncos under new coach Gary Kubiak won nail-biter after heart-stopper. With a resurgent Peyton Manning returning at quarterback in the second half of the 2015 regular-season finale against the Chargers, Denver used its No. 1 AFC playoff seed to pass through the first round with a bye, rallied in the fourth quarter to beat the Pittsburgh Steelers in the second round, and host Tom Brady, Bill Belichick, and the Patriots in the AFC Championship.

Ware hit Brady not once. Not twice. Not three times. Not four times. DeMarcus Ware hit Brady seven times in the AFC Championship Game.

And then he was about to hit him again to blow up Brady's game-tying, 2-point conversion attempt with 12 seconds remaining to preserve the Broncos' 20–18 win.

Which turned out okay, because in the next game, Super Bowl 50, Ware registered four quarterback hits and two sacks on Carolina's Cam Newton in the Broncos' 24–10 victory. Von Miller stole the show with two strip-sacks that led to two touchdowns and the Super Bowl 50 MVP award.

All Ware did was combine for 12 quarterback hits (we'll give him his 2-point strike on Brady) and 2.5 sacks in the final two games of the Broncos' magical 2015 season.

"His run at the end of '15 was ridiculous," Marshall said. "He helped power us through those playoffs. Our defense set the tone for our team and the pressure he put on the quarterback made it easier on our DBs, easier for me to cover the running backs and tight ends."

Ware may be considered primarily a Cowboy as he posed for his bronze bust that will be forever placed in Canton. But the Broncos would not have won their third Lombardi Trophy without Ware's play at the end of the 2015 season. He played three seasons in Denver, registering 7.0 sacks through his first six games in 2014, before his back acted up and slowed him to 3.0 in his final 10 games.

He had 7.5 sacks in his injury-riddled 2015 season—with 3.5 more sacks in the postseason run to the world championship. Forced to take a pay cut in 2016—general manager John Elway was known to put business ahead of sentimentality as Manning had discovered the previous year—Ware managed just 4.0 sacks in 10 games in his final year before conceding his back could no longer hold up.

Another Hall of Famer, safety Brian Dawkins, also played his final three seasons in Denver after a distinguished career with the Philadelphia Eagles. Dawkins forgot to mention the Broncos in his Hall of Fame speech. Ware promised the Broncos would get mentioned in his remarks during the Hall of Fame ceremony in August 2023 in Canton.

"Yes. It's one of those places in my life where it was life-changing," Ware said of Denver during an interview for 9NEWS. "To where it was the rebirth of me. When the Dallas Cowboys released me I was able to become a leader in a new locker room and do something that I didn't get to do with the Dallas Cowboys, and that's win a championship. There were some amazing players that goes down in . . . when they say etch your name in stone in a team, I feel like we did that. Me and Peyton [Manning]."

Ware then held up his Super Bowl ring for the television viewers.

"Broncos Country, it's . . . See this? There's no other words, that's it."

Mature and handsome with a big smile and an immaculately shaven bald head, Ware was also instrumental in mentoring Miller, whose enormous talent was sometimes negated by his rambunctious youth.

"Von is like my brother, I'm just going to start there," Ware said. "And to be able to come and mentor Von and then him doing the same thing and going to win that championship with the Rams and then [trying] to do the same thing with Buffalo. It was like that little seed I planted and it's still living."

Ware officially ranks ninth all-time with 138.5 career sacks. Among those on the NFL's top-15 sack list, all who are eligible have already been inducted into the HOF (Julius Peppers and Terrell Suggs are not yet eligible).

A Cowboy, first? Sure, he was. But DeMarcus Ware also had his Hall of Fame moments with the Broncos.

TOM JACKSON (1973–1986)

A Broncos Ring of Famer, Jackson belongs in the Hall of Fame, too, as a combo candidate for not only his 14-year playing career as a Broncos outside linebacker but also his 30-plus years as the NFL's top studio analyst. Jackson was given the prestigious Pete Rozelle Radio-Television Award by the Pro Football Hall of Fame in 2015.

But Jackson deserves a bronze bust with the legends in Canton, Ohio, for his 45 years as a player and contributor— during a time when football eclipsed all other sports as the game best suited for television.

He was inducted into the Broncos Ring of Fame in his first year of eligibility, in 1992.

"What you call flamboyant or colorful personalities, there were two guys," said Randy Gradishar, who played inside linebacker alongside Jackson. "The first was Lyle Alzado. And also

Tommy Jackson. They were the guys with the biggest personalities in my 10 years.

"Tommy stayed all 10 years I was there. He got in your face. He was always talking to the opponent, different players. He was yelling at coaches. He was our emotional, inspirational kind of guy. Tommy was a good outside linebacker. He competed. He was All-Pro a couple of times. He was certainly the big voice and emotional voice of our team with [Bob] Swenson and Billy Thompson."

In 1981, the Broncos started the Bob Peck Memorial Award in honor of the team's beloved public relations director who died of brain cancer the previous year. The Bob Peck Award would be given to the team's most inspirational player.

Jackson was voted by his teammates as the most inspirational player the first six consecutive seasons of the award. He had to retire before another player could receive the honor (Keith Bishop in 1987).

"Tommy was the heart and soul and swagger of our defense," Foley said. "And he was a hitter. He wasn't that big, 215, 220. But he could run and he could hit. That legendary hit on, I think it was Clarence Davis, and he runs up to Madden— and I'm behind him, I'm playing right corner, and he's playing the weak side and I'm running up and I hear him go, 'How do you like that, Fat Man!' And the Raiders are ready to jump on him. But that was Tommy."

Ah yes, one of the most famous smack-talk moments in Broncos lore. It occurred during the 1977 regular-season game on October 16 in the Oakland-Alameda County Coliseum. Context is important here. Going into the 1977 season, the Broncos had won just 2 of their previous 28 games against the Raiders going back to 1963: 2-24-2.

In this game, the Broncos took out 14 years of Raiders frustration by dominating Oakland, 30–7. The Orange Crush intercepted Raiders quarterback Kenny Stabler not once, not twice, but seven times. The most stinging moment, however, was reserved for Raiders coach John Madden.

"There is a turnover that takes place right on the sideline," Jackson said for the book, *The 50 Greatest Players in Denver Broncos History*. "And we kind of ended up rolling up on the sideline. And when I got up John Madden was literally standing within four or five feet of me. It wasn't meant to be derogatory, but what it was, was this relief of all of the things that had gone on with the Raiders' success and the Broncos' failures up to that time. And all of a sudden here I was face-to-face with the guy who stood for what the Oakland Raiders were about. I just remember standing up and saying, 'It's all over, Fat Man.' It was quite the moment."

Here's how Madden referred to that moment in his autobiography, *One Knee Equals Two Feet (And Everything Else You Need to Know about Football)*:

> *Tommy Jackson of the Broncos wasn't very big, but he was a quick linebacker before there were quick linebackers. And he was the wildest linebacker I've ever seen. You never knew where he was going to turn up. He was tough, but not disciplined, which made him that much harder to figure out. Against a disciplined linebacker, you knew that if you did this, he would do that. But with Jackson, you had no idea. One time he might run in there, the next time he'd run out there. And for some reason he didn't like me.*
>
> *"Take that, Fat Man," he would yell.*
>
> *He was the only player who ever yelled at me like that.*

In 1976, as the Orange Crush was formulating, Jackson had 7 interceptions with 136 return yards. As a linebacker. It's a single-season record among Broncos linebackers that will likely never be broken, and only one other linebacker in the 95-year history of the NFL had more—Baltimore's Stan White, who had 8 interceptions in 1975.

More than one of Jackson's former Orange Crush teammates referred to him as the Von Miller of his day.

Besides 20 career interceptions, Jackson also had 44 sacks. And this was as Jackson was finishing up his career in 1986, as Lawrence Taylor was taking over the game that year and transforming outside linebackers into the league's preeminent pass-rushers.

Jackson never got to pin his ears back and go after the quarterback play after play the way Miller, DeMarcus Ware, and Derrick Thomas did a few years later.

"No, our responsibilities back then were twofold," Jackson said. "You had to not only be a player who could pass-rush, but you had to play the run as well. You had to play well in coverage. I think as complicated as the game has become, it's also gotten a little bit simpler."

Really? Meaning more specialized? Some guys are good against the run and play on first down while other guys are better going forward and play on third down?

"It's gotten specialized," Jackson said. "Guys in our day had to play every down. Guys don't do that anymore. I respect Von so much. What a superior talent he is."

While watching the Broncos during their Orange Crush years from the Chicagoland area and at college in Murray, Kentucky, I always thought Jackson was Denver's best player, not Gradishar or Louis Wright.

It wasn't until I moved to Colorado in October 1984 that I heard people occupying the local barstools state the case for Gradishar and Louis Wright as the best players on that famed Broncos defense of the late 1970s.

I came to realize why I always thought Jackson was the best. One, he was a great player. A first-team All-Pro in 1977 and '78. A playmaking linebacker. The first player to play 14 seasons with the Broncos, as he lasted one more year than Billy Thompson and Barney Chavous.

"Tommy was my roommate. We'd just lay in bed and talk about football all night long," Thompson said. "One of the best weakside linebackers I'd ever seen. Played with tremendous heart, tremendous effort."

The second reason was that Dick Enberg, Curt Gowdy, and Merlin Olsen, the NBC announcers for AFC games in the 1970s and '80s, often spoke, and relayed more anecdotes, about the engaging Jackson than any other Bronco. One can only imagine how smitten the announcers must have been with Jackson during their production meetings on the eve of the Broncos broadcasts.

"He was the greatest storyteller I've ever been around," said Steve Foley, a cornerback, safety, and longtime Jackson teammate in Denver.

The Orange Crush years were to the Broncos what Neil Armstrong was to astronaut moon walkers. The first. Football fans had begun to take the Broncos for granted because they pretty much won every year from the mid-1970s until the late 2010s. But there was a time when they never won. As in their first 13 seasons.

The Broncos' 14th season featured a rookie from Cleveland and the University of Louisville named Thomas Louis Jackson III. It also marked the franchise's first winning record. Jackson's final season was 1986, otherwise known as the year of The Drive.

It's no coincidence the Broncos took off during the Tom Jackson years.

"Earlier you asked me about the highlight of my career," Jackson said. "The highlight really is that we managed to go from losers to winners. The hardest thing to do in sports is to try and figure out how to take a losing mentality that has existed for 13 years and turn that into a jumping-off point for winning. It's something we believe we're part of to this day. We figured out how to teach this franchise to win. That's probably something we're most proud of."

STARTERS

Von Miller and Tom Jackson
Miller was the best edge-rusher from his outside linebacker position in Broncos history. Jackson was perhaps the best

Von Miller © ERIC LARS BAKKE

three-way outside linebacker of stopping the run, dropping back in coverage to make plays, and rushing the passer.

A strong case can also be made that the two most outgoing, fun-loving personalities were the two starting outside linebackers among *The Denver Broncos All-Time All-Stars.*

OTHERS

Jim Ryan (1979–1988)

Undrafted out of William & Mary, Ryan was smaller than most left outside linebackers at 6-foot-1 and anywhere between 215 and 225 pounds. But he was as tough and smart as they come. And durable. Counting the postseason, Ryan played in 159 of a possible 162 games in his 10-year career.

A special teams captain in two of his first three years, Ryan became a starting linebacker in the strike season of 1982. He had at least 100 tackles in five seasons, leading the team with 127 in 1987 and registering a career-most 130 in his final season of 1988.

In 1989, head coach Dan Reeves cut several veterans in a team youth movement, and Ryan, receiver Steve Watson, and offensive tackle Dave Studdard all held a retirement press conference together in September. Ryan, Watson, and Studdard all came in together as undrafted rookies in 1979 and went out together 10 years later.

Bradley Chubb (2018–2022)

Through no fault of his own, Chubb will be remembered for two things in his Broncos career. One, the Broncos selected him with their No. 5 overall pick in the 2018 draft, and not quarterback Josh Allen, who went two picks later to Buffalo.

And two, the Broncos got a first-round draft pick back for Chubb after trading him midway through the 2022 season to

Miami—a first-round pick Denver used after the season to acquire head coach Sean Payton from the New Orleans Saints.

As for his four and a half seasons with the Broncos, Chubb was a good player but fell short of the sizable expectations that came with his No. 5 overall selection in the 2018 NFL Draft. His career began well as he posted 12.5 sacks in his first season to break Von Miller's previous team rookie record of 11.5 sacks.

But then came a series of injuries that hindered Chubb's performance over the next three seasons. He had one sack through four games in his second season of 2019 when tests the morning after game 4 revealed a torn ACL—the same ACL he'd torn earlier in high school.

He rebounded some in 2020 when he recorded 7.5 sacks through the Broncos' first 11 games, a run that led to getting enough votes to receive his first Pro Bowl berth.

But an ankle injury that eventually led to surgery caused him to have no sacks through the final five games of 2020, and none in 2021, as he suffered an injury to his other ankle that also required surgery.

Chubb returned on a $12.716 million, fifth-year option in 2022 and he responded with his career-best start, with 5.5 sacks through the Broncos' first five games. He did not record a sack in his next three games for the Broncos, and with the team sitting with a 3-5 record and no draft picks in the first or second round coming after the season, Chubb was dealt to the Dolphins in exchange for that first-round pick that Denver would later use to get Sean Payton.

Chubb, by the way, immediately signed a five-year, $110 million contract extension—$22 million per year—with the Dolphins, so all's well that ends well.

Ian Gold (2000–2003, 2005–2007)

A second-round draft pick out of Michigan, Gold was a five-year starter mostly at right linebacker in the Broncos' 4-3 defense. His best season was 2002, his first as a starter, when he had 100 tackles and 6.5 sacks, both of which were career highs. Gold was small at 6-foot, 220 pounds, but he was fast and played with emotion and great energy on game days.

He made the Pro Bowl as a special teamer in 2001.

Mike Croel (1991–1994)

A No. 4 overall selection out of Nebraska in the 1991 draft, Croel was the highest-drafted defensive player in Broncos history (starting with the 1967 common draft) until 20 years later when Von Miller was taken No. 2 overall. Croel was sensational as a rookie, recording 10.0 sacks to earn the NFL's Defensive Player of the Year.

But he declined drastically from there, as he had just 5.0, 5.0, and zero sacks in his final three seasons with the Broncos.

Bob Swenson (1975–1983)

A tackler, not a pass-rusher, in the true, 4 linebackers across, 3-4 set who lined up next to Randy Gradishar on the left side, and opposite Tom Jackson. Swenson was a first-team All-Pro in 1981—when he had 3 interceptions, and a 93-yard fumble return for a touchdown. He got three votes to finish seventh for NFL Defensive Player of the Year in 1979, thanks to 3 interceptions, 3 sacks, and 3 fumble recoveries.

Swenson was only a four-year starter, but they were during the height of the Orange Crush Defense, from 1977 to 1981. According to the Broncos media guide, Swenson claimed he was "the greatest Monopoly player in the world."

SAFETIES

From the very beginning, the Broncos have been incredibly strong at their safety position.

It's easily been the deepest defensive position of standout players and it arguably has been the top collection of greats on either side of the ball in Broncos history.

The case starts with the Broncos Ring of Fame. Of the 35 men who have been inducted through the 2022 season, the quarterback and safety position lead with 5 each. A distant second on defense is outside linebacker and inside linebacker, with two each.

And it can be argued the Ring of Fame committee has been somewhat lenient with its quarterbacks (Charley Johnson was 20–18, with 52 TD passes and 52 interceptions) and restrictive with its safeties (Steve Foley, the Broncos' all-time interceptions leader, is not yet included).

The positional breakdown of the 35 Broncos Ring of Famers:

Quarterbacks (5): Frank Tripucka, Charley Johnson, Craig Morton, John Elway, Peyton Manning

Safeties (5): Austin "Goose" Gonsoulin, Billy Thompson, Dennis Smith, Steve Atwater, John Lynch

Coaches (3): Red Miller, Dan Reeves, Mike Shanahan

Kickers (3): Gene Mingo*, Jim Turner, Jason Elam

Receivers (3): Lionel Taylor, Haven Moses, Rod Smith

Owners (2): Gerald Phipps, Pat Bowlen

Running backs (2): Floyd Little, Terrell Davis

Cornerbacks (2): Louis Wright, Champ Bailey

Outside linebackers (2): Tom Jackson, Simon Fletcher

Inside linebackers (2): Randy Gradishar, Karl Mecklenburg

Tight end (1): Shannon Sharpe

Returner (1): Rick Upchurch*

Center (1): Tom Nalen

Offensive tackle (1): Gary Zimmerman

Defensive end (1): Rich "Tombstone" Jackson

Defensive tackle (1): Paul Smith

*Mingo was also a halfback and returner; Upchurch was also a receiver.

Furthermore, the best player during the Broncos' historically bad six-year losing skid entering the 2023 season has been another safety, Justin Simmons.

Thus, the process of picking two safeties for *The Denver Broncos All-Time All-Stars* involved more candidates than usual.

THE CANDIDATES

Dennis Smith
Steve Atwater
Austin "Goose" Gonsoulin
Steve Foley
Billy Thompson

Justin Simmons
John Lynch

Dennis Smith (1981–1994)

There are freak athletes and there is Dennis Smith. In high school, and later at USC, he was a 7-foot-2 high jumper.

"As high as I ever got," he said with a tinge of disappointment, but not a trace of conceit. "I couldn't clear higher than 7-2."

Growing up in Santa Monica, where his ancestors bought property in the 1930s, Smith excelled at track, basketball, and receiver and defensive back.

Smith's superior athleticism was encapsulated in one NFL game played November 17, 1985, against the San Diego Chargers. Smith was all over the Mile High Stadium field on defense, plus blocked two field goals in a 30–24 overtime victory.

Smith first blocked a 47-yard field goal by Ralf Mojsiejenko in the first quarter, keeping San Diego's lead at 7–0. This was the drive after the Chargers' Gary Anderson returned the opening kickoff 98 yards for a touchdown.

With the score tied, 24–24, after four quarters, Dan Fouts led San Diego to the Broncos' 23-yard line on the first drive of overtime. Bob Thomas lined up for a 40-yard field goal, but his kick was blocked.

Many thought it was Smith who blocked it, but while he did storm up the middle with his arms raised, he said years later: "I didn't block that one."

Daniel Hunter did. Didn't matter, because Broncos safety Mike Harden had called a timeout just before the snap, as he thought that's what coach Dan Reeves was signaling from the sideline.

The Chargers got another chance to kick the game-winner. Improbably, Smith blocked the next one, too. Thomas's kick banged off Smith's forearm. Broncos cornerback Louis Wright picked up the ball and ran it 60 yards for a touchdown as old Mile High Stadium trembled from the upper deck to the playing field.

Per the Broncos' legendary public relations director Jim Saccomano, Smith was the only player in NFL history to lead his team in tackles (nine) and passes defensed (three) while blocking two field goal attempts in the same game. It was also the only game in NFL history when the first and last touches of a game resulted in touchdowns.

"He did stuff other people couldn't do," Wright said of Smith.

"If Dennis Smith had a memorable name, he'd be in the Hall of Fame," said Karl Mecklenburg, a linebacker who retired with Smith following the 1994 season.

Smith is one of just five players who played 14 seasons with the Broncos (Elway, Jason Elam, Tom Nalen, and Tom Jackson are the others). A six-time Pro Bowl selection, Smith's most accomplished season was 1989, when he was also named second-team All-Pro and finished fifth in the NFL Defensive Player of the Year voting. He had a well-rounded year with 82 tackles, 6 forced fumbles, 3 fumble recoveries, 2 interceptions for 78 return yards, and a blocked kick.

He had five 100-tackle seasons and finished with 1,158 to go along with 30 career picks and 15.0 sacks.

During his college days at USC, Smith in his four years played in the same secondary with the likes of Dennis Thurman, Ronnie Lott, Jeff Fisher, and Joey Browner. Smith said Marcus Allen also started out as a defensive back, but in his freshman training camp, a bunch of Trojan running backs got hurt and he was switched to the offensive backfield.

Of all those USC stars in the late 1970s, none meant more to Smith than Thurman.

"Dennis Thurman went to my high school and he went to USC," said Smith, who was three years younger than Thurman.

"So it was not a hard choice for me to go to USC, because he was my hero when I was growing up. He was the first person I looked up to as an athlete. He's one of my best friends now."

Smith was the Broncos' first-round draft pick, No. 15 overall, in the 1981 draft. His college teammate Lott went No. 8 overall to the San Francisco 49ers.

A right cornerback his rookie season, Smith shifted to safety in his second season of 1982 while also dropping down to the nickel position on third down.

"Dennis invented the nickel blitz," Wright said. "I shouldn't say Dennis, it was [defensive coordinator] Joe Collier who came up with it. But Joe Collier had Dennis cover the wide receiver and then blitz the quarterback. Joe Collier invented that against the LA Rams."

The Broncos were playing the Rams in Anaheim in a December 1982 game. Vince Ferragamo was the Rams quarterback.

"Dennis started going out on the slot because people started going three wide receivers," Wright said. "He was such a good blitzer he would be there. Sometimes you worry when you're on the blitz there's no one back there to help. He would be there. He did that against the Rams and we won the game.

"So, like, two weeks later, the Rams were doing the same thing. They started doing it. Pretty soon the whole league was doing it. But it all started with that game against the Rams. That had never been done."

Smith was inducted into the Broncos Ring of Fame in 2001, his second year of eligibility.

STEVE ATWATER (1989–1998)

Selected by the Broncos with their No. 20 overall pick in the 1989 draft, Atwater was moved to the box by Broncos defensive coordinator Wade Phillips, while Dennis Smith played free safety.

As a rookie, Atwater had an astounding 129 tackles and 3 interceptions, and he would have been the NFL Defensive Rookie of the Year if it hadn't been for the pass-rushing exploits of Kansas City's Derrick Thomas.

In his next four seasons, Atwater was credited with 173, 150, 151, and 141 tackles—unheard-of totals for a safety.

The eight Pro Bowls in Atwater's 10 seasons in Denver were tied with Champ Bailey for second-most in franchise history, just one behind John Elway's nine. Atwater was inducted into the Broncos Ring of Fame in his first year of eligibility, in 2005.

Atwater was also a key figure in the Broncos' back-to-back Super Bowl titles to cap the 1997 and 1998 seasons. His play in Super Bowl XXXII would have been worthy of MVP consideration had it not been for the sensational performance of running back Terrell Davis.

It took longer than expected for Atwater to draw serious Hall of Fame consideration, but once he made it to the 15 modern-era finalists, he began to build momentum. Atwater was elected to the Pro Football Hall of Fame in 2020—his 16th year of eligibility, but only after his third time as a top 15 finalist.

"I played with him and I tell ya, I'm glad I didn't have to play against him," John Elway said of Atwater's Hall of Fame election. "He changed that position. He was big and physical and could move around. He was like a linebacker playing safety and had great range. Was also a great leader."

Until he ran into Steve Atwater on a Monday night 33 years ago, Christian Okoye could have been nicknamed "The Nigerian Dream." It was Atwater's blast on the NFL's biggest and best running back in 1990 that gave Okoye nightmares.

Okay, just kidding about Okoye's nickname. He was the NFL's defending rushing champion in 1989 and played with moniker "The Nigerian Nightmare" throughout his career. But

Okoye would agree that all these years later, Atwater deserved his election into the Pro Football Hall of Fame.

Atwater was eventually elected in part because he had a signature play with his Monday-night, 1990 blast of the 253-pound Nigerian Nightmare, Christian Okoye.

"It's been neat that [this] play is still alive today, especially with YouTube and all the other methods that people use to keep up with videos forever and replay them forever," Atwater said. "I'm amazed that it is still out there. But, yeah, we have a tremendous amount of respect for one another, and whenever people ask me about it, I always tell them the other side of the story: 'Yeah, I got him on that play, but that still doesn't take away from him as a player, but more importantly, him as a man.'"

One play also does not top back-to-back Super Bowl rings—especially when Atwater was arguably the Denver D's MVP in their first Super Bowl–winning game against Green Bay.

"I definitely think it was a huge part of my career," Atwater said. "I think that was certainly the highlight of my career. Especially after having gone [to the Super Bowl] my rookie year and we played against the 49ers and they beat the mess out of us.

"I remember trying to tackle Jerry Rice on a play that was set up perfectly, and I ran and slammed into him and he just bounced off me and ran into the end zone. Oh my goodness, one of the worst days of my life. [The 49ers beat the Broncos in that Super Bowl, 55–10.] And to be able to finish up with the two Super Bowl victories, it was truly special, and I think that's played a part in this honor of getting inducted into the Pro Football Hall of Fame."

Atwater became the eighth Bronco elected into the Hall of Fame, following Elway, Gary Zimmerman, Floyd Little, Shannon Sharpe, Terrell Davis, Champ Bailey, and owner Pat Bowlen. During Atwater's HOF induction ceremony in Canton,

Ohio—which was pushed back a year because of COVID—he had former safety mate and mentor Dennis Smith serve as his presenter.

"Steve was an intimidating force on the field who made plays at big times, and that's the type of player you want in the Hall of Fame," Smith said during his presentation.

It started to drizzle at Tom Benson Hall of Fame Stadium in the seconds prior to Atwater taking the stage. It stopped by the time he had thanked everyone. The highlight of the speech was when Atwater asked for all of his former Broncos teammates to stand and be recognized.

"John Elway, Terrell Davis. Dennis Smith," Atwater said.

Alfred Williams, Rod Smith and Neil Smith, Ray Crockett and Mark Schlereth, among others. There were close to two dozen former teammates who showed up to help Atwater celebrate his special moment.

"It was truly an honor to play with each and every one of you," Atwater said.

He thanked coaches and teammates from high school to college to the pros, including those in his one season of 1999 with the New York Jets. He especially had kind words for late Broncos owner Pat Bowlen.

"Mr. B was a kind, generous man who knew how to make you feel special," Atwater said. "I appreciated all he did for our team. What a phenomenal leader he was."

He then thanked his Broncos defensive coaches and strength and conditioning coaches and trainers, especially Steve "Greek" Antonopulos. A special salute was directed at former head coach Mike Shanahan.

"The most organized and disciplined person I ever met in my life," Atwater said. "And obviously the coach who led us to those back-to-back Super Bowl victories."

A few years ago, the Broncos brought Atwater back to serve as the team's ambassador, where he has been the team's most front-and-center-and-available alumnus.

"I'm not a guy looking for notoriety or wanting to be a celebrity, but it's amazing how being in the spotlight, being a Denver Bronco, being a member of a team that won the first two Super Bowls here, how people look up to me and more than anything look to me for leadership, look to me for encouragement, and I take that role seriously," Atwater said. "I want to bring people together. I want to unite people. I like being happy, I like being around happy people and I like making people happy, and I'm fortunate to be in this role with the Broncos where I can do that."

Austin "Goose" Gonsoulin (1960–1966)

With seconds left in the first half of the first game the Broncos ever played, on September 9, 1960, safety Goose Gonsoulin intercepted a pass thrown by Boston Patriots quarterback Butch Songin to preserve the Broncos' 7–3 lead heading into the break.

It was the first interception in Broncos history. Gonsoulin also came up with the Broncos' second interception, picking off Songin again in the fourth quarter, this time at his own 2-yard line, to preserve the Broncos' 13–10 victory. For a game 2 encore, Gonsoulin had four interceptions against the Bills—three off quarterback Tommy O'Connell, and the final one, with just seconds remaining, off Bob Brodhead.

Through week 2 of the first American Football League season in 1960, Gonsoulin had six interceptions. There have been full seasons when the NFL's interception leader had six.

Gonsoulin compiled an incredible 43 interceptions through his first six seasons with the Broncos—by far the most of any AFL player through 1965—when mysteriously the picks stopped coming his way. A switch to playing one-on-one cornerback in 1966, plus injuries that forced Gonsoulin to miss four games, contributed to the fact that he didn't record an interception that year.

"I remember how tough Goose was," said Gene Mingo, a Broncos halfback and kicker through the team's first four and a half seasons. "Our trainer Fred Posey used to carry these tongs as part of his sideline medical bag. Once Goose got hit so hard he nearly swallowed his tongue. Thank God we had Fred Posey there and he pulled it out. It was quite a sight to see. Goose Gonsoulin to me—I put him in the same category as Lionel Taylor. Goose loved the game. He played the game hard."

To begin the 1967 season, Gonsoulin was still a team captain, but as he drove from his Texas home to Denver for training camp, he learned he had been waived. Gonsoulin had played out his option the previous season and was hoping to negotiate a no-cut clause in his contract upon arriving.

New head coach Lou Saban, in one of his many regrettable decisions, decided instead to cut Gonsoulin. That same off-season, Saban traded cornerback Willie Brown to the Raiders.

Gonsoulin was picked up by the San Francisco 49ers, who held his rights after drafting him in 1960 in the 17th round. He recorded three more interceptions in just seven starts for the 49ers in the National Football League and retired after that season.

Had Gonsoulin, who averaged an astounding 7.2 interceptions through his first six seasons, recorded just four more picks with the Broncos, he would have gone down as the all-time AFL interception leader.

As it is, Gonsoulin finished tied for third with Kansas City safety Johnny Robinson, and trailed only David Grayson and Jim Norton. Gonsoulin was a first-team all-AFL selection in 1960, '62, and '63, and was named to the second team in 1961 and 1964.

Gonsoulin held the Broncos' career interception record from the team's first game in 1960 until Steve Foley broke it with his 44th interception in game 4 of the 1986 season. It was Foley's last interception, but enough to still be holding the record nearly 40 years later. Gonsoulin still holds the team's single-season record with the 11 he picked in that first Broncos season of 1960.

What did the AFL interception king do after that great first season? He spent six months serving in the US Army Reserves, which he did again after the 1961 season. After his third season of 1962, Gonsoulin worked on teammate Bud McFadin's Texas ranch.

When the All-AFL team was selected after its final 1969 season, Gonsoulin was a second-team safety.

In 1960, Goose was not only drafted out of Baylor in the 17th round by San Francisco, but also by the American Football League Dallas Texans. He signed with the Texans but was quickly traded to the Broncos, along with end Don Carothers in exchange for Jack Spikes.

In his first day of Broncos' training camp at the Colorado School of Mines in Golden, Colorado, head coach Frank Filchock put Gonsoulin at safety. An AFL All-Star was made.

Gonsoulin was single through his first four NFL seasons, then married Nickie on Monday, September 28, 1964. The date was mentioned because it was a Monday, the day after the Broncos lost at Bears Stadium to the Houston Oilers. Goose broke up two passes and had three tackles on the eve of his wedding.

The next day, teammate and fellow Texan Bud McFadin was his best man, and Bob Scarpitto—a Broncos do-everything running back / flanker / punter—also stood up in the wedding.

After football, Gonsoulin ran a successful construction company and invested in land. He wound up with a 167-acre farm outside Port Arthur, Texas. The Gonsoulins had two children, Angela and Greg, and four grandchildren when he died at 76 on September 8, 2014, in Beaumont, Texas, after a long battle with prostate cancer.

When Pat Bowlen bought the Broncos in 1984, he started the Broncos Ring of Fame, and Gonsoulin was one of the four original inductees, along with Floyd Little, Rich "Tombstone" Jackson, and Lionel Taylor.

STEVE FOLEY (1976–1986)

Foley was the epitome of consistency as evidenced by the year-by-year breakdown of his career interception totals. Foley never had more than 6 interceptions in a year, but he had 3 of those six-pack seasons along with two seasons of 5 picks, two of 4 interceptions, and two of 3 picks. He finished as the Broncos' all-time interception leader with 44—a mark that is still standing 37 years after he retired.

Defensive coordinator Joe Collier liked to turn a cornerback into a safety every few years, and the versatile Foley—a quarterback in high school and in college at Tulane—was a natural to convert halfway through the 1980 season. He finished with 21 interceptions in his first four and a half seasons at cornerback, 23 in five and a half seasons at safety. (He missed all but one and a half quarters in 1982 because of a broken arm suffered in the opener.)

Foley got his first interception as a safety in his third game at the position against San Diego's Dan Fouts, returning it 30 yards. He got another the next week against the Jets' Richard Todd, returning it 18 yards.

That was the thing about that Orange Crush defense in the late 1970s, early 1980s. They didn't just force turnovers, they did something with them. Foley had 622 return yards with his 44 interceptions, including a 40-yard touchdown return against Seattle's Dave Krieg in the final game of the 1984 season.

Earlier that year, in a memorable mid-October game against the Green Bay Packers played in an incredible blizzard at Mile High Stadium, Foley on the first play of the game returned a fumble 22 yards for a touchdown. On the second play of the game, Broncos cornerback Louie Wright returned a fumble 27 yards for a touchdown.

The Broncos were up, 14–0, with 37 seconds gone in the game without their offense putting a sliding step on the field. The Packers dominated the rest of the game, but that fast defensive start held up in a 17–14 Broncos win.

"That had to be the most fun game I had ever played in," Foley said. "It was the closest thing to a Little League, sandlot game that you ever played in. You were falling all over. I remember hitting a 235-pound tight end and he felt like he weighed 180 pounds. I said, 'This is great.'"

As a cornerback, Foley averaged 62 tackles a year in his four full years. But it was after Billy Thompson retired following the 1981 season that Foley really came on as a run enforcer. He was third on the team with 124 tackles in 1983, compiled a career-best 167 stops in 1984, and 92 in his final season of 1986.

In all, Foley had 877 tackles in his 11 NFL seasons. Take away his injured 1982 season and that's 87 tackles a year. Not bad for a defensive back who was listed as 6-foot-2, 190 pounds.

It was Foley's ball-hawking skills, though, that made him unique among Broncos defenders. Unlike Goose Gonsoulin—who had been the Broncos' interception leader from the first game in franchise history in 1960, and got his picks in bunches—Foley got his interceptions at a steady pace.

Gonsoulin had 43 interceptions through his, and the Broncos', first six seasons, an average of better than 7 per year. Foley strung together a bunch of 6-, 5-, and 4-interception seasons.

After 10 seasons, Foley had 42 picks, one shy of Gonsoulin's team record, heading into his final season of 1986.

"I remember around game 10, 11 every year, you'd get injuries," Foley said. "Once you'd get injuries that hobble you—you're playing with a sprained ankle, you can't make good plays—it would limit you. And you knew the guy was going to have to throw the ball right to me [to get an interception]. I'm not at that full speed I was in the first half of the year. There were a few years where you're just playing injured the last half of the season. You're not making as many plays as you were in the beginning."

Foley tied Goose's career record in game 2 of 1986, intercepting Pittsburgh's Mark Malone with 48 seconds remaining—and returning it 24 yards, of course—to clinch a 21–10 victory.

The record-breaker came in game 4 against New England, and was probably the key play in the Broncos' rallying for a 27–20 victory. It didn't look that way at the 2-minute warning of the first half. The Pats were up 10–3 and had first down at the Broncos' 11.

New England tried tricking the Broncos by having Craig James throw a halfback pass. Foley intercepted it at the 3-yard line. And yes, he returned it 15 yards, to the 18.

For the first time in 36 years, Austin "Goose" Gonsoulin was No. 2 on the Broncos' all-time interceptions list.

After starting in Super Bowl XXI against the New York Giants, Foley notified coach Dan Reeves he would retire. All his Orange Crush teammates were going, too. Barney Chavous had retired the year before. Rubin Carter got hurt in game 5 of the 1986 season and didn't play again. Jackson and Wright also played their last game in Super Bowl XXI, a 39–20 loss.

They were the last of the Orange Crush players.

"It was a special time in Denver's history," Foley said. "It was Orange Crush defense and it was the coming of age of the Denver franchise. And getting to play Pittsburgh and Oakland [in the 1977 season playoffs], who were in the midst of their Super Bowl years. Domination years. Pittsburgh was in the midst of their four Super Bowls and we caught them in the middle there.

"As long as we had home-field advantage and beat them and Oakland to go to that first Super Bowl, that was a special, special time. We had some special defenses. Pittsburgh had the Steel Curtain. Joe Collier was the architect of the Orange Crush. Everybody loved Joe Collier. We were just excited to be playing in Joe Collier's defense, knowing we could play with anybody in any game."

Foley never made a Pro Bowl, although it was a joke he didn't make it in 1984 when he had six interceptions with the pick-six and two fumble recoveries, one he returned for a touchdown in the Blizzard Game against Green Bay. His problem was all those great defenders around him often hogged the honors, players like Randy Gradishar, Lyle Alzado, Louis Wright, Tom Jackson, Billy Thompson, and later, Rulon Jones and Dennis Smith.

Foley has come up for discussion among the Broncos Ring of Fame committee members in recent years, and he should have a decent chance of getting elected sooner rather than later.

BILLY THOMPSON (1969–1981)

Had Thompson been eligible in these modern times of looser HOF elections, he might have been elected in his first or second year on the ballot. But in the late 1980s to early 1990s, Hall of Fame classes were often just four or five inductees deep—modern-era, seniors, contributors, coaches, whatever.

The result was an incredible backlog of Hall of Fame talent, and players like Thompson fell through the cracks to the lake of the forgotten.

Check this out about Thompson: He was a 13-year starter who was not only a tackling safety, he had 7 defensive touchdown returns—3 off 40 career interceptions and 4 scores off 21 fumble recoveries. His 4 fumble returns for touchdowns rank No. 3 all-time in the NFL. His 21 fumble recoveries are tied for 26th all-time. His 40 interceptions are tied for 78th.

"Bronco Billy" was the team captain of the Orange Crush defense. He also is the only player in NFL history to lead the league (AFL) in kickoff returns (28.5-yard average) and punt returns (11.5) as a rookie (1969).

No safety in today's game makes the kind of big plays Thompson delivered on a consistent basis. Game in and game out. Even while playing in an era of 14-game seasons, Thompson still holds the Broncos' record, with 156 consecutive games started.

A college teammate of Hall of Famer Art Shell, Thompson was no less than the captain of the famed Orange Crush defense that went 12-2 and reached the franchise's first-ever Super Bowl in 1977. Thompson was a first-team All-Pro that season.

He began as a cornerback but he elevated his game after he was switched to strong safety, from where he scored six of his seven defensive touchdowns.

It was as a strong safety that Thompson made his mark as Bronco Billy. His defensive backs coach in 1969 was Joe Collier, who was also in his first year of coaching for the Broncos. Collier would stay through the 1988 season in Denver, and among his trademark strategies was converting some of his best cornerbacks to safety later in their careers.

"When Coach wanted to change me, I said, 'Why?'" Thompson said. "He said, 'Well, we're going to make you a better player. You're going to be my guy that moves on defense and you're going to be the run enforcer. And you've got to take care of yourself because you're going to be facing guys bigger than you.'"

NFL tackle stats were sketchy prior to 1982—and still are today, for that matter—but in his final 12 seasons, from 1970 through 1981, Thompson was credited with 891 tackles.

A member of the Broncos Ring of Fame, Thompson worked another 29 years for the team after his retirement as a player before retiring in the spring of 2022.

JUSTIN SIMMONS (2016–PRESENT)

In the long line of Broncos safety greats, Justin Simmons is more Goose Gonsoulin than Dennis Smith, more Billy Thompson than Steve Atwater, more Steve Foley than John Lynch.

Simmons is more playmaker than bone crusher.

"If I have the opportunity to separate somebody from the ball or go for the interception, I'm going for the interception," Simmons said. "That's just the type of player I've been since I started playing football. I think it's important to stick to what you know and what you do best. Those are some of the things I do best."

Simmons had at least two interceptions in each of his first seven seasons with the Broncos, with a career-most six despite missing five games because of injury in 2022. His 27 career picks already put him No. 8 on the Broncos' all-time list. He has been named to one Pro Bowl and twice was a second-team All-Pro.

Simmons now has a real good chance to one day have his banner draped inside the Pat Bowlen Fieldhouse, his name hung on the Broncos stadium Ring of Honor, and his plaque positioned in the Ring of Fame Plaza. His first seven seasons with the Broncos were so good he at one time, even if it was for a short time, was the NFL's highest-paid safety, with a $15.25-million-a-year contract.

"There are some players that are good players that need a caddy out there," said former Broncos coach Vic Fangio. "He's a good player and he caddies for others. Those are hard to find."

Sometimes there's debate about whether a team should pay a player. In Simmons's case, there was universal acceptance among the fan base he should get his money. One reason is fans who work hard every day appreciate that while there is finesse to Simmons's game, there's also grit. He not only shows up for every game—66 in a row in a four-season stretch, from 2018 to 2021, plus the opener of the 2022 season—but also for darn near every single snap—3,388 in succession from the 2018 opener until he was removed in a 26–0 week 3 rout of the Jets in 2021.

The Iron Man streaks are something Simmons took pride in.

"Since I got in here, the vets my rookie season were telling me the best ability is availability," Simmons said. "Learning how important it is to invest in your body. Missing a couple games, not being out there with your team, I've experienced that and it really stinks. Especially when you think you can contribute to the team's success when you're out there."

JOHN LYNCH (2004–2007)

It took a while, but John Lynch is a Pro Football Hall of Famer, once and forever.

It was on his eighth consecutive try as a top-15 modern-era finalist that Lynch, a former Tampa Bay and Broncos safety, was elected into the Hall of Fame.

Lynch, who is now general manager of a San Francisco 49ers team that has been to three NFC Championship Games in a four-season span, from 2019 to 2022, played 11 seasons for Tampa Bay, where he was named to the NFC Pro Bowl team five times and helped the Bucs win the 2002-season Super Bowl. He then played four seasons with the Broncos and was named to the AFC Pro Bowl team all four times.

Lynch's 9 Pro Bowls are tied for second with Ed Reed and Brian Dawkins among safeties, trailing only Ken Houston's 12. Reed and Dawkins had previously joined Houston in the HOF.

With Lynch and Champ Bailey anchoring the Denver D from 2004 to 2007, the Broncos were fourth in total defense in 2004, and ranked third in scoring defense in 2005, when the

Broncos went 13-3 during the regular season, beat Tom Brady and the Patriots in a second-round playoff game at Mile High, and hosted the AFC Championship Game.

"The Broncos were a blessing," Lynch said. "Eleven years is a long time to be in one place. I kind of was the idealist who wanted to play his whole career in one spot, but I hurt my neck and we parted ways.

"The Denver situation transpired at the exact right time. Reenergized my career and came in with Champ. Our defense was all-time in Tampa but it was our thought, 'Let's make that the case in Denver.' We didn't become one of those type [of] defenses—we didn't have all those pieces—but I think we were top 10 a bunch of those years, and we took a lot of pride in it."

Lynch was more than just a four-time Pro Bowler in his four years with the Broncos. He and his wife, Linda, gave out more than $1 million in college scholarships to local high school scholar-athletes through their John Lynch Foundation for 14 years, from 2004 to 2017.

As part of his Hall of Fame induction speech in August 2021 in Canton, Ohio, Lynch said: "To the late great owner Pat Bowlen, a true Hall of Famer, and to the Bowlen family, Mike Shanahan, and everybody at the Denver Broncos, thanks for giving me such a great landing spot to play the final four years of my career."

STARTERS

Steve Atwater and Dennis Smith
It's a shame that such stalwarts as Billy Thompson and Goose Gonsoulin couldn't make the starting lineup. Or the team's all-time interception leader, Steve Foley. But we told you this was easily the deepest defensive position in Broncos history.

Smith and Atwater were such a dynamic safety tandem for the Broncos in the six-year period between 1989 to 1994—the back end of Smith's career and beginning of Atwater's—that it was difficult to differentiate between them.

Both were large by safety standards.

"Our games were pretty similar," Smith said. "I liked the way they played Atwater his whole career. They played him where they took advantage of his strengths.

"For me it was a little different because I was able to do more as far as covering. I was more like an all-around DB. Atwater was more of a pure safety. And they took advantage of that. He was able to do great things playing safety. I was able to do great things with whatever they told me to do. Being able to do a lot of things kind of hurt you sometimes because you couldn't specialize on one thing you were best at.

"But when Wade Phillips came in [as defensive coordinator in 1989], he played us primarily at safety and he did some things with us that really made us shine. I credit Wade Phillips, too, for the development of Steve Atwater."

Smith and Atwater were equally bone-rattling hard hitters.

"When he hit Christian Okoye, he hit him early in the game and he was a non-factor after that," Smith said of Atwater's iconic Monday-night hit. "When you hit them early, usually they're dizzy or you knock them out of the game for a while. And they don't want to play anymore. You don't want to injure or kill anybody but you do want to take their heart away."

There are die-hard Broncos fans and longtime observers who say Smith was better than Atwater, no matter what the Hall of Fame says. Atwater himself has long said Smith was better because he was faster. And Smith was more versatile than the Hall of Fame safety mate he helped mentor.

"It seems like I've been overlooked," said Smith, who has moved to the expansive, overflowing senior pool of Hall of

Fame candidates. "I've never been overlooked by the Broncos community, though, so that's a good thing."

Smith has said there is one area where Atwater had it over him: Super Bowl victories. Both started in three Super Bowls. But Smith's Broncos lost all three Super Bowls, first to the New York Giants, before they were blown out by Washington and San Francisco.

Atwater was part of the loss to the 49ers following his rookie season of 1989, but he also was key in the Super Bowl

Steve Atwater © ERIC LARS BAKKE

THE DENVER BRONCOS ALL-TIME ALL-STARS

wins against the Packers and Falcons in 1997 and 1998. And Atwater played well in both those Super Bowl victories.

"That was the difference," Smith said. "That's what I tell him that separates us. Super Bowls are important. And they're more important—for me, personally, I'd much rather have two Super Bowl rings over the Hall of Fame, any day."

OTHERS

Kareem Jackson (2019–present)

There were 53 defensive backs selected in the 2010 NFL Draft.

Only two were still playing 13 seasons later in 2022: the Patriots' Devin McCourty and the Broncos' Kareem Jackson.

And from those two survivors only one has never been elected to the Pro Bowl.

"I know, right," Jackson said. "Crazy."

The University of Alabama product may eventually retire with the distinction as one of the best players to never make a Pro Bowl.

"Might have to," Jackson said. "The thing about it is, I'm completely fine with that. The Pro Bowl is a [bleep] show anyway, with the way they pick guys, but that's no indication on my career."

No, it's not. A better indication are Jackson's 193 games played and 185 starts, more than 900 tackles and 100 pass breakups, plus his 20 interceptions.

And also that two teams gave him big-money contracts.

It was the Houston Texans who drafted Jackson in the first round and after five years gave him a four-year, $34 million extension. Most of those nine seasons in Houston were as a cornerback. When Jackson became a free agent in 2019, he signed with the Broncos with the idea of making a full-time conversion to safety, even though he still has a cornerback's build at 5-foot-10,

183 pounds. He got $23 million over his two years with Denver, then accepted pay cuts the next two seasons, but still wound up making $30 million in his four seasons with the Broncos.

Overall he's made nearly $77 million in career earnings.

"For me it's all about being accountable and being consistent," Jackson said. "I feel like I've done that throughout my career and I'm still here and I believe I'm still playing at a high level."

The switch from cornerback to safety has partially helped extend the careers of Jackson and McCourty, who made the transition in his third season. McCourty announced his retirement after the 2022 season. Jackson turned 35 in 2023 while McCourty played his last season at 35, and there aren't many cornerbacks playing at that age. In fact, there are none. Safety, though, is no walk in the park.

"It's still kind of taxing on the body," Jackson said. "Depending on what scheme you're in, it's a different skill set. It's a little bit more physical at safety, [you] help more in the run game."

Still, a lot of safeties from that 2010 draft class—like Eric Berry (whose career was interrupted by Hodgkin's lymphoma), Earl Thomas, and T.J. Ward, a trio that combined for 14 Pro Bowl berths—have long been retired while Jackson plays on.

Darian Stewart (2015–2018)
The least known from the Broncos' famed No Fly Zone in 2015, Stewart also may have been the secondary's steadiest influence. He had at least 60 tackles in each of his four seasons as a free safety and recorded 8 interceptions.

Upon announcing his retirement in a Zoom press conference in December 2020, it was arranged so that his No Fly Zone secondary members—T.J. Ward, Aqib Talib, Chris Harris Jr., and Bradley Roby—entered into the galley.

"There'll never be another group like that," Stewart said. "[Super Bowl 50] was definitely the highlight. Can't beat that."

Here was the exchange between Talib and Stewart:

Talib: "Hey, congrats. One of my all-time favorite team-mates, man. The way you played the game. I really admired that and you already know that, I told you that plenty of times. My question, man: What makes you play like that? What lit that fire under you? I've seen you from South Carolina to the Rams to the Broncos. You play a certain way. I need my kids to hear it. What makes you play that way?"

Stewart: "I always knew that if I second-guess anything on that field from making a tackle—because I always wanted to let them feel me any time I came into a tackle. So I always tried to go for the big hit. You don't always get that, but for me it was to not even think twice, man. If you're going to do it, go do it, you feel me, because that's how you end up getting hurt."

Stewart had been an oft-injured journeyman who had played with the St. Louis Rams and Baltimore Ravens before signing a modest two-year, $4.25 million deal with the Broncos in 2015.

He became one of Elway's most underrated free-agent signs. After helping the Broncos win their third-ever Super Bowl in his first year with the team, Stewart was playing good ball again in 2016 when a spectacular three-turnover perfor-mance against New Orleans—two interceptions on two con-secutive defensive plays off Drew Brees and a 28-yard recovery return off a Michael Thomas fumble—earned him a four-year, $28 million contract extension.

He collected $17.5 million from his new contract before he was released. He played one more season with Tampa Bay before retiring.

"I got some money in my pocket—I'm thankful for every-thing Denver gave me and my family," Stewart said. "My daugh-ter was born in Denver, so I have so much love for Denver.

Super Bowl ring, my firstborn child, there's a lotta love for Denver. But it's time for a change. I'm in a good place."

T.J. Ward (2014–2016)

A box safety, Ward's reckless-abandon playing style exemplified the personality of the Broncos' great Super Bowl 50 defense in 2015.

During his eight years in the NFL, Ward was known as a fearless, hard hitter who belied his smallish, 5-foot-10, 200-pound frame.

Drafted in the second round out of Oregon by the Cleveland Browns in 2010, Ward was a Pro Bowler in 2013, which helped him receive a four-year, $22.5 million contract as a free agent from the Broncos in 2014. Ward joined DeMarcus Ware, Aqib Talib, and Emmanuel Sanders as the Broncos' dream free-agent class of 2014. All four made the Pro Bowl that year and played huge roles in the Broncos' Super Bowl 50 championship in 2015.

As a team, Denver put it all together in 2015 when under first-year head coach Gary Kubiak and first-year defensive coordinator Wade Phillips the Broncos went 12-4 during the regular season, then swept the postseason with wins against Pittsburgh and New England in the AFC playoffs and Carolina in Super Bowl 50. Ward helped ice the Lombardi Trophy with a fumble recovery and stumble to the Carolina 4-yard line, setting up a touchdown run by C.J. Anderson.

The tenacious Denver defense was still very good, but not quite the same, in 2016 after losing defensive lineman Malik Jackson and inside linebacker Danny Trevathan to free agency. It also hurt that Ward's body started to become banged up. Ward was released as the Broncos were setting their season-opening roster prior to the 2017 season.

Nick Ferguson (2003–2007)

A starter for three and a half of his five seasons in Denver, Ferguson was a classic overachiever. Undrafted out of Georgia Tech in 1996, Ferguson was cut by the Bengals, Bears, and Bills before catching on with the Jets to play in his first game at 26 years old in 2000. Primarily a special teamer and backup defensive back for three years with the Jets, Ferguson became a starter six games into his first season with the Broncos in 2003.

He then became John Lynch's safety mate for the next four seasons, highlighted by 2005 when he had a career-most 81 tackles and 5 interceptions, 12 pass deflections, and 2 forced fumbles. It was Ferguson who came on a zero blitz that hurried New England quarterback Tom Brady into throwing an end-zone interception to Champ Bailey, who returned it 100 yards to set up a touchdown—a 14-point swing that was the difference in the Broncos' 27–13 win that dethroned the two-time Super Bowl champs in an AFC second-round playoff game.

After his career, Ferguson got into coaching with the 49ers, Broncos, Seahawks, and Texans before moving into Denver sports media.

Brian Dawkins (2009–2011)

Dawkins was one of the most electric and popular NFL safeties during his first 13 seasons with the Philadelphia Eagles, from 1996 to 2008. During that time, he earned five Pro Bowl appearances and four first-team All-Pro selections.

His best season, though, may have been his first with the Broncos. Released to free agency, Dawkins signed with the Broncos and new head coach Josh McDaniels in 2009. Dawkins was terrific that season, helping the Broncos to a 6-0 start.

"I had such a block on my shoulder," he said. "Not a chip. I had such a block. I was so filled with anger and rage along with my normal passion that there was nothing you would be able to put in front of me that year that was going to prevent me from having a good year."

Dawkins's leadership reached its apex during the off-season lockout leading into the 2011 season. He organized, and paid for, workouts for Broncos players with local performance coach Loren Landow—who later became the Broncos strength and conditioning coach.

The Broncos went from 4-12 in 2010 to winning the AFC West title in 2011.

"The thing that I knew is, my first couple years I did not have a plan for the off-season," he said. "So you're telling me there's a lockout with guys who don't have a plan? No. In order for us to stay together and have any chance to have any type of success, somebody needs to do something to bring people together."

Elected in 2018 into the Pro Football Hall of Fame, Dawkins was enshrined mostly as a Philadelphia Eagle, but to the man, the Broncos will always hold a special place in his heart.

"Eagles fans don't like it," Dawkins said. "They don't like to acknowledge that time ever existed. But my time in Denver, I cherish that. Everything we dealt with, I know what we went through, I know it was tough, but that last year making the run that we had to make it to playoffs . . . The way we played on defense, giving up 12 points a game, something like that, that's tremendous ball. The way we won some games [rallying from behind late], I'm very proud to have been a part of. That's not a throwaway.

"I tell people all the time there's a certain peace that I got off of the chaos of how I departed [from Philly]. I needed that peace. I needed that ability to kind of find myself a little bit. To go through some of the pain of the breakup that I had with the Philadelphia Eagles—I have more to give today because of that.

"Would I have loved to have stayed in Philadelphia forever? Yes, I would tell you that. But, I would [also] tell you this: I would not be the man that you see standing in front of you today had I not gone through that and come to Denver to explore that peaceful time so I could gain more of myself so that I can give now."

Charlie Greer (1968–1974)

Drafted in the 13th round out of the University of Colorado, Greer was a seven-year starter for the Broncos. He started as a cornerback his first year, then was moved to safety in his second season of 1969 by first-year defensive backs coach Joe Collier.

An outstanding athlete with great leaping ability, Greer played one year of varsity basketball for the CU Buffs. He finished with 17 interceptions and 11 fumble recoveries for the Broncos.

Tyrone Braxton (1987–1993, 1995–1999)

It was during the second part of Braxton's tenure with the Broncos that he became a strong safety. He was a left cornerback for much of his first seven years in Denver, then signed with Miami as an unrestricted free agent. Released by the Dolphins after one season, Braxton signed back with the Broncos on a one-year, $300,000 contract as a safety.

He was a starting safety alongside Hall of Famer Steve Atwater in two Super Bowls.

Extremely popular within Broncos Country, Tyrone Braxton got an official day named in his honor as proclaimed by Denver mayor Wellington Webb and the city of Denver.

"I'm so shocked," said the recipient of "Tyrone Braxton Day" during the ceremony.

Braxton grew up in Madison, Wisconsin, in a family where two of his brothers wound up in prison from crimes related to drugs. Scouts said Braxton was too small at 5-foot-10, 180 pounds, coming out of tiny North Dakota State to play safety. With a 4.7 time in the 40, he was too slow to play cornerback.

Yet, Braxton not only played 13 seasons in the NFL, 12 with the Broncos, the city of Denver gave him his own day.

Five days after playing in his last game, Mayor Webb announced that January 7, 2000, was "Tyrone Braxton Day," in a ceremony in front of City Hall that included balloons, posters, flags, and short speeches by teammates, coaches, and owner Pat Bowlen.

"He being so low in the draft and making it, and me being so [low] in the polls and getting elected, I kind of draw a parallel," Webb said at the ceremony. "Tyrone Braxton is a survivor."

Nicknamed "Chicken" by his Broncos teammates because of his skinny legs, Braxton wound up starting at both cornerback and safety for so long, only four defensive players—Tom Jackson, Dennis Smith, Barney Chavous, and Billy Thompson—played more seasons with the Broncos than his 12.

His 34 interceptions are tied with none other than Champ Bailey for fourth on the team's all-time list. And that total doesn't include Braxton's three interceptions in 17 postseason games—numbers that rank second in the team record books in both categories. There was a first-quarter interception Braxton had of Green Bay's Brett Favre in the Broncos' Super Bowl XXXII upset. He then recovered a fumble in the Broncos' rout of Atlanta in Super Bowl XXXIII.

Snubbed annually by Pro Bowl voters, they finally couldn't ignore him in 1996 when he tied for the NFL lead with nine interceptions.

Braxton may not have had the stature or speed, yet his awareness brought him to the ball. He was in on 905 tackles in his 12 seasons, and 4 of his 34 interceptions were pick-sixes. Including his first one. In his very first NFL career start in the 1989 season-opener, Braxton intercepted a pass from Kansas

City quarterback Steve DeBerg and returned it 34 yards for a score.

Although "Tyrone Braxton Day" was a glorious sendoff to retirement, Braxton's post-playing days weren't always easy. In 2007 he pled guilty to cocaine and marijuana possession stemming from his arrest on December 2, 2006, and received a two-year deferred sentence. But Braxton turned his embarrassing moment into a positive, becoming a Denver court drug and alcohol case worker.

As Mayor Webb said, Braxton is a survivor.

SPECIAL TEAMS

KICKER

Kickers. That's what some of football's tough guys call the one player who has the greatest impact, play per play, on a game's outcome. Kickers.

It's sometimes said in a derisive manner, as if kickers aren't really football players because they don't block or tackle. And even if they are brought into a tackle situation, it's a cataclysmic event. There is so much open space between the kicker and the returner, about all the untrained tackler can do is make the ball carrier turn a bit.

The Broncos have been fortunate with their kickers, though. From the beginning with Gene Mingo, to more recently with Brandon McManus, with the likes of Jason Elam, Jim Turner, and Matt Prater in between, they've had men at the kicker position who were widely respected by their teammates. Not pampered guys who watch practice except for their 10-minute segment. Rich Karlis made kicks with a bare right foot through Denver's inclement weather. They were all men who faced interrogation with courage if they missed a crucial kick in a loss and exhibited humility by sharing credit if they came through in the clutch to win it.

Pound per pound, no football position confronted more pressure than kickers.

There have been many good to great kickers in Broncos history—where home games played at 5,280 feet above sea level make for longer, and therefore more exciting, field-goal attempts—and there was just one kicker. Until we get to the

starting kicker on *The Denver Broncos' All-Time All-Stars*, we
have six candidates worthy of consideration:

THE CANDIDATES

Matt Prater
Jason Elam
Rich Karlis
Brandon McManus
Jim Turner
Gene Mingo

MATT PRATER (2007–2013)

You can pick from any kicker in Broncos history. Game in the
balance, 50 yards or so field-goal attempt, final seconds. Miss
and you lose, make and you win.

I'd pick Prater. He was streaky early in his career, and there
was a time when he was better from the 50s than he was from
the 40s.

But Prater was as clutch as it gets.

"I think Matt, especially beyond 50, he's probably the best
of all time," Brandon McManus, the Broncos' current kicker,
said in 2021.

Just ask Tim Tebow during his magical 2011 season. Down
15–0 with 3 minutes remaining in Tebow's first start of the season at Miami, Tebow miraculously engineered 15 points in the
final 2:44 to tie the game (thanks in no small part to a successful onside kick by Prater), and Prater won it with a 52-yard field
goal in overtime.

Prater made another overtime field goal to beat the Chargers that year, followed by two field goals in the final 1:33 of
regulation (one from 46 yards) to beat the Vikings.

The kicker (ahem) to Prater's clutch run was the Broncos' 13–10 win against the Chicago Bears, the sixth of the Tebow-led six straight wins. Prater nailed a 59-yard field goal with 3 seconds left in regulation to tie it, and then a 51-yard field goal in overtime to win it.

All those clutch, long-range kicks helped to ignite Tebow-mania in 2011.

In 2013, Prater was simply the best kicker in the NFL as he converted 25 of 26 field goals for 96.2 percent—including an NFL-record 64-yard field goal on an 18-degree, December day at what is now called Empower Field at Mile High. The record-setting boot as the first half expired against Tennessee broke the iconic 43-year record set first by the New Orleans Saints' Tom Dempsey in 1970 and tied three other times, once by the Broncos' Jason Elam.

Prater's 64-yard kick held for eight years before Baltimore's Justin Tucker hit a 66-yard field-goal game-winner at Detroit in 2021 that bounced high off the crossbar and over.

Prater was on his way to challenging Elam as the best kicker in Broncos history, but off-field issues led general manager John Elway to release him following the 2014 preseason. But to Prater's credit, he got his life in order and was still kicking 10 years later as he spent seven seasons with the Detroit Lions and two more with Arizona heading into the 2023 season.

Prater's .829 field-goal percentage with the Broncos is the best in the team's history, and his 21 of 27 conversion rate on 50-yard-plus field goals is by far the best.

JASON ELAM (1993–2007)

Elam grew up in the suburbs of Atlanta, Georgia, playing soc-cer while also competing in swimming and track. As of Jason's freshman year at Brookwood High School in Snellville, he had not yet played football. And then one day he went out to watch his high school football team play. They weren't very good. And the kicker didn't have it that day.

"I thought: I can do that," Elam said for the book, *The 50 Greatest Players in Denver Broncos History.* "So I went out in my driveway and at the end of our driveway there was a power line at the other end and I would kick over that power line. That's how I first started."

From that unusual start came the most accomplished kicker in Broncos history. When he made his last boot for the Broncos following the 2007 season, Elam had set franchise records with 395 field goals, an incredible 601 of 604 extra point tries over 15 seasons, and 1,786 points over a team-record 236 games—marks that won't be broken anytime soon, if they're surpassed at all. Brandon McManus is a distant second, with 223 field goals and 946 points. Elway was a close second with 234 games played. But in today's transient era of player movement via free-agency and salary-cap restrictions, players simply don't last 15 seasons with one team.

Elam added a 51-yard field goal in the Broncos' first-ever Super Bowl championship to cap the 1997 season, a 31–24 win against the heavily favored Green Bay Packers in XXXII, and two more field goals in an easier Super Bowl XXXIII victory against the Atlanta Falcons for the 1998 Lombardi Trophy repeat.

For his feats, Elam was inducted into the Broncos Ring of Honor in 2016 in only his second year of eligibility.

Elam owes much of his success to his father, Ralph, a World War II veteran who went through France, Germany, and Austria. After the war, Ralph had a lengthy career in law enforcement, including a stint as chief of police in Fort Walton Beach, Florida, where Jason was born.

"I'm king of the black sheep," Elam said. "I'm the only one in generations that wasn't a policeman. My brother, my dad, my grandpa, everybody was in law enforcement."

Elam played some receiver as a high school junior for the 1-9 Brookwood Broncos, but then Dave Hunter took over as coach and not only did he immediately transform Brookwood into a 10-2 team, he made sure Elam understood his special gift was kicking the ball. Elam went to Hawaii on a scholarship, where he set school records, then was taken in the third round—an extraordinarily high position for a kicker—by Broncos' first-year coach Wade Phillips in 1993.

Elam's fondest memory during his 15 seasons with the Broncos can be summed up in two words: Toro! Toro!

Most people would think Elam's top moment would have been his 63-yard field goal in an October 25, 1998, game that tied Tom Dempsey's long-standing NFL record. Sweet as it was, the record-tying boot to end the half stretched a 24–10 lead to 27–10.

The Toro! Toro! kick from 42 yards away at Buffalo to open the 2007 season turned defeat into stunning victory at the gun.

"Yeah, that would probably be even above the 63," Elam said prior to his Ring of Fame induction. "Because that was for a win. The 63-yarder was more an individual thing. We were winning at the time and that was just a fun kick. But the Toro! Toro! thing, that was awesome. Just the way the whole thing went down. The season-opener, on the road, everything about it was just a fun kick."

The Buffalo Bills, behind the rookie debut of running back Marshawn Lynch, had mostly outplayed the Broncos. They were trying to protect a 14–12 lead with 1:08 left when Denver coach Mike Shanahan was forced to take his final timeout with the ball on his side of the 50.

Broncos quarterback Jay Cutler eventually threw an 11-yard completion to Javon Walker with 18 seconds left, moving the ball to the Buffalo 24.

Toro! Toro! was the call from the Broncos' sideline, which meant fire drill. The field-goal team had to run onto the field and set up for Elam's kick while the offensive team sprinted off the field. The clock was ticking.

"The fans were counting it down." Elam said. "They were loud. Ten, 9, 8 . . ."

What the fans didn't realize is that their countdown helped the Broncos field-goal team. They knew how much they had to hurry, and how much they didn't.

"They didn't think for a second we were going to be able to get that kick off," Elam said.

There was 1 second left when Elam struck the ball. The gun went off as the ball carried beyond the crossbar. Good! Broncos win, 15–14. Bills fans suddenly went silent. It was one of 24 game-winning or game-saving field goals Elam kicked for the Broncos. He added another 15 field goals in the postseason.

"He was just money as a kicker," said John Lynch, a Broncos safety who was inducted into the team's Ring of Fame along with Elam and pass-rusher Simon Fletcher in 2016. "Throughout my career, I played with some really good kickers. Down in Tampa, Martín Gramática comes to mind, but it was always exciting. You always watched. I hate to say it, but with Jason, you took him for granted. You just [turned] your head and [went] back about your business—'Kickoff team, get ready'—regardless of where he was kicking from. That's how much faith we had in him."

Elam's contract expired after the 2007 season, and while he wanted to finish his career with the Broncos, his hometown Atlanta Falcons offered a longer and more lucrative contract. He had the best individual season of his career with the Falcons in 2008, when he made 29 of 31 field goals and went 42 of 42 in extra points.

Elam suffered through injuries in 2009, though, and called it a career. In the 16 years and counting since he made his last kick with the Broncos, no one has approached his career kicking records.

RICH KARLIS (1982–1988)

The last of the barefooted kickers, Karlis first got the job as the Broncos kicker after winning a 478-player tryout camp in May 1982. He was given a Broncos T-shirt with No. 192. He still has it. Karlis barely kicked in high school but walked on at the University of Cincinnati as a punter. In the spring of his freshman year he experimented with kicking barefoot because he was intrigued by Tony Franklin's barefoot, soccer style at Texas A&M, especially after Franklin once nailed a record-setting, 65-yard field goal.

"I noticed when I hit it good I had a good feel for it and it went far," Karlis said in a 2017 Broncos podcast with longtime public relations maven Jim Saccomano. "And if I hit it bad it really hurt. So it taught me to concentrate very quickly."

It's difficult to believe now with some kickers going full seasons without missing more than a kick or two, but heading into the 1980s, kickers rarely made 80 percent of their field goals. In fact, Karlis was the first kicker in Broncos history to convert 80 percent of his field goals in a single season—and he went back-to-back in his first two seasons of 1982 (84.6 percent, 11 of 13) and 1983 (84.0, 21 of 25). He followed his first two seasons with three consecutive 100-point seasons.

Karlis made the cover of *Sports Illustrated* after he leaped for joy following his game-ending, and winning, 33-yard field goal in overtime of the AFC Championship Game at Cleveland—known forever more as The Drive game—to send the Broncos to Super Bowl XX. His 48-yard field goal—the longest in Super Bowl history at the time—off the Broncos' opening drive gave them a 3–0 lead against the New York Giants.

The combination of a contract dispute and talented rookie kicker David Treadwell helped escort Karlis out of Denver in 1989, but he wound up having one more great season with the Vikings. Karlis finished as the Broncos' second-leading scorer all-time to Jim Turner, with 655 points, and still ranks No. 5 on the team charts.

During his active and post-playing career, Karlis was one of the more community-oriented Broncos, volunteering his time and financially supporting organizations like Family Tree, the Special Olympics, Children's Hospital, the YMCA, and National Sports Center for the Disabled.

BRANDON MCMANUS (2014–22)

The long, tall Philly native knows he will finish his career in Denver with the No. 2 ranking to Jason Elam in field goals, extra points, and points scored. He ranks second to Matt Prater in field-goal percentage.

But only McManus got a shout-out from the president of the United States.

McManus was clutch during the Broncos' 2015 postseason run to their Super Bowl 50 title as he was 10 of 10 in field goals and 3 of 3 in extra points in the Broncos' three games. Notice the mere 3 extra points in three postseason games. In a 24–10 Super Bowl win against Carolina, McManus kicked three field goals and an extra point.

During the Super Bowl celebration in June 2016 at the White House Rose Garden, President Obama in his speech mentioned several prominent offensive players, purposely keeping star quarterback Peyton Manning, who was standing directly behind him, in suspense. Finally Obama mentioned all the key offensive starters but one.

"And we can't forget to mention the heart and soul of this team's offensive firepower," Obama said. "Kicker Brandon McManus."

That brought roars of laughter, including one from the good-natured Manning.

Easygoing McManus has been making kicks ever since he replaced Matt Prater in 2014. Prater was sensational as the Broncos kicker from 2011 to 2013, setting an NFL record that held for eight years, with a 64-yard field goal in December of 2013.

But after Prater was slapped with a four-game suspension to start the 2014 season, for violating the league's substance-abuse policy, the Broncos acquired McManus from the New York Giants for a conditional seventh-round draft pick. The condition was McManus had to stick with the Broncos after Prater's suspension elapsed.

The seventh-rounder was sent to New York.

"I was happy to finally have an opportunity," McManus said. "At the time there [were] not a lot of young kickers and it was really tough to get your foot in the door, whereas now there [are] a lot more younger guys. The previous year I was with the India-napolis Colts, [and] I didn't miss a field goal. I led the NFL in kickoffs [touchback percentage]. Same year with the Giants, I didn't miss a field goal and I led the NFL in kickoff stats.

"I couldn't understand why I wasn't getting an opportunity. It was difficult to get your foot in the door, so I was really happy to [get] at least get four games out there and potentially show-case what I could do, and I was able to perform pretty well.

"I can say it now six years later: They were pretty easy kicks I had the first four games. But I was happy I was able to stick around here and continue to perform here in Denver."

McManus was surprisingly released by the Broncos in May 2023. He signed with Jacksonville a few days later. Leg strength is McManus's forte. Through the 2022 season, he kicked the most field goals in Broncos history from 50 yards–plus, with 40—three more than Elam. And take away kickoff specialist Brad Daluiso's lone season with the Broncos in 1992, and no one was close to McManus's 69.3 percent touchback percentage—a rate that would have been higher had he not been occasionally ordered to purposely keep the kickoff in play during his last three or four years with the team.

McManus missed just two games in his nine seasons with the Broncos.

Jim Turner (1971–1979)

One of the last of the straight-on, toe kickers, Turner's 742 points for the Broncos' off field goals, extra points—and one memorable 25-yard catch-and-lumber touchdown reception off a fake field-goal pass from holder Norris Weese against the Oakland Raiders during the magical Orange Crush season of 1977—stood as the team record for 20 years until Elam surpassed the mark during the 1999 season.

Before he became a Bronco, Turner kicked three field goals that were the difference in the New York Jets' famed 16–7 victory in Super Bowl III against the heavily favored Baltimore Colts—still considered the greatest upset in NFL history. He was traded from the Jets to the Broncos straight up for kicker Bobby Howfield prior to the 1971 season—one of Lou Saban's better swaps as head of Denver's football operations.

Turner retired as the NFL's No. 2 all-time leading scorer to George Blanda with 1,439 points and with the second-most field goals (304). Turner was inducted into the Broncos Ring of Fame in 1988.

Incredibly, Turner never missed a game in his 16-year career, a streak of 236 consecutive games counting the postseason. Turner went into broadcasting both on TV and radio after his playing career, then became an active leader in football's "Play It Smart" program that helped at-risk students get into college. Turner passed away on June 10, 2023, at the age of 82. Upon learning of Turner's death, Broncos head coach

Sean Payton paid tribute by having his kickers boot straight-on, 9-yard field goals in practice.

GENE MINGO (1960–1964)

An original Bronco, not only was Mingo the first Black kicker in the AFL/NFL, he was among the league's best during his four and a half seasons in Denver.

In the AFL's first season, Mingo led the league with 123 points on a league-most 18 field goals (and AFL-best 64.3 percentage), 33 extra-point kicks, and 6 touchdowns. Like the league's other best kickers at the time—George Blanda, Paul Hornung, Lou Groza, and Lou Michaels—Mingo doubled as a position player, in his case a running back and returner.

Mingo also led the AFL with 27 field goals in 1962 and a 66.7 field-goal percentage in 1964, when he was traded at mid-season to the Oakland Raiders.

But it's the historical element of his career that makes him the most proud.

"I love being able to say that I was the first Black kicker in the NFL," Mingo said.

Mingo grew up in Akron, Ohio, where he barely attended school. He didn't graduate from high school. He didn't attend college.

His football skills were honed while playing for the US Navy service team. After his football career, Mingo struggled with personal addiction demons, but he overcame them and wound up doing great work as an alcohol and drug counselor.

In October 2014, Mingo became the fourth "original Bronco" to be elected into the Broncos Ring of Fame, joining Frank Tripucka, Lionel Taylor, and safety Goose Gonsoulin.

"It means a lot to me," Mingo said for the book, *The 50 Greatest Players in Denver Broncos History*. "The Broncos gave me a start. They gave me my chance and I took advantage of it. As they say, I took it and ran with it. I did the best I could."

STARTER

The nod for top placekicker goes to Jason Elam in one of the easier starter choices for this project. No one was more consistent over a longer period of time. This project of choosing *The Denver Broncos All-Time All-Stars* can be repeated 50 years from now and Elam may still be the team's career field-goal and scoring leader.

OTHERS

David Treadwell (1989–1992)

A star high school soccer player who didn't play football in Jacksonville, Florida, Treadwell walked on at Clemson where in three seasons he was noted for coming through with several clutch field goals that turned defeat into victory. He was a consensus All-American as a senior in 1987, when he also earned his electrical engineering degree.

Unable to beat out veteran Rich Karlis in his rookie preseason of 1988, Treadwell eventually returned to the Broncos in 1989—via trade from Phoenix in exchange for a conditional draft choice. With Karlis in a contract holdout, Treadwell beat out Rafael Septién for the job. In his first season, Treadwell led the AFC in scoring with 120 points and was named to the Pro Bowl team.

Treadwell was the Broncos' most accurate kicker following his fourth and final season with the team in 1992, with a 78 percent field-goal percentage.

But Treadwell didn't have the strongest kickoff leg, prompting new head coach Wade Phillips to select Elam in the third round of the 1993 draft. Elam beat out Treadwell in training camp and the preseason and became the Broncos' kicker for the next 15 years. Treadwell kicked two more years for the New York Giants and former Broncos head coach Dan Reeves.

Following his playing career, Treadwell had a stellar sports broadcasting career in the Denver market before moving on to the health and medical field.

Fred Steinfort (1979–1981)

Born in West Germany, Steinfort moved to the United States when he was 13. A left-footed sidewinding kicker, he was a kick-off specialist late in the 1979 season for the injured Jim Turner, then had a good, two-year run as placekicker in 1980–1981.

Steinfort made five of eight field goals from 50-plus yards in 1980, including one from 57 yards—an unheard-of success rate from that distance more than 40 years ago.

Bobby Howfield (1968–1970)

Howfield was a powerful-legged English soccer player who had never played football when he came to the United States at 32 years old in 1968 to kick for the Kansas City Chiefs. But he wasn't about to beat out Jan Stenerud, and after Howfield was cut, he signed with the Broncos.

He was brilliant on extra points in his three seasons in Denver, making 93 of 95, and converting 50.6 percent of his field goals—which was middle of the pack in the AFL/NFL at the time. He also consistently was near the top in the league in kickoff touchbacks.

Howfield became a much more consistent kicker after he was traded to the New York Jets straight up for kicker Jim Turner prior to the 1971 season. Howfield was the NFL's second-best kicker in 1973 when he converted 73 percent of his field goals and fourth-best in 1974 with a 70.8 percent conversion rate.

PUNTER

Chances are, not many Colorado kids have worn Broncos punter jerseys to school.

Punters don't do commercials or make much money compared to position players. They are asked to perform the invaluable, if unappreciated, task of setting up good field position for their defense.

Despite the position's relative obscurity, the Broncos have had an interesting set of punters over the years. Bob Scarpitto and Billy Van Heusen were receivers as well as punters. Big Jim Fraser was a starting linebacker who was the American Football League's best punter all three years he was with Denver.

Tom Rouen was a two-time Super Bowl champion punter who married an Olympic Gold Medalist swimmer. Britton Colquitt is a descendant of the first family of NFL punters.

The punted ball at Mile High, where the thin air adds 9 percent to a ball's flight according to an early 1990s baseball study, makes for a wondrous view for those sitting in the stadium's upper deck. But because the ball travels farther at 5,280 feet, a premium is placed on placement for Broncos punters— those long boot touchbacks are no-no's.

For *The Denver Broncos All-Time All-Stars*, here's a look at the best punters in team history:

THE CANDIDATES

Tom Rouen
Britton Colquitt
Bob Scarpitto
Billy Van Heusen
Jim Frazer

TOM ROUEN (1993–2002)

Rouen was the sixth player in Broncos history to accomplish the Colorado Holy Trinity of playing at a Colorado high school (Heritage in Littleton), college (Colorado State and Colorado), and the NFL (the Denver Broncos) when he signed with the Broncos as a free agent in 1993.

It took him a bit to break into the NFL. As a rookie Rouen was cut from the New York Giants' training camp, then punted for the World League of American Football's Ohio Glory in 1992.

But once he caught on with the Broncos in 1993, Rouen lasted nine and a half seasons with his hometown team, more than any punter in the team's franchise history. Besides helping the Broncos win back-to-back Super Bowls in 1997 and 1998 (when he had a career-best 46.9-yard average), Rouen led the NFL in 1999 with a 46.5-yard gross average.

More than 20 years after his last punt for the Broncos, Rouen is still the franchise's all-time leader in career punts (641) and punts inside the 20 (182). He was also an exceptional placeholder for kicker Jason Elam for eight seasons of Elam's Ring of Fame career with the Broncos.

In February 2001, Rouen married six-time Olympic Gold Medal swimmer Amy Van Dyken.

BRITTON COLQUITT (2009–2016)

The son of former NFL punter Craig Colquitt, brother of former NFL punter Dustin Colquitt, and nephew of another former NFL punter, Jimmy Colquitt, Britton Colquitt initially signed with the Broncos in 2009 out of Tennessee. He didn't make the opening-day roster, but was signed back in the final week of the Broncos' 2009 season and stayed until his release for salary considerations in training camp of 2016.

Colquitt finished his six seasons with the Broncos as the franchise leader in gross average (45.2 yards per punt) and net (39.1)—records he holds for those who have punted more than two seasons with the team. (The two-year averages for both Sam Martin and Riley Dixon eclipsed Colquitt in both gross and net punting.)

Colquitt's two best seasons were in 2011, when he helped set up quarterback Tim Tebow's late-game heroics with an astounding 47.4-yard gross average (seventh in the league), and in 2012, when he netted a then franchise-record 42.1 yards (third in the league).

After Colquitt put together terrific back-to-back seasons in 2011 and 2012, he received a three-year extension at an annual average of $3.9 million that in "new money" made him the NFL's highest-paid punter.

Although Colquitt's performance slipped in subsequent years, he found his rhythm during the Broncos' 2015 postseason run to Super Bowl 50 when he had an NFL-most 23 punts for a 42.7-yard average that was also the league's best among those who made at least eight punts. He also had nine punts land inside the 20 against just one touchback.

"It's easy to say the Super Bowl, but there was so much of the building process that led to that," Colquitt said when asked about his top highlight with the team after he was released in 2017. "When I was young, I guess you could call them the Tebow years (2010–2011). That was eight, nine punts a game and you wound up helping out winning the game. Kind of like how the Super Bowl ended up. It feels good to know you're part of that."

Colquitt wound up punting three more years for the Cleveland Browns and two more years for the Minnesota Vikings. He finished his 11-year career after the 2020 season with an impressive 45.2-yard gross punting average and 39.2-yard net.

BOB SCARPITTO (1962–1967)

One of the most versatile and overlooked players in Broncos history, Scarpitto was acquired by the Broncos as a flanker in 1962 in a trade from the San Diego Chargers.

He then had a five-year run from 1962 to 1966 with the Broncos when he averaged 29 catches for 485 yards (16.8 yards per catch) and 5 touchdowns. He also mixed in 9 rushing attempts during that span (mostly off fake punts) for 209 yards and a remarkable 23.2-yard average.

In his final three seasons with the Broncos he handled the punting duties and he led the AFL with a league-record 45.1-yard average in 1966 when he was named to the AFL All-Star team. He topped the league again in 1967 with a 44.9-yard average—off a whopping 105 punts, a single-season team record that still stands even though he did so in a 14-game season.

He had the AFL's longest punts all three seasons he was the Broncos punter, with 74 yards in 1965, 70 in 1966, and 73 in 1967. He had a league-best 87-yard punt for the Boston Patriots in 1968, his final season.

BILLY VAN HEUSEN (1968–1976)

Scarpitto was a flanker first who could also punt. Van Heusen was a punter first who could mix in a catch or two a game. Usually an impact catch.

Van Heusen still holds the team record, with 20.5 yards per reception, which he compiled off 82 career catches, 11 of which went for touchdowns. He also ran out of the punt formation 13 times for 171 yards for an incredible 13.2-yard average. He ran 66 yards for a touchdown off one fake punt. He also completed two passes off the fake.

Oh, and he was a good punter, too. In 1973, there was Jerrell Wilson's 45.5-yard average for the league lead. Hall of Famer Ray Guy was second, at 45.3. Billy Van Heusen was third, at 45.1. Van Heusen's 78-yard punt was the longest in the NFL that year.

In his nine years as the Broncos punter, Van Heusen ranked seventh overall in the NFL in that span, with a 41.7-yard average, and he finished five seasons ranked in the top nine.

His well-rounded athleticism was on display at Maryland where he played halfback, quarterback, flanker, and defensive back. And, no surprise, he was once a near-scratch golfer, winning the 1971 Brian Piccolo Cancer Fund Tournament in Lake Geneva and 1974 Quarterback Club title.

He did all this despite undergoing seven knee operations during his career.

His 574 career punts held as a team record for 25 years until Tom Rouen booted past in 2001.

JIM FRASER (1962–1964)

One of the most underrated players in Broncos history, Fraser not only was a three-year starting linebacker—huge for his time, at 6-foot-3, 240 pounds—he led the American Football League in punting in each of his three seasons with the Broncos—with a 44.4-yard average in 1962, then a league-record 46.1 mark in 1963, and a 44.2-yard average in 1964.

To show how good Fraser was, he was traded prior to the 1965 season to the Kansas City Chiefs straight up for running back Abner Hayes, who was the AFL's all-time leading rusher through the league's first five seasons.

STARTER

Tom Rouen

An easy choice for many reasons. One, he had the longest service time among Broncos punters, with nine and a half seasons. Two, he recorded the most punts for the most yards with most punts dropped inside the 20. Three, Rouen punted for two of the Broncos' three Super Bowl championship teams. And four, Rouen forever will have crossover popularity because of his marriage to Van Dyken.

OTHERS

Mike Horan (1986–1992)

Not the first of the coffin-corner punters but among the first to master the art form, the left-footed Horan didn't have the strongest leg, but he was the first to succeed with the nuances of punting, particularly in placement.

Only 29 of his 374 punts in his seven years as the Broncos punter resulted in touchbacks, a 7.8 percentage that was below the NFL norm in his era. After his final season in Denver in 1992, Horan was among several players who followed coach Dan Reeves to the New York Giants, where he punted another four years before finishing with the Chicago Bears and, at 40 years old, the St. Louis Rams in 1999, where he punted nine times in the Greatest Show on Turf's postseason run to the Super Bowl XXXIV championship.

Bucky Dilts (1977–1978)

Undrafted out of Georgia in 1977, he made the NFL's All-Rookie team after he punted a staggering 91 times in a 14-game season, finishing fourth with 20 punts inside the 20. First-year head coach Red Miller played to his Orange Crush defense that year and wasn't afraid to punt, making Dilts an invaluable contributor to the Broncos' first Super Bowl-appearing team.

He had 96 punts in the NFL's first 16-game season of 1978 and again finished fourth with 23 punts inside the 20. At the time, directional punting was all aimed at the sidelines, not high and down the middle as punters do now.

He was beaten out by seventh-round drafted rookie Luke Prestige in 1979.

Luke Prestridge (1979–1983)

A large-sized punter at 6-foot-4, 235 pounds, Prestridge was tremendous in the Broncos' otherwise abysmal 2-7 season of 1982, when he led the NFL with a 45.0-yard average to earn first-team All-Pro and Pro Bowl honors.

Sam Martin (2020–2021)

Only punted two seasons for the Broncos but recorded the two-best single-season net punting averages in team history, with 42.8 net yards in 2021 and 42.1 in 2020.

RETURNER

This may be a stretch, but the thin air that is part of 5,280 feet of altitude may be at the elevated root of why, outside of a sensational punt return season from Rick Upchurch in 1976, the Broncos haven't featured many world-class returners.

Especially at kickoff return, where touchbacks for kickers at altitude carry the same degree of non-difficulty as a layup in basketball.

Through the 2022 season, Cordarrelle Patterson, a part-time running back and receiver who had played for five teams through the first 10 seasons of his NFL career, had the league record with 9 touchdowns off kickoff returns. There have been another 55 players with at least 3 kickoff return touchdowns through the 2022 season.

The most touchdowns by a Broncos kick returner is 2, shared by Goldie Sellers and Trindon Holliday, who both spent just two seasons in orange and blue. Holliday added a third touchdown off a kickoff return in a 2012 playoff loss to the Baltimore Ravens.

But the Broncos have been far better at punt returning. Upchurch, Holliday, Darrien Gordon, Floyd Little, and Deltha O'Neal were all explosive punt returners who scored multiple touchdowns.

As for kickoff returners, Vaughn Hebron, a backup running back to Terrell Davis in the team's three-year sweet spot, from 1996 to 1998, was the Broncos' most consistent. But Hebron only played those three seasons in Denver.

That's the thing about Broncos returners: Aside from Upchurch, few of the Broncos' best returners handled the duty very long. Either they didn't stay with the team for long, like Hebron, Gordon, O'Neal, Glyn Milburn, and Holliday, or returners like Little and Billy Thompson relinquished the return duties after a couple years to concentrate on their full-time position work.

A look at the candidates for the No. 1 returner who belongs on *The Denver Broncos All-Time All-Stars*:

THE CANDIDATES

Rick Upchurch
Glyn Milburn
Billy Thompson
Deltha O'Neal
Darrien Gordon
Floyd Little
Eddie Royal
Trindon Holliday
Vaughn Hebron

RICK UPCHURCH (1975–1983)

The NFL's All-Decade returner in both the 1970s and '80s, Upchurch was primarily a punt returner. In fact, when he retired in 1983, Upchurch was tied with Jack Christiansen for the all-time NFL lead with eight touchdowns off punt returns, and those two are still tied for fourth.

As the Broncos were finally becoming relevant in the mid-1970s, Upchurch was arguably the most dangerous weapon on a team otherwise dominated by defense. Upchurch was such a prolific returner that he made the NFL All-Decade team not only in the 1970s, but in the 1980s as well.

It was the 1976 season when Upchurch gained national attention as one of the league's most electrifying players as he brought back four punts for touchdowns—73 and 47 yards in one game against the Cleveland Browns at old Mile High Stadium; 92 yards in a 26–0 win against the San Diego Chargers, also at Mile High; and 55 yards to give the Broncos the lead for good in a 35–26 victory against the Kansas City Chiefs at Arrowhead Stadium.

Howard Cosell on the *Monday Night Football* halftime highlight show became extremely familiar with Upchurch's exploits.

Upchurch burst onto the NFL scene immediately in his very first game as a rookie in 1975. He caught a 90-yard touchdown pass from Charley Johnson as part of his 153-yard receiving game, rushed once for a 13-yard touchdown, returned one punt for 30 yards, and three kickoffs for another 88 yards in an exhilarating 37–33 win against the Kansas City Chiefs. What an all-purpose debut.

Yet, Upchurch said years later during his Ring of Fame media call in 2014 that his first game was not as auspicious as his stat line would suggest.

"The first time I touched the ball, I got knocked out," he said. "As a matter of fact, they cracked my helmet and I had a big knot over my eye, my lip was all jacked up. And they said, 'Welcome to the NFL, little guy.' Then Haven Moses, he gets jacked up, his facemask just explodes . . . Then all of a sudden I'm thrust in as a starting wide receiver.

"At the game's end, we come back and we beat Kansas City and I ended up with 284 yards and two touchdowns of total offense."

Besides his prowess as a returner, Upchurch averaged 42 catches during a five-year stretch from 1979 to 1983, a time when the Broncos were a running team. But make no mistake: It was his return ability that made him special.

For 25 years, Upchurch was often considered the best player who was not in the Broncos Ring of Fame. He gladly lost that distinction when he was finally elected, along with head coach Dan Reeves and 1960s all-purpose performer Gene Mingo, in the class of 2014.

"To look and feel slighted, I really didn't feel [or look at it] that way," Upchurch said in his Ring of Fame conference call. "I often looked at statistics and wondered why it took so long for me to get there when you look at everyone else's statistics, but once again, I don't have control of that."

Later, it was revealed in a memoir written by former US Secretary of State Condoleezza Rice that she and Upchurch had dated for more than a year.

They met in 1975, Upchurch's rookie year, through a mutual friend.

"It was a typical initial conversion: 'How you doing? It's my pleasure to meet you,'" Upchurch said.

They dated for one and a half to 2 years, Upchurch recalls. He would not say whether they became engaged. Rice mentioned Upchurch as her boyfriend in the mid-1970s, in her memoir *Extraordinary, Ordinary People* that was published in 2010.

The dating part of their relationship ended when life, still in the early years for both, took them separate ways.

"She went on to do something in Washington and got started with her career," Upchurch said. Indeed, Condoleezza first worked in the State Department under President Jimmy Carter's administration in 1977. "And then her career took off from there."

Rice eventually became secretary of state in George W. Bush's second term, from 2005 to 2009. She was announced as a new Broncos owner, joining the Rob Walton–Greg and Carrie Penner group, in August 2022.

"I wasn't surprised," Upchurch said. "Was not surprised because I knew she had the ability. She's very smart business-wise, she's good with people, she gives her opinion. I think Condoleezza Rice joining the Broncos ownership group is going to culturally help the NFL. It's good to have a woman in a leadership position. Women are so organized. And women are not going to be afraid to fight the fight."

As for Upchurch, he found the right woman in Donna.

"Happily married for 26 years," he said.

They live in Las Vegas. He has four children; Donna has a son who's a firefighter in Las Vegas. Upchurch was diagnosed with leukemia in 2011, and while he takes three pills a day, he is a survivor.

"I wake up every day and the moment my eyes open I say, 'Thank you, Lord, for all you have given me,'" Upchurch said.

GLYN MILBURN (1993–1995)

He maybe wasn't great at any one thing at the NFL level, but he was good at everything. Milburn still ranks No. 5 all-time in the NFL with 12,772 combined punt and kickoff return yards—375 yards more than Dante Hall and 1,744 more than Hall of Fame finalist Devin Hester.

Where Milburn was great at everything was during his three years at Stanford, accounting for 2,358 yards and 14 touchdowns rushing; 1,508 receiving yards and 7 touchdowns off 143 catches; 1,182 yards with 4 touchdowns off punt returns; and 1,321 yards off kickoff returns.

The Broncos' second-round draft choice in 1993, the plan was for Milburn to play the Eric Metcalf/Mel Gray role. And in 1995, Milburn was just that as he made the Pro Bowl as a returner and was second-team All-Pro after he ranked No. 5 in the NFL with an 11.4-yard punt return average and No. 2 with a 27.0-yard kickoff return average.

He also averaged 5.4 yards per carry and 8.7 yards a catch as a scatback-sort out of the backfield.

Milburn had 77 catches in 1994. But with rookie running back Terrell Davis established as the Broncos' bell-cow ball carrier in 1995, Milburn through his agent Mike Sullivan—who years later became the Broncos' salary capologist and contract negotiator—asked for a trade to a team that played on an artificial surface to best utilize Milburn's speed and quickness.

Nice thought, but perhaps too smart for his own good. Milburn was traded to the Detroit Lions prior to the 1996 season in exchange for second- and seventh-round draft picks. In Detroit, Milburn was used almost exclusively as a returner and he never again was used out of the backfield as he was during his first three seasons in Denver. He did have a nice comeback season with the Bears in 1999, when he was first-team All-Pro as a punt and kickoff returner.

BILLY THOMPSON (1969–1981)

Thompson was the second-most-productive punt returner in Broncos history, with 157 returns for 1,814 yards. Only Rick Upchurch had more in each category. And Thompson's 25.1-yard-per-kickoff return is best in franchise history among those with at least 65 returns.

Thompson famously led the American Football League in both punt returns (11.5-yard average) and kickoff returns (28.5) as a rookie in 1969, as he mostly relieved Floyd Little, aka, "The Franchise," from his return duties so he could expend his efforts on running back.

After his rookie year, Thompson only occasionally returned kickoffs. He returned punts off and on through the 1975 season, at which point he was able to focus on serving as captain and strong safety for the Orange Crush defense.

DELTHA O'NEAL (2000–2003)

The Broncos' first-round draft pick, No. 15 overall in 2000, out of Cal, O'Neal seemed to be on his way to a Ring of Fame career after his second season in 2001, when he earned his first Pro Bowl by registering 9 interceptions for a league-most 115 return yards, plus another 25 pass deflections while returning a punt 86 yards for a touchdown.

O'Neal followed that up the next year in his third season of 2002 with five more interceptions, two of which he returned for touchdowns as he continued to serve as a consistent punt returner.

But midway through his fourth and final season with the Broncos, in 2003, O'Neal was surprisingly moved by coach Mike Shanahan from cornerback to receiver, where he finished the season with just two catches for 4 yards.

An unhappy O'Neal was traded to the Bengals prior to the 2004 season in exchange for a flop of first-round draft picks. The Broncos used their pick in the deal (No. 17 overall) to select linebacker D.J. Williams. O'Neal led the NFL with 10 interceptions in 2005 with the Bengals to earn his second Pro Bowl, although his returning days pretty much expired after the Broncos' trade.

O'Neal's three touchdowns combined off punt (2) and kickoff (1) returns are tied for third in Broncos history, behind Upchurch's eight and Trindon Holliday's six (including two in a playoff game).

DARRIEN GORDON (1997–1998)

One of the most underrated playmakers in the annals of Broncos history, Gordon didn't return kickoffs but he was special as a punt returner. His 12.5-yard punt return average was best in Broncos history among those with at least 10 returns, and his 3 touchdowns were second all-time to Upchurch's 8. Gordon also averaged an impressive 14.7-yard-per-punt return in the Broncos' back-to-back postseason runs to Super Bowl XXXII and XXXIII titles.

A starting cornerback both of those world championship years, Gordon also had 13 interceptions, with 5 coming in the postseason.

He became a free agent after that season, and that's when Shanahan made the regrettable decision of signing Kansas City free-agent cornerback Dale Carter—a chippy player who was not well-liked inside the Broncos' locker room as Denver was winning Super Bowls—instead of Gordon, who signed with the Oakland Raiders.

FLOYD LITTLE (1967–1975)

For many reasons, Floyd Little was, and forever will be, known as the "The Franchise" for the Denver Broncos. One of those reasons was because after Little became the Broncos' first-ever, first-round draft pick to sign with the AFL team in 1967, he did everything for the franchise—run, catch, return punts, and return kickoffs. He even threw a 35-yard halfback touchdown pass in a rare win against the Oakland Raiders in a 1972 game.

Little was especially busy as a returner in the first two years of his career.

As a rookie in 1967, Little returned a Curley Johnson punt 72 yards for a touchdown to help upset Joe Namath's New York Jets at Shea Stadium. He also had a 60-yard kickoff return that year and an 89-yard kickoff runback in his second season of 1969, when he also had a 67-yard punt return score against the Houston Oilers.

While Little, who was born on the Fourth of July and died at 78 on New Year's Day, was elected into the Pro Football Hall of Fame primarily for his running back exploits, he still ranks No. 2 in Broncos annals with 2,523 kickoff return yards, and his combined punt and kickoff return yardage of 3,416 ranks No. 2 only behind Upchurch (5,366).

All these return yards were primarily compiled in Little's first two years, as rookie Billy Thompson—who soon became "The Franchise's" best friend—took over primary return duties in 1969. Little did return a punt or kickoff later in his career, though, whenever his team was shorthanded from injury.

EDDIE ROYAL (2008–2011)

Among the dozens of draft strategies teams employ, one is to use the second round to select an all-purpose speed player with return ability. Most famously, the Bears took Devin Hester in the second round of the 2006 draft. He returned a combined 9 punts and kickoffs for touchdowns in his first two seasons, and a 10th opened the 2006-season Super Bowl.

Mel Gray, Glyn Milburn, and Kevin Williams were other top-10 returners, in terms of combined punt and kickoff return yardage, who were taken in the second round.

And in 2008, Broncos head coach Mike Shanahan took Eddie Royal from Virginia Tech in the second round with the idea of making him the team's returner that season.

Royal had other plans his rookie season: catching 91 passes as a receiver. Royal did have a 95-yard kickoff return as a rookie in 2008 and a 93-yard kickoff return for a touchdown in 2009, the same season he also returned a punt 71 yards for a score.

He added an 85-yard touchdown return off a punt in 2011, giving him three combined return touchdowns in his four seasons with the Broncos to tie with Darrien Gordon and

Deltha O'Neal for No. 3 all-time in team history behind Rick Upchurch (8) and Trindon Holliday (6).

TRINDON HOLLIDAY (2012–2013)

If not for just one flaw, Holliday could have gone down as not only the best returner in Broncos history, but also the best the NFL had ever seen. The flaw: ball security. Holliday dropped or fumbled the ball too much.

A former sprinter standout on LSU's track team, Holliday was among the NFL's fastest players in the early 2010s. And for a while, he was the league's most electric returner. Claimed off waivers from Houston after week 5 of the 2012 season, Holliday had a punt and kickoff return for touchdowns during the regular season for the Broncos, then added a 104-yard kickoff return and 90-yard punt return for touchdowns in Denver's second-round, overtime AFC playoff loss to Baltimore.

Holliday was also terrific early in the 2013 season, returning a punt 81 yards for a touchdown in a game 2 victory against the New York Giants and a kickoff 105 yards for a score in a game 4 victory against Philadelphia.

That gave Holliday three touchdowns off punt returns and three touchdowns off kickoff returns—six total TD returns—through his first 15 games with the Broncos.

But Holliday was mostly ineffective as a returner the rest of the 2013 season, as he first lost two fumbles, then seemed hesitant in his returns as he became preoccupied with ball security.

He was limited to a kickoff return role by the 2013 postseason and he was non-tendered as a restricted free agent after the season. Holliday only had two more punt returns and five more kickoffs, none for touchdowns, with San Francisco and Tampa Bay in 2014, his last season in the NFL.

VAUGHN HEBRON (1996–1998)

Hebron only played three seasons, but that was enough to easily become the team's all-time kickoff return yardage leader, with 3,324 off a team-record 134 kickoff returns for an impressive 24.8-yard average. He returned another 20 kickoffs over the Broncos' three postseasons from 1996 to 1998, for 460 yards.

He had a 95-yard kickoff return for a touchdown in a late-1998-season game at Miami. Between kickoff returning and spelling Terrell Davis for a couple carries a game at running back, Hebron played a significant role in the Broncos' back-to-back Super Bowl championships in 1997 and 1998.

STARTER

Rick Upchurch

Some decisions on naming the starters for *The Denver Broncos All-Time All-Stars* were easier than others. Then there was picking Upchurch as the team's all-time top returner. A five-time Pro Bowler and All-Pro in the five seasons of 1976 through 1979, and again in 1982, Upchurch is not only the best returner in Broncos history, he's arguably among the top 10 in NFL history.

OTHERS

Goldie Sellers (1966–1967)

Goldie made an impact in the short time he was with the Broncos, returning two kickoffs for touchdowns in 1966 and coming up with seven interceptions as a cornerback in 1967.

Born January 9, 1942, in Winnsboro, Louisiana, Goldie Sellers played football for legendary coach Eddie Robinson and ran track (clocked at 9.4 seconds in the 100-yard dash) at Grambling State University, where as a freshman he was a teammate of future Pro Football Hall of Famers Buck Buchanan and Willie Brown.

Rick Upchurch DENVER BRONCOS HISTORICAL
ARCHIVES

Sellers was a sophomore when he started dating one of the
school's cheerleaders. Two years later, on New Year's Eve, 1965,
Goldie and Vasa, known as "Peaches," were married.

Denver's eighth-round draft choice in 1966 (he was also
drafted by the NFL Chicago Bears), Sellers had three interceptions as a cornerback, but where he really made his mark in his
rookie season was as a kickoff returner, scoring touchdowns of
88 and 100 yards while leading the American Football League
with a 28.4-yard return average.

In his second year, Sellers had seven interceptions, one of
which he returned for a touchdown. After the 1967 season,

Sellers was traded to the AFL's more successful franchise, the Chiefs, where in his first season of 1968 he had three more interceptions and a punt return for a touchdown.

Sellers's first professional experience was at the Broncos' 1966 training camp at the Colorado School of Mines in Golden.

Two years later, Goldie and Vasa bought a "short acre" parcel of land for $6,500 in Applewood Mesa, part of unincorporated Jefferson County, and started to have their home built there in January 1970.

"The area was so green and plush, it reminded him of the South we grew up in," Vasa said.

Sellers also played on the Chiefs' Super Bowl IV team in 1969, which turned out to be his final season.

Sellers suffered a thigh injury in training camp of 1970 and spent the entire season on the Chiefs' injured reserve list. He was then traded to Houston, where he balked at a position switch to receiver. Released and picked up by the Boston Patriots, Sellers decided to come home to his family in Applewood and worked for Chuck Stevinson Chevrolet rather than accept a pay cut. (In those days, it wasn't uncommon for a portion of the US workforce to earn near, if not more, than what professional players were making.)

Sellers was then hired away by Mountain Bell as a Yellow Pages salesman, where he was in charge of a 14-state territory.

"He made more money in that job than he could have ever dreamed [of] making in football," Vasa said.

He was with Mountain Bell and Qwest for 29 years, 5 months, when he retired just before the Joseph Nacchio insider trading scandal hit in the early 2000s.

Sellers died at 78 in March 2020.

"He was very proud of being a Denver Bronco and just as proud of being a Kansas City Chief," Vasa said.

Rod Smith (1995–2006)

There were two seasons when Smith—the Broncos' all-time career leading receiver in catches, yards, and touchdowns—dropped back to help the team by returning punts. The first time was 1996, when Smith was a seldom-used No. 3 receiver behind Anthony Miller and Ed McCaffrey. The second time was 2004, when Smith was the Broncos' No. 1 receiver.

Even though he had 79 catches for 1,144 yards and 7 touchdown receptions that year, Smith also brought dependability to the punt return game by returning 22 punts for better than a 10-yard average.

In all, Smith ranks No. 2 in team history with a 12.2-yard-per-punt return average among those with at least 10 returns.

Gerald Willhite (1982–1988)

Let's call him the fifth-best punt returner in Broncos history, as he ranks No. 5 in punt returns (101) and punt-return yardage (1,102), which included a 70-yard touchdown runback.

An all-purpose running back who returned kickoffs as a rookie, Willhite's best season was 1986—"The Drive" season—when he rushed for 365 yards and 5 touchdowns, compiled 64 catches for another 529 yards and 3 touchdowns, and returned 42 punts for 468 yards (a career-best 11.1-yard average) and a touchdown.

In all, Willhite combined for 1,362 yards and 9 touchdowns in those three categories.

THE DENVER BRONCOS
ALL-TIME ALL-STAR TEAM

Head Coach: Mike Shanahan

OFFENSE
Quarterback: John Elway
Left Tackle: Gary Zimmerman
Left Guard: Keith Bishop
Center: Tom Nalen
Right Guard: Paul Howard
Right Tackle: Ken Lanier
Running Backs: Terrell Davis, Floyd Little
Wide Receivers: Rod Smith, Demaryius Thomas, Lionel Taylor
Tight End: Shannon Sharpe
Fullback: Jon Keyworth, Howard Griffith (tie)

DEFENSE
Cornerbacks: Champ Bailey, Louis Wright
Defensive Tackles: Trevor Pryce, Rubin Carter
Defensive Ends: Rich "Tombstone" Jackson, Rulon Jones
Inside Linebackers: Karl Mecklenburg, Randy Gradishar,
  Al Wilson
Outside Linebackers: Von Miller, Tom Jackson
Safeties: Steve Atwater, Dennis Smith

SPECIAL TEAMS
Kicker: Jason Elam
Punter: Tom Rouen
Returner: Rick Upchurch

ABOUT THE AUTHOR

Mike Klis has been a reporter covering the Denver Broncos since training camp of 2005, first with the *Denver Post* and since 2015 with 9NEWS TV. Previously, he covered the Colorado Rockies baseball team from 1990 (*Colorado Springs Gazette Telegraph*) until the 2005 All-Star break (*Denver Post*). He is married to Becky and they have four children, Brittney, Kaitlyn, Blake, and Johnny. This is Mike's seventh Broncos-related book.